LANCASTER TO BERLIN

LANCASTER TO BERLIN

Walter R Thompson
DFC & BAR, MA, LL.B, QC

A Goodall paperback
from
Crécy Publishing Limited

Published as a new edition by Goodall, 1997

First published by Goodall in 1985

ISBN 0 907579 37 X

A Goodall paperback

published by

Crécy Publishing Limited
Southside, Manchester Airport,
Wilmslow, Cheshire. SK9 4LL

Printed and bound by
The Guernsey Press Company Ltd,
Guernsey, Channel Islands.

Contents

	Foreword	7
Chapter One:	Service Flying	9
Chapter Two:	England	19
Chapter Three:	A Backward Step	30
Chapter Four:	Ready for War	42
Chapter Five:	Neophytes	55
Chapter Six:	The Dangerous Period	67
Chapter Seven:	Young Warriors	82
Chapter Eight:	Pathfinders	97
Chapter Nine:	Attrition and Hamburg	112
Chapter Ten:	Tame Boars and *Schrage Musik*	132
Chapter Eleven:	H2S and 'Abortions'	154
Chapter Twelve:	Night and Day	179
Chapter Thirteen:	The End Game	195
Chapter Fourteen:	Checkmate	205
Appendix A:	Monthly Tables of Sorties and Aircraft Missing	211
Appendix B:	Bomber Command Aircrew Killed, 1939-1945	214
Appendix C:	The Author's Operational Flights	215
Appendix D:	Squadron Aircraft and Crews Missing	217
Appendix E:	83 Squadron Operations Record Book	219
Appendix F:	Summary of 83 Squadron's History	228
	Bibliography	230

To my wife Eunice and to our children,
Jane, Judy, Jill and David,
I dedicate this book

Foreword

by Air Vice-Marshal D. C. T. Bennett, CB, CBE, DSO

TO be asked to write a Foreword to Walter Thompson's 'one man's saga' LANCASTER TO BERLIN gives me a chance to emphasise the tremendous courage and sacrifice of Bomber Command crews. About 25% of them survived!

In a matter-of-fact, straightforward way Walter Thompson has given an insight into the life of a pilot in the RAF in World War II. He makes no attempt to glorify those, like himself, who put their heads on the chopping block every time they went on a Bomber op. – and hoped that the axe would not fall. He simply tells us that they did so. He gives factual statistics of the degree of their sacrifice.

For a large part of the war Bomber Command was our only means of hitting back – our only weapon capable of defeating the enemy. Bomber Command was the biggest part of the Air Force and its contribution included not only strategic bombing to destroy the enemy's ability and will to fight, but also to hit tactical targets, flying bombs and military and naval miscellanea. Bomber Command lost 55,500 (dead) – Welsh, Irish, Scots, English, Australian, South African, Canadian and New Zealanders – in a fight to set the European nations (and ourselves) free. We won the war, but we have not yet won freedom. The flak is of a different and dirtier nature, but for humanity's sake we must win. We must be worthy of Walter Thompson and men like him.

DON BENNETT
Leader of the Pathfinders

CHAPTER ONE

Service Flying

THE winter snows had arrived and settled when we reached Yorkton in East Central Saskatchewan on November 8th, 1941 but clouds were absent and wisps of smoke from the town and the farms could be seen to the horizon as we approached by rail. The tracks were pencil lines of steel on the white, flat land extending for miles, as far as one could see to the light blue sky. The snow crunched and squeaked to the walk, the tiny crystals flashing like diamonds. We were loaded into trucks at the station, our worldly possessions squeezed into a light blue kit-bag, with a name and service number painted on the side. W. R. Thompson R-106592 was mine. The total strength of the RCAF for both air and ground crew was about 90,000 at this time. I suspected that our service numbers were started at several thousand just to confuse the enemy.

The attention of the enemy was elsewhere however as he paused for what was to be the final assault upon Moscow. The formidable panzer divisions, elite of the German Army, had taken Kharkov and pushed into the Crimea. They were snorting in the snow, thirsty for the oil of the Caucasus. Yasnaya Polyana, Tolstoy's home had been over-run but a month later, on December 6th, the Russians counter-attacked before Moscow. The daylight air was quiet in West Europe, save for the fighter sweeps over France. Much of the Luftwaffe's strength had been removed to the East. Major Hans-Ulrich Rudel, who was to become Hitler's favourite airman, was beginning his remarkable assault on Russian tanks – in excess of 500 put out of action during the war by this one airman! Rudel flew in combat for six years, mostly in Stuka dive bombers He was the only Luftwaffe pilot to be awarded the order known as the Knight's Cross with Golden Oak Leaves, Swords and Diamonds.

Sergeant Fogarty was a pilot too, but he was of that great majority of early graduates of the British Commonwealth Air Training Plan who were themselves immediately trained as instructors in order to pass on to a larger group the skills they had acquired. This seemed analogous to the division of cells so as to provide a sufficient concentration that some could be spared for a different function. Fogarty was obviously not enraptured with this role but with his strong sense of duty and dry wit he was determined to be a competent instructor, which he was. He introduced two of us to the Cessna Crane. Frail in appearance, with its metal tubular skeleton visible behind a yellow fabric exterior, its stilt-like undercarriage legs looked exceedingly weak for the pounding it must be receiving from ham-fisted student pilots. It had, of course not a cockpit but a cabin, not a joystick but a control column, a wheel like that of a car for control of the ailerons. This was attached to a metal stick which went, not into the floor but in and out of the dash in front of the pilot for control of the elevators. There was a second control column beside the first for use by the instructor in demonstration, or in moments of panic when forced to take control from the student. The only thing I found to admire about the machine was the appearance of the two 225 horse power Jacobs air-cooled engines protruding aggressively forward of the cabin from the main wing spar. A most unmilitary looking aircraft it was, I rationalised, not designed for any but a training function and in this it was faithful to its designers.

The living quarters at Yorkton were of the usual steel hut style but there was ample room for sleeping and studying. We were impressed with the dining hall and its food content. These were often critical factors in the lives of young men living in accommodation and consuming food similar to that in logging and mining camps; if good they were taken for granted, if bad they elicited loud complaints.

The Air Force knew enough to feed us and to house us properly. It knew something else as well; conspicuously displayed in the dining hall were four large oil paintings of four Canadians from WWI: Bishop, Collishaw, McLaren and Barker. If this was indoctrination we approved it. Bishop with a Victoria Cross and a history of utterly fearless attack, he of whom the American Rickenbacker had said that he didn't know what fear was – and this was true of Bishop – most men swallow their fear but Bishop seemed devoid of it – not because he was insensitive or unimaginative – (many people can push fear aside while it nevertheless persists in looking over their shoulder) but with Bishop fear would not have dared try to influence his actions. And Barker too, a man of such valour as legends are made of who, although grievously wounded, fought a brilliant single handed battle with German scouts over France in October, 1918 and also won the VC. And Raymond Collishaw from the West Coast, the third highest scoring British scout pilot of WWI. Yes indeed, the Air Force knew what it was doing when it put those portraits before the eyes of young warriors. I will have more to say of Collishaw and of meeting him on a snowy windswept night in Scotland. But in November, 1941 at Yorkton we admired the portraits and ate our meals. The one of Collishaw was familiar because I could see the family resemblance to his cousin whom I knew well and to his sister whom I had met – the same ruddy complexion and angular-faced good looks. I thought, 'Why, they were only boys!'

We were Course No. 42 – Red Section and the aircraft we flew were of 'D' Flight, No. I Hangar. Military authorities love numbers and letters and the organisation techniques of industry. They are particularly fond of organisation charts which look like family trees, with the title at the top of the chart showing the office of the person who ordered the chart to be drawn up. Our first day at Yorkton required a word or two from the top of the chart.

'You will do some of your dual instruction two at a time, two pupils to the instructor; one will observe while the other is under active instruction. When Red Section is flying, Blue Section will be at Ground School. You will do 50 hours dual and 60 hours solo. Included will be six cross-country navigation flights and some night flying and formation flying. If either your flying or your ground school is sub-standard or if you disobey orders you will be washed out. Upon graduation the upper 20% of you will be commissioned as officers and the remainder will become non-commissioned officers of Sergeant rank.' This was the Chief Flying Instructor speaking. 'Your success here and your chances for officer status upon graduation will be determined as follows: take this down, so that you won't forget it. (I took it down so I wouldn't forget it, as you can see below). Your performance will be evaluated under three main heads, Ground School, Flying and Qualities of Leadership. We allot 750 marks to each of these for a total of 2,250 marks. Flying Officer Heslop will explain to you the Ground School.'

'Thank you, Sir', said Heslop. 'In the Ground School you will require a 60% mark to pass, with a minimum of 50% on any one course. The subjects covered and the time of instruction will be:

Airmanship	10 hours	150 marks
Aircraft maintenance	2 hours	50 marks
Armaments	35 hours	200 marks (100 of these will be oral and 100 written)
Navigation	54 hours	150 marks
Meteorology (weather)	10 hours	50 marks
Signals	19 hours	150 marks (100 marks written 50 marks oral)

TOTALS	130 hours	750 marks

The 54 hours spent on Navigation will be further broken down into:

Maps and Charts	6 hours
Compasses	6 hours
Instruments	6 hours
Dead Reckoning Navigation	36 hours

An audible sigh passed through the room. There would be much work to do.

Fogarty wasted no time in getting us flying. You have seen no doubt, pilots making a tour around an aircraft, examining its external features and controls before getting in. Fogarty showed Woodhouse and I the points of interest on this tour. Not only did he determine that a finch had not built a nest in the air intake or that a chipmunk had not chewed a hole in the wingtip, he established that there were in fact two propellers, each firmly attached to its drive shaft and he exhibited that the control surfaces were not locked and had been spared from sabotage; he established that the pitot head was uncovered, was free of dirt and ice and had not been bent. What is a pitot head? (pronounced pea-toe). It is a little tube sticking out from the wing or fuselage which provides a source of outside air for the airspeed indicator, that it may register changes in speed.

Fogarty made a special point of checking the level of extension of the undercarriage oleo legs. The Crane, as I have mentioned, had long and delicate legs which it was advisable to check periodically lest one find oneself in the nesting position prior to take-off. These things done one entered a Crane by the side door, careful not to kick a hole in the fabric. I thought I had seen stronger looking box kites.

Most of a pilot's concern is in getting an aircraft safely on and off the ground and all his early training is directed to that end.

What happens in between is, in many cases, not even 'flying'. Once the aircraft controls are trimmed for a journey or put on automatic pilot it is only a matter of correct navigation and steering and, where possible, avoiding inclement weather, ground obstructions and other air traffic. This sounds simple and it is, but flying itself, even without hostile action, has a habit of eliminating both the undesirable and the unlucky. And sometimes it is difficult to tell which is which.

On December 7th, my 21st birthday, Japan attacked Pearl Harbour. While tactically this was a brilliant operation, strategically Japan could not have done a more stupid thing. Germany, if she had reflected, would also have regarded it as stupid. Until now it was clear that Britain alone could not have launched a counter-attack in the West, whether assisted by the Commonwealth or not. But with the United States at war against Japan, Germany considered herself bound by the axis treaty and on December 11th declared war on the U.S. She was stupid in not ensuring that the slumbering giant stayed asleep. We in Canada were keenly aware of these facts, having for years slept next to the giant. So although shocked by Japan's attack we were relieved as well. We knew now that we would win the war.

Meanwhile, as you might expect, the course of training was not uneventful. There was the problem that Fred Stevenson had for example. Fred was a fine pilot who took off one day in an easterly direction to fly a cross-country. When he returned a few hours later the wind had shifted 180° from the East and was now blowing out of the West. Fred mis-read the windsock and landed facing East. This was one of the things no one did, that is to land down wind, although frankly it was an error anyone could have made. But flight cadets are merciless. For a month or so Fred had to put up with 'Downwind Stevenson'. Or take the worse case of another who took off on a cross-country and forgot to raise his undercarriage after take-off. He unknowingly flew for two and a half hours with undercarriage down and upon returning to Yorkton moved the undercarriage lever to the opposite position to lower the wheels, only of course it had the reverse effect. His wheels came up and he made a surprised belly landing, surrounded by red flares with which the control tower tried to warn him.

We even learned to navigate. The student would take off and climb to the selected height, set the directional gyro to read the

same as the compass and fly over the centre of the airfield at the
correct height and airspeed on the pre-calculated course. He would
note down the exact time of departure. Good, he's on his way,
patting himself on the back for efficiency. The books then told him
to 'maintain the course accurately until the position of the aircraft
can be checked in relation to a landmark'. This was Air Force
language for taking a bearing or as we broadly interpreted it, for
noting where the nearest railway line went and thence peering at
the grain elevators to see if this was perhaps Springside, Foam
Lake, Yellow Creek, or some other point on an aerial line to Prince
Albert. Going to Saskatoon was even easier. But the books also said
that one should estimate wind drift, correct the course and calculate
the ground speed. So there was a nice amount of computation and
genuine effort necessary to bring back a log coherent enough to
dazzle the navigation instructors. They had been there too and were
expert at detecting fraud. There existed however a manually
operated device called a Dalton computer which, like a circular
slide rule, would yield quick answers to such computations. After
a while Navigation became simple.

    In addition at Yorkton we did some formation flying. To a pilot
who has never done formation flying it comes as something of a
shock to find how much manoeuvring of throttles and controls is
necessary to stay in formation with two or three other aircraft. Just
as you've caught up with and taken a proper station next to the
aircraft on your right, he finds it necessary to speed up in order to
catch the man on his right, who meanwhile thinks he should slow
down a bit, and so on. It is exhausting. One's throttle arm gets tired
moving the throttles back and forth, but with practice it becomes
less exhausting, until ultimately three or four can fly in a gaggle
like geese. But I was never satisfied with 'V' formations and was
pleased to hear later that fighters had switched to two pairs in a
'finger four' formation. This sounded a great deal freer, more
sensible and easier to fight from.

    My sister Ivy bought me a diary for Christmas in 1941 and
inscribed it: 'To a future William L. Shirer'. If I did not follow
Shirer as a war correspondent, I was grateful to my sister that she
thought I might have. I faithfully kept the diary for a month, after
which other matters intervened and no further entries were made. It
had a clasp lock for privacy and I lost the key, so it was kept locked
until now, when I prised it open. I have set out here, quaint though
they now seem, some excerpts as they were then written.

'Jan. 3: 1942 I've been looking at pictures on my locker two are 'Petty' pictures. (Of what else? Girls!) The other is of Jean Willcock. I'm buying her a watch for her graduation from business college. Sometimes I think I'm in love with her. Yet I imagine if I really were I'd want to marry her. As it is I want to travel round the world and satisfy this infernal thirst for adventure. We started night flying last night and I managed to get in an hour solo after dual instruction by Flying Officer Patterson.

Jan. 4: My flying is coming along satisfactorily but it's not as good as I'd like it to be. It's a marvel to me that someone else's carelessness combined with my own hasn't led to an accident. We got hell for not turning back when we met fog on the way to Weyburn today. What with night and day flying we haven't time to go down town. I'm disappointed too – I did so want to see a certain lovely, young blond who makes my heart jump. Ah, me!

Jan. 5: We fly two hours every night now and it certainly is fun. The instructors insist that we depend entirely upon our flight instruments but it's usually too well lit by moonlight to do so.

Jan. 8: My instructor is pretty grumpy these days. He just got back from a couple of weeks' leave. He sure ate my ass out all around the circuit today. And I was growling back at him and mumbling objections as I came in to land. We were both like bears with a sore hind foot.

Jan. 9: We had a fire on the station last night. The 'bombing teacher' building burnt down. There was an improvised aircraft on the top floor of this building and on the ground floor was a moving mosaic of a section of ground, simulated to look like a target and its surrounding country. You sit in the aircraft, the controls of which are so synchronised that the ground pattern seems to change beneath you as the aircraft responds to the controls. A bombsight and a system of lights is hooked up so that a light flashes when the bomb is gone and another shows where and when it hits the ground. We feel that the loss is deplorable but not irreparable.

Jan. 10: Nothing much of interest. We went down town tonight. Same old routine. Movie-show, a bottle of pop or grog and perhaps a game of pool, then sit in the local restaurant which is the cafe society of the village. It seems that this blonde I was so ardently pursuing has gone somewhere with her girl friend. They were evidently craving something besides the monotony of their life here, so they have gone down to the States.

Jan. 11: I had my 'wings' navigation test today. I passed it all right but made a couple of silly little mistakes in computation. My partner for the trip had bad luck in his test. He followed the wrong railroad and got himself completely lost. (We were not allowed to assist each other). We were even off the map sheet that we were using. This kid is a Hollander, named Speeljens. He's only been in Canada a year and a half – left Holland when the Germans advanced. He seems quite determined to fight for the freedom of his homeland. The testing sergeant isn't very amiable but I managed to endure him without getting angry – which fact was a great surprise.

Jan. 12 & 13: Exams.

Jan. 14: More exams. We write them and then hold a post-mortem. It's funny to see guys kicking their ass for some silly mistake, and believe me some of them are silly-things which if they only re-read their paper they would know are silly. But they don't. They write it feverishly, sign their name and get out.

Jan. 15: Still more exams. I scratched my head over Navigation all morning. Radius of action interception – course and airspeed, track and groundspeed. I poured the whole works onto the paper.

Jan. 16 & 17: Just flying now. They're getting the exams corrected. I was first in Armaments – oral and written.

Jan. 18: Had a wonderful time last night. I was in the local cafe with the best looking girl in town. She really is lovely – she drinks a little but then what girl doesn't these days? She treats most of us with a great deal of justified suspicion.

Jan. 19: More exam marks. I only got 50% in meteorology but everyone got low marks. Question: 'What effect have convection currents upon the smoke conditions in Central

England?' Now how the hell do we know what happens to smoke in Central England? Of course I put a lot of bullshit down but I'll bet I lost some marks on that one.

Jan. 20: 'Signals' marks are out now. I got 48 out of 50 on the written exam and 95 out of 100 on Morse sending and receiving. My mark in Navigation was 129 out of 150. It was a comprehensive exam, quite characteristic of Flying Officer Heslop. He's a thoroughly intelligent, clear thinking man. He used to be a mining engineer, and I'll bet he was a good one.

Jan. 21: Now all we need to know are our 'Airmanship and Maintenance' marks. There were four repetitious questions on the Airmanship exam. If we did badly on one, the same will be true on the other three. They all dealt with the loss of an engine. Of course we gave them the story of, 'Full throttle, fine pitch, hold straight with rudder, maintain height and trim the machine for single engine flight'. Same old stuff all the way, but it must be right – it's what they've been pounding into us, day after day in the air.

Jan. 22: I got 139 out of 200 on Airmanship and Maintenance. That isn't very good but then the others were very much worse. That gave me a total of 615 out of 750 and an average of 82%, which seems to be pretty good so far. I'll know tomorrow where I stand in relation to the rest of the class.

Jan. 23: What do you know? I finished second in the class on the examinations. Second out of sixty-four. I can hardly believe it.

Jan. 24, 25, 26 & 27: Haven't been flying much lately. A low pressure area has moved in and brought with it the usual bad weather, low ceiling, fog and snow. We just sit around the crew room when we can't sneak out. Using the parachutes for pillows, it's a good opportunity to catch up on our reading – I've read two books in the last two days. 'The Stray Lamb' by Thorne Smith and 'The Jungle' by Upton Sinclair. I also read the gospel according to St. Matthew. I've always wanted to read the teachings of Christ but hitherto scorned Christianity because I judged the religion by its exponents in the pulpit.

Jan. 28: More bad weather – no flying – I'm enjoying it no end.
The rest of the fellows have just come from the show.
They're all extolling the amorous advantages of a
posting to the Bahamas. The movie was 'Bahama
Passage'. They say that the hero didn't want to play
Adam to her Eve and they doubt if any sane man really
has that much self control.

Jan. 29: It's snowing like hell. The aerodrome is unserviceable
but there is one ray of sunshine. We're going to get four
days leave. I guess I'll try to stall off some of my urgent
creditors so that I can go to Winnipeg. We're certainly
going to rip that town apart.'

And so ends the diary. I think we actually got two days in
Winnipeg. I remember the snow blowing in my eyes and against
my greatcoat at the corner of Portage and Main. The city must have
withstood our onslaught.

On February 28, 1942 we graduated from SFTS. The sun shone.
We shined our shoes, polished our buttons, cleaned up the barracks,
pressed our uniforms and had a hair trim. Clean shaven and full of
goodwill we formed up to march according to flights, in columns
of three, past the station headquarters to one of the hangars where
the instructors and station staff had been mustered to act as
audience while the Station Commander pinned a cloth badge, four
inches long and shaped like wings to the left chest of each of us.
We were officially pilots in the RCAF. We were made sergeants
and sent to our homes on leave, equipped with rail vouchers, some
money and in the case of twenty percent of us, with a warrant to
buy an officer's uniform. We were also issued with rail vouchers to
Halifax and instructions to report there on March 14th. With two
days travel to the West Coast and five days by train from there to
Halifax, this meant a week at home. No one of course travelled by
air. The Rocky mountains had been crossed in late 1939 by Trans-
Canada Airlines but the service was limited and expensive.

CHAPTER TWO

England

WHILE home on embarkation leave I was drafted. I waited to respond until my officer's uniform had been made up by a Vancouver tailor and then walked into the draft registration office. I suppose the sergeant at the desk didn't see too many Air Force officers. He almost upset his chair getting to attention and saluting. That was the first salute I ever received. I explained that I was reporting for the draft and the sergeant's smile became broad as he said, 'I think the army can spare you, sir.' He took down the necessary particulars and checked my identity, then as I was leaving he snapped to attention and said, 'Good luck sir, and good hunting.' Embarrassed, I thanked him and left.

Upon boarding the train for Halifax the usual sad farewells were in progress. Women, old and young, and fathers too, were tearfully embracing young men, each no doubt silently wondering if they would ever see the other again. My thoughts turned to my home and loved ones. I was glad to see the night fall. I pulled the curtains as we speeded East up the lush Fraser Valley. I'd been through all this before, it seemed, in several movies and in the descriptions of WWI I had heard as a boy. Here we were, twenty-four years after 'All Quiet on the Western Front' and 'Wings' and 'Mademoiselle from Armentieres', going over to do what had been done before.

At each stop across the prairies we picked up members of the Yorkton graduating class until at Winnipeg about a third of the class was aboard. The other two thirds were even now scattering across Canada, some to be instructors, some to be staff pilots at gunnery and navigation schools and some to Coastal Command for submarine hunting.

Upon reaching Halifax we could see at last the grey Atlantic and hear the corvettes hooting and yapping around the harbour, waiting for the convoy to form up. Halifax was a busy port. We noted the old Lewis machine guns on the merchant vessels. Oh well, they might bolster morale.

But we did not join a convoy. We were soon aboard the 'Capetown Castle', a fast mail boat of 20,000 tons normally on the run from England to South Africa. Loaded with soldiers, including General MacNaughton the Canadian Army Commander-in-Chief, we set out alone to cross the Atlantic. The theory was that a fast ship could outrun submarines – whereas in convoy it would be more apt to be attacked. I did see a destroyer the second day out and it was a vast relief to think that the navy was keeping an eye on us. There was little to do on the ship except try to meet a small contingent of Army nurses. But with several thousand men aboard, occupying every available space, the competition was keen. One of our group was very upset at leaving Canada. A small man, I had seen him crying as he looked back over the stern at Halifax Harbour. Apparently one or two of our group had seen him as well and assumed that he was afraid to go overseas. I heard Vincent telling him, 'What you have to do is check the sea temperature every day. If you are torpedoed when it's close to 32°, as it is now, you can only last about fifteen minutes in the water. When it warms up a few degrees you'll be safer.' That must have been a great comfort to him.

I observed General MacNaughton at dinner. He looked thin and careworn; I expect he felt that way too. He certainly had his problems trying to keep the Canadian forces intact. A week after we landed in Britain, that is on April 6th, 1942, the first Canadian Army was formed under his command. It was ultimately to consist of five divisions and two armoured brigades. On April 9th the Americans surrendered at Bataan in the Philippines. On April 27th a national plebiscite was held in Canada on the question of imposing overseas conscription 'if necessary'. The plebiscite passed but Quebec voted a resounding 'No'. Two weeks later two ships were torpedoed in the St. Lawrence. I doubt that an earlier torpedoing would have changed the vote; Quebec had its mind made up to stay out of Europe.

The RAF at this time had only thirty-eight fully operational bomber squadrons, with about 16 aircraft per squadron. Of these, most squadrons were still operating the tough twin-engined Wellingtons; three were using the cumbersome four-engined Stirlings; four were using four-engined Halifaxes and three were flying the four-engined Lancaster. The rest was a motley collection of twin-engined Whitleys, Bostons and Hampdens. What with drains to the Navy and to the Middle East there were perhaps 300 aircraft available for attacks on Germany. A massive assault on Germany was in the planning stage but as yet Bomber Command was quite incapable of carrying it out. The first squadron of Lancasters, No. 44 Squadron, had been equipped in January at

Waddington and took off on March 3rd on a 'feeler' operation to try out the aircraft. Crews led by Squadron Leader Nettleton went 'gardening' as it was called, laying mines in enemy waters off Heligoland Bight. On March 20th, the second Lancaster Squadron, No. 97, made its first operation.

The bombing results of 1941 had been unproductive and incapable of influencing the war. Navigation at night, target location and actual bombing were ineffective. A detailed analysis from photo-reconnaissance reports showed that only about a third of the crews who claimed to attack any target had come within five miles of the aiming point. Losses had averaged twenty-one aircraft and crews a week.

But on February 20th, 1942 Air Marshal Arthur Harris took command of Bomber Command with a directive from the War Cabinet to commence a 'prolonged, specific offensive against Germany with the morale of the enemy civilian population and particularly of the industrial workers to be its chief focal point.' This policy was to remain in force for two years. Harris believed that the war against Germany could be won by application of 'the big fist'. With 4,000 and 8,000 lb. High Capacity bombs now available Harris conceived the 'Operation Millennium' or 'Thousand Plan', which was that by putting every available bomber in Britain, including the strength of the operational training units, over a particular city on one night it could be attacked by 1,000 bombers and so ultimately Germany would be smashed into submission. On May 30, 1942 one thousand and forty-six bombers attacked Cologne. Prior to this time no RAF bomber force had exceeded 230 in number on a single operation. German casualties amounted to nearly 5,000, of whom 469 had been killed. The city had been left blazing and belching columns of smoke. Forty-one bombers were missing; 250 men were missing or killed. The trend had started. Churchill had been 'prepared to lose 100 bombers' on this raid. The attack fired public imagination as it spurred government efforts in Britain to speed the production of bombers. But two other 1,000 bomber raids which followed, against Essen and against Bremen were not as effective.

On March 28th the overseas contingent of Yorkton Course 42 arrived at Liverpool where the expectations of that group of Canadians were realised by the sight of a sea of chimneys above smoke-darkened brick houses, crammed as in a huge amphitheatre round the harbour. We remarked to each other, 'I suppose it's all like this. If you have fifty million people in a small island there can't be room for open spaces.' There were surprises in store for us, commencing the next day when on a fast English train heading South, we saw miles of cultivated green fields and scattered deciduous trees arranged in pleasant patterns, with domestic animals placidly feeding in lush pastures. I could understand the line, 'Oh, to be in England now that April's there.'

We arrived at a railroad station marked 'Bournemouth', which none of us had heard of and, throwing kit bags on a truck, a squad of between twenty and thirty young pilots with 'Canada' badges sewn on their shoulders marched in bright sunshine down the main thoroughfare of Bournemouth, overlooking the sea in Hampshire. I for one was amazed. The building and store fronts were white and clean and modern; the place was a mass of hotels, large and small, all new or in good repair. It had a large pavilion near the beach and a park close by was filled with shrubs and flowers; huge rhododendrons formed high hedges for the privacy of fine-looking brick houses. There was a live theatre, a dance hall, tea shops and a large indoor swimming pool on the beach. The naval base at Poole was close by. But most of all there were young women! Pretty ones in bright print dresses lined the sidewalks and smiled as we marched to the Royal Bath Hotel where we received our allotted quarters in Burley Court, one of the attractive hotels on the sea cliff. We could put up with this we thought, if the war wasn't ready for us.

The war indeed was not quite ready. We heard gossip that the supply of pilots was catching up to the supply of aircraft and we would, in any event, have to complete an Advanced Flying Unit before going to an Operational Training Unit. The purpose of the AFU, we were told, was to give us some eighty hours flying over the unfamiliar terrain and different conditions of visibility of England. But first there were the delights of Bournemouth to explore. Coming from windswept Yorkton and the winter ridden plains of Canada, Bournemouth in April was a delight. We swam in the pool, walked the parks and learned to behave with a modicum of decorum at tea dances. At one of these I approached a lovely, young girl with long, golden hair; she could not have been more than seventeen and the assistance given to the natural gold of her hair could not mask her innocence, 'Would you care for a dance Miss?' I had not danced since those thirteen year old attempts at a May Day Ball, where one approached the May Queen and with her permission, stiffly placed a perspiration-stained paw on the back of a pristine white dress and waltzed. One-two-three, one-two-three. I wondered now if Meryl Barge, the May Queen, ever thought of those days and of hiding under an upturned row-boat on the beach and of the hungry, shy kisses of adolescence. I danced with the blonde girl who seemed as interested as if dancing with a mechanical man. There had been other groups of pilots ahead of us, I reflected, and she's been learning the techniques of coquetry from her older sisters. Little did I realise that she really wasn't interested in who she was dancing with, so long as it was someone presentable. 'One-two-three, One-two-three; the band sounds good! But what does one do when we get to the corner of the dance floor?' With a reverse One-two-three I triumphantly navigated the corner.

Thus began a sporadic association with a young woman, frequently to be broken by flying duty and only occasionally containing moments of happiness. Her name was Jean Gaffikin and she lived at Boscombe on the outskirts of Bournemouth. We could not have spent many hours in total in each other's company, always only brief moments before quarrelling; most of my memories of her are unhappy. But I did learn to dance properly.

One night a few of us went to a small pub outside Bournemouth and the war intruded for a moment. Packed in a smoke-filled bar, jammed with servicemen and women I found myself sharing elbow space with a Canadian Naval lieutenant whose small glass of whisky literally shook on the bar as he grasped it. I watched him drink it neat and compose-himself. He was Lieutenant Dave Killam from Vancouver. Based at Poole he commanded a motor-torpedo boat; an hour earlier he'd come in from a sweep at night to the French Coast where he'd had the bridge of his vessel literally shot from underneath him by the combined fire of German Channel batteries and E-Boats. He had managed to deliver an attack on an E-Boat and get out of there. Delayed shock was now striking a very brave man. I bought a round and he relaxed to see and talk with someone from BC.

The next day we were given leave to go to London for a few days. My first night in London, staying in a hostel for overseas personnel I received the fright of my life. Having just gone to sleep in an upper bunk I was awakened by the most godawful crashing explosion I had ever heard; the building shook terribly and I actually fell out of the bunk on to the floor. Unknown to us, outside our window was the biggest anti-aircraft gun I had ever seen and certainly the biggest I had ever heard. Someone had flown over London's air space. I was to find later that these gunners didn't much care who owned the aircraft they shot at, so long as there was an aircraft to be shot. The next night we all went, as everyone did, to the 'Windmill Theatre' which, with its stunning and scantily clad females and bawdy humour, had never closed during the blitz. We were grateful it had stayed open. After the show we looked around at the stage door where, to our amazement, was a long line-up of officers, all higher in rank than we, waiting to see one or other of the young women. We thought we would come back some time in the future when we had enough clout to get to the front of the line. In fact I did, as I will tell you later.

Meanwhile the Air Force was puzzled about what it should do with many high spirited young men to keep them out of mischief for a few days. Someone hit upon the idea of a course with the Army or Navy; 'Good for them – find out what the other services do – make proper officers of them.' So for the last two weeks of April I was the lone Air Force officer with the 34th British Army Tank Brigade, training at Salisbury, Wiltshire for expected North African combat duties. I lived as a subaltern of the 34th and the Regimental Sergeant Major was assigned the task of showing me around and keeping me from getting myself killed. A splendid NCO, he did this easily in addition to his regular duties. I became quite spoiled after only two days of having a 'batman' wake me each morning with a 'good morning sir' and a hot cup of tea. We junior officers were daily drilled in the operation of the Churchill tank and its 6 pound gun, a paltry weapon with a range of 1000 yards; we thought it no match for the superb German all-purpose 88 mm gun.

One day we went to an artillery demonstration at nearby Larkhill and learned that the 34th was to be equipped with the new 17 pound anti-tank rifle which we there saw lovingly demonstrated by an artillery crew. Everyone was delighted but I don't think that the 34th was in fact equipped with this weapon before going to Africa. The colonel twice took the junior officers on what was called a TEWT, tactical exercise without troops. This I found to be rather like playing cowboys and Indians. We sat on a knoll overlooking a valley while the Colonel set the scene with his swagger stick and a map of the terrain. 'Well here you are chaps,' he said. 'You are here alone in one tank hunched behind this knoll and you look at that road, there across the valley. From around that hill emerge four *Sturmgeschutz* short-barrelled 75 mm assault guns mounted on tank chassis and six *Schutzenpanzerwagens*, each carrying twelve men. What do you do?' One of the British subalterns said, 'Well sir, I expect we'd let the bastards have a packet.' The Colonel shook his head, turned to me and said 'What do you say, Canada?' I said, 'Well sir, maybe I'd take a shot at them too but I hope this tank has a radio so I can tell someone else before I do.'

'Absolutely correct', said the Colonel. 'We're trying to win a war not create dead heroes. It would be better to have more firepower than your single tank, Watkins. Get some help.' With the arrogance of ignorance I thought, 'By golly, maybe I should be in the tank corps.' Little did I realise that in two months time I would come very close to having to make good that boast.

At lunch I asked the Colonel what would have happened if England had been invaded at the time of the Battle of Britain. He was quite frank. 'Well they could have taken Britain if they had landed an armoured division. Of course', he added, 'they'd have had a few casualties, perhaps three or four divisions and they'd have lost one *luftflotte* (air fleet) and half their navy and no end of support vessels. But if they'd landed one armoured division and kept it supplied they could have taken Britain.'

I don't know how accurate that assessment was but I had no reason to doubt it. The defence of Britain, even then, seemed somewhat tenuous. We noted that only persons who had business there or whose homes were in the South Coast area were permitted to be there. Tank traps were in the roads and concrete gun emplacements were strewn about at country road intersections. The beaches had been barricaded and mined and the 'Home Guard', a motley group of young and elderly civilians, were mobilised throughout England but I saw no real power, nothing but the Canadian Army cooling its heels, which could not for long have stopped an efficient, determined armoured attack. Most of the British Army was clearly not at home and that which was at home was hardly armed to the teeth. It seemed likely to me that the Colonel was right.

When I left the 34th it was in high spirits at the thought of combat duty. I returned to Bournemouth for a further few days' frivolity and strolls through apple blossoms in the park, of tea

dances, movies with Jean and swimming at the beach in the early
summer heat. The beaches were lined with obstacles made of pipe
placed below low water to discourage landing craft. The centre
section of the Boscombe pier had been blown out by sappers and
certain areas of the beach front were mined but we knew the safe
areas and went there to frolic in the waves. I loved the cool green
surf and wallowed in it, snorting and blowing like a walrus. The
water was not as clear as in my youthful swimming club days but
we soaked up the warm sun and forgot the Air Force. While I'd been
away with the Army two Focke Wulf 190s had come over from
France, low level across the Channel to escape radar detection one
Sunday morning and had sprayed the main square of Bournemouth
with cannon shells. I saw where a steel light standard had been cut
in half by a cannon shell. The Fw 190 was a fine aircraft, faster than
the Messerschmitt 109 with a speed of 400 MPH at 32,000 feet and
armed with two 20 mm cannons and 13 mm machine guns, it could
out-perform the Spitfire V. During the Dieppe raid two months later
in August, 1942 it was to shoot down allied planes at a rate of two
to one and wasn't to be matched by an allied fighter until the
introduction of the Spit IX and Spit XIV in 1943.

While at Bournemouth I saw my cousin Bill Sherry who had just
completed an Advanced Flying Unit. He was full of stories of what
was in store for him and I was envious. He was going to be flying the
twin-engined Beaufighters. Three months later he was killed landing
one on the Isle of Man. He had a total of 275 hours flying time.

On May 12th we left Bournemouth in the morning by train,
changed trains in London and arrived at Grantham in Lincolnshire
in the late afternoon. We were five Canadians, three officers and
two sergeants. We found ourselves among a group of twenty-three
pilots for the course at the Advanced Flying Unit; the rest of the
twenty-three, with the exception of one Australian, were British. In
all there were sixteen sergeants and seven officers. My good friend
Murray Taylor from Lloydminster, Alberta was among them.
Murray claimed to be a pig farmer and both he and the animals
brightened noticeably if we were ever in the vicinity of hogs; he
claimed he could talk to them. He had a wonderful sense of humour
and was a delight to be on course with. For reasons which you will
soon see I lost track of him on leaving Grantham and he was killed
about a year later flying Beaufighters. But at Grantham we often
flew together. My first flight came two days later in an Airspeed

Oxford. They were smaller but more powerful than the Cessna, having two 350 HP Cheetah engines. Their wing-load was high and we were told they had a nasty habit of flicking inward if you lost speed in a turn. I later tried this out at a safe altitude and found it to be a far from nasty habit. In fact after flying it for some time I thought the old Oxford a pleasant aircraft to fly provided you respected its limitations, which were many.

On my first flight in England the day was sunny but there seemed a lot of smoke haze around the airfield. I took off with Sgt. Letts, an instructor, in the left seat and myself beside him in the right. When we reached 1,000 feet Letts looked out ahead and said, 'Eeh, what a wizard day!' in a Yorkshire accent so strong that my Canadian tuned ears could barely understand what he was saying. I looked out at the supposedly 'wizard' day and could see nothing but smoke. After a few minutes however I began to make out fields below like a patchwork quilt of greens and browns and here and there a group of houses. We did an hour and twenty-five minutes of circuits and landings and later a further hour and a half before I went solo. There followed the usual dual instruction, including some low flying in a farm area, which was fun; this was one of the few times till then that I had done low flying legally. Then followed precautionary landings, single-engined flying, steep turns and navigational exercises. Then we did night flying from a satellite airfield called Harlaxton. This I enjoyed until one night, when I'd flown there about eight hours, Letts told me of an incident which had occurred a few weeks earlier.

I will let him tell it without his accent, he said, 'We were in radio contact with the tower when I was told to fly a few miles away and circle at 2,000 feet over the beacon – there was a 'bandit' in the area. I thought, they can't be serious. What would a bandit be doing here? I was to do a left hand circuit round the beacon with my navigation lights off and watch for other aircraft circling at heights above me. After ten minutes of this I was bored. Then I saw what appeared to be a large yellow flare. That is all I saw. In another ten minutes we were told to return to Harlaxton and land. I was the lowest in the stack and the first to land. I was signalled over to the parking area, flying was finished for the night. It was then that I learned that there really had been an intruder. A Ju 88 had shot down two Oxfords above me, one containing a pupil and the other a pupil and an instructor. The yellow flare was a burning aircraft. The Ju 88 was shot down by one of our night fighters before crossing the English coast on his way back to Holland.' The war was getting closer it seemed.

About this time too another incident occurred to remind us that there was a war on. Our routine of night flying was broken when a Handley Page Hampden, one of a rather elderly species of bomber, returning from an operation made a belly landing on our grass field. He'd been shot up and couldn't make it to his own airfield, so he put down at the nearest available place. The ground crew had to work to get the pilot free of the seat in which he was jammed, uninjured. We gazed with admiration at the unperturbed pilot, an American in the RCAF.

At Grantham the airfield was called Spitalgate and there we were exposed to the peculiar practice of hood flying. This consists of night flying in the daytime. A canvas hood is placed around the pilot so that he can see nothing outside the aircraft but can see the instruments in front of him. The instructor, who is not hooded, taxies the machine to the take-off position where the take-off check is done; he lines up the aircraft down the middle of the runway, asks the student to uncage the directional gyro and says, 'You have control'. About this time you are apt to break out in a light sweat. You open the throttles, hope that the directional gyro is working properly, get yourself airborne, get the gear and flaps up and pray that the artificial horizon and the rate of climb indicator are truthful instruments. You pull back on the two throttles to the correct boost. You still can see nothing outside. Pull back on the two pitch-control levers to the correct revs for climbing. All the while you are watching the directional gyro, the artificial horizon, the air speed indicator and the vertical speed indicator and correcting on the controls as necessary. Glance too at the turn and bank indicator; check the altimeter. When at the correct altitude, level off on the selected heading on the directional gyro. You can stop perspiring now until you get round to reverse the process and do the landing approach. Soon you find that you can take off, fly a circuit and do a landing approach without seeing anything. I never did it however without thinking of hunting falcons; they are hooded while sitting on the falconer's arm in order that they will not fly; we were expected to fly hooded. There was a variation of the hood technique for the actual landings. It was a heavily tinted sheet of plastic placed on the windows on the student's side of the cockpit

with a curtain between him and the instructor. Special runway
lights were turned on in the daytime so as to be barely visible
through the tinted windows and off you went. You could see
nothing but the lights. Down the runway, get airborne, around the
circuit and do an approach and landing with those barely visible
lights; nothing else but the instruments inside was visible at all.
After an hour or two of this the English haze seemed crystal clear
when you raised the plastic. So when it came time to do night
flying the transition was simple. All you needed to see was a lane
of blue runway lights and off you went, into the high, black yonder.

CHAPTER THREE

A Backward Step

WE WERE living now on a British station with British staff and instructors; I liked them and admired them. We were almost finished there when the chief instructor, Squadron Leader Kinnear, one day demonstrated how to waltz a Hurricane fighter at a local Air Force display. He tuned his radio to a Strauss Waltz, got the ground people to broadcast the same music on the loudspeakers and came over the airfield at low level waltzing the Hurricane's wings from side to side and rolling to the music. We were impressed with Kinnear and with the British; they even asked us to list our several preferences for the type of flying we hoped to do. They said that those who did best would have first choice. I chose night fighters first, Coastal Command ship-fighters second and bombers third. I had worked diligently at flying and ground school and graduated first in the class. On the 10th day of July, 1942 my flying log book was endorsed by Squadron Leader Kinnear, 'Proficiency as pilot on Type – Above Average'. What more could one ask?

Then the world collapsed! I was told that I had received a high mark in Navigation and was therefore posted to commence a Navigation Instructor's course at the Central Navigation School at Cranage. As simple as that! This was unbearable! But I did report to Cranage as ordered on July 12, 1942, and next day reported as ordered to the classroom and took the day's lectures before making up my mind that I would refuse the posting, resign my commission, face whatever charges resulted, and join the Tank Corps. I could not become a Navigation Instructor. There seemed no alternative but to return to Grantham immediately, which I did. There I asked the Flying Wing Adjutant, a Flight Lieutenant, for an interview with the Station Commander.

This was arranged immediately. I told the Station Commander that I had returned from Cranage because I could not be a Navigation Instructor. He was a large man of Wing Commander rank who immediately informed me, 'Thompson, I don't give a damn if you come from Canada or from Timbuctoo, you'll do as you're told.' Conscious of the triteness of my words, I replied, 'Sir, my conscience will not permit me to be a Navigation Instructor. If I'd wanted to be an instructor I could have been one in Canada. I

will join the Tank Corps first.' The Wing Commander got very red
in the face and said, 'You are under arrest. Do you think that the
rest of us like this type of duty?' I held my tongue while he got
redder. He continued, 'We would rather be fighting the war too but
we go where we are ordered – you will too. You will confine
yourself to the officers' quarters in custody until further dealt with.'
I left his presence with a light heart. I didn't care what happened.
After all I wasn't going to be shot for wanting to fight the enemy
and I could fight equally well in the Army. My opinion of the
British was changing. All this trouble because some jackass had
created such a stupid order in the first place and having created it
could not back down. I had no doubt that my Air Force career was
over and that I might serve a little time in jail. But I thought to
myself, 'We'll soon see if "Theirs is not to reason why" – If I'm
going "to do and die", I'll do it my way.'

I was kept under arrest. I had the freedom of the officers'
quarters and the mess for two and a half months but was socially
ostracised. One of the duties of the Orderly Officer twice each day
was to check on my whereabouts. No one spoke to me, which was
fine with me. It took all that time for the legal machinery to roll its
ponderous path. 'My God', I thought, who can bear 'the law's
delay, the proud man's contumely'?

As a souvenir of those tedious days I kept the official Charge
Sheet and Summary of Evidence. It was as follows:

CHARGE SHEET

The accused Pilot Officer Walter R. Thompson No. J. 10506,
Central Navigation School, Cranage, a member of a Dominion
Force subject to the Air Force Act as an officer of the Royal
Canadian Air Force, is charged with:

First Charge: WHEN ON ACTIVE SERVICE FAILING TO APPEAR AT
Section 15(2), THE PLACE OF PARADE APPOINTED BY
Air Force Act   HIS COMMANDING OFFICER

in that he, on Wednesday, 15th July, 1942, at
Cranage failed to appear at No. 8 Lecture Room
at the said RAF Station at 0830 hours, the place
of parade duly appointed by Wing Commander
R.G. Musson, his commanding officer.

Alternate Charge: WHEN ON ACTIVE SERVICE CONDUCT TO THE
Section 40,   PREJUDICE OF GOOD ORDER AND AIR FORCE
Air Force Act   DISCIPLINE

in that he was at RAF Station, Grantham, on
Wednesday 15th July, 1942, when his duty
required him to be with his unit, the Central
Navigation School, RAF Cranage.

Wing Commander, Commanding
Central Navigation School
9th September, 1942   CRANAGE

SUMMARY OF EVIDENCE
in the case of
J.10506. Pilot Officer W.R. Thompson,
Central Navigation School, Royal Air Force, Cranage.

The Commanding Officer has directed that the evidence be
taken on oath.

1st Witness: Squadron Leader John Bentley Weightman,
Central Navigation School (being duly sworn) states:

I am Chief Instructor, Central Navigation School RAF
Cranage. Pilot Officer W.R. Thompson J.10506 was
posted to No. 2 S. of A.N. (now C.N.S.) on 12th July
1942 for No. 38 S.N. Instructors' Course and reported to
this Unit on 12th July 1942. At 0900 hours on Monday
13th July, Pilot Officer Thompson applied for an
interview with the Chief Instructor, during which he
stated that he had no desire to become a Navigation
Instructor and that he had informed his Instructor at his
previous unit (No. 12 P.A.F.U.) to this effect. Pilot
Officer Thompson failed to report for lectures at 0830
hours on Wednesday 15th July and after searching in
camp, it was ascertained that he had left the station on
the previous evening, leaving no information as to his
movements. At 1430 hours on 15th July the Chief
Instructor was informed by the Adjutant RAF Station
Grantham that Pilot Officer Thompson had reported to
that unit and that he had been interviewed by the Station
Commander, Headquarters No. 21 Group had been
informed, and it was intended to return Pilot Officer

Thompson by air immediately. These details were communicated by telephone to Headquarters Flying Training Command (Squadron Leader Palmer) and instructions were received to the effect that Pilot Officer Thompson was not to return to Cranage, but was to remain at Grantham and await further instructions. Pilot Officer Thompson was instructed to return to RAF Cranage on the 4th September 1942, and reported on the 7th September 1942.

First Question: Was the signal re-posting me to Cranage dated the 4th September, or was the posting effective on the 4th September.

First Answer: The date of the signal (P.224, 21 Group) was the 4th September and the text is as follows: 'P/O Thompson to report to 2 S. of A.N. forthwith'. The time of origin was 1710.

The accused declines to make any further cross-examination of the witness.

(Sgd.) M.O. Thompson A/S/O. (Sgd.) J.B. Weightman S/Ldr.

2nd Witness: Flight Lieutenant Howard Gordon Rhys Thomas 82778 (being duly sworn) states:

I am School Adjutant Central Navigation School, RAF Cranage. On the evening of Tuesday 14th July 1942, I was having tea outside the Officers' Mess about 1715 hours and I saw Pilot Officer Thompson leave the Mess in a taxi. The accused declines to cross-examine the witness.

(Sgd.) M.O. Thompson A/S/O (Sgd.) H.G.R. Thomas F/Lt.

3rd Witness: Flight Lieutenant Cyril Allen Whitmore 62450 (being duly sworn) states:

I am Flying Wing Adjutant, RAF Grantham. On the morning of July 15th 1942, about 0900 hours, Pilot Officer W.R. Thompson reported to my office stating that he had just returned from RAF Cranage. On questioning him I ascertained that he had, in fact, absented himself without leave from RAF Cranage. I immediately contacted RAF Cranage by telephone and advised the acting Chief Instructor of the position, indicating that we were returning Pilot Officer Thompson immediately. I was, however, instructed to retain Pilot Officer Thompson at this unit pending further instructions.

The accused declines to cross-examine the witness.

(Sgd.) M.O. Thompson A/S/O (Sgd.) C.A. Whitmore F/Lt.

The accused is warned in accordance with R.P.4(E).

The accused declines to make any statement or give evidence.

CERTIFIED that the foregoing Summary of Evidence consisting of three pages (two typewritten sheets) was taken down by me at RAF Cranage and RAF Grantham on 8th September 1942, in the presence of the accused, and that R.P.4 (C), (D) and (E) were complied with.

(Sgd.) Margaret O. Thompson A/S/O

Officer detailed to take this Summary of Evidence

ADDITIONAL SUMMARY OF EVIDENCE
in the case of
J.10506 Pilot Officer W.R. THOMPSON,
Central Navigation School, Royal Air Force
CRANAGE

The Commanding Officer has directed that the evidence be taken on oath:

4th Witness: Flight Lieutenant Maurice Max Wallenstein 44926 (being duly sworn) states:

I am Navigation Instructor at Central Navigation School, RAF Cranage, detailed as Officer i/c No. 38 S.N.I. Course. Pilot Officer W.R. Thompson was a member of this course and appeared in Lecture Room 8 on the morning of July 13th 1942 at 0830 hours till 1630 hours daily. On July 15th Pilot Officer Thompson did not arrive for lectures at 0830 hours, and on enquiry I discovered his bed had not been slept in the night previously. The matter was reported to the Chief Instructor a.m. on 15th July. The accused declines to cross-examine the witness.

(Sgd.) M.O. Thompson A/S/O (Sgd.) M.M. Wallenstein F/Lt.

The accused is warned in accordance with R.P.4(E).

The accused declines to make any statement or give evidence.

CERTIFIED that the foregoing Additional Summary of Evidence consisting of one page was taken down by me at RAF Cranage on 9th September 1942, in the presence of the accused, and that R.P.4 (C), (D) and (E) were complied with.

(Sgd.) Margaret O. Thompson A/S/O

Officer detailed to take this Additional Summary of Evidence.

As you see, it took from July 15th until September 9th to lay the charges and gather the evidence. This involved flying back and forth from Grantham to Cranage and later to Training Command Headquarters. I suppose they wondered, 'Why waste the services of another pilot on these duties, we'll make Thompson do it.' So it became my job to fly administrative and legal personnel to the places where they investigated my disobedience. This was a good sign. His Majesty had a lot of money invested in my training and intended to get something for it. I flew people on other tasks around England as well and soon found that, although I could now be talked to by most people, they felt that they had to be circumspect in dealing with an outlaw, lest it be contagious. In particular the Section Officer detailed to take the evidence, a rather attractive young woman only slightly older than I and with the same surname, appeared to have a problem deciding whether to hold her nose in my presence or to encourage my mildly flirtatious advances. She finally decided on the former.

All of this culminated in the presentation of myself, together with the Charge Sheet and Summary of Evidence on or about September 25th 1942 to the Air Officer Commanding, Training Command Headquarters. The AOC was an Air Vice-Marshal. I had never seen such a high ranking officer and was quite certain we could have had only one such in Canada. The Headquarters, as you would expect, was an old ivy covered stone mansion with round battlements at the gate. This was approached by a spacious roadway of light-coloured crushed rock which ran through well manicured lawns, shrubs and trees. The greeting committee was anything but hospitable; I was still under arrest. Two RAF police officers took stations on either side of me; I felt like Lord Essex going to the Tower. With a Squadron Leader in command they marched me through several corridors and up one of the towers to a roomy well-lit office. There behind a wide desk, placed so that its occupant could see if an aeroplane flew by, was an elderly pilot with many ribbons below his wings who, it was apparent, had long ago left the sky for the desk. I was marched in, I saluted, the escort was excused and except for the Squadron Leader we were alone.

'Well', said the Air Vice-Marshal, looking at the charge sheet in his hand, 'What's this all about? Don't want to be an instructor? Is that it Thompson?'

My voice was squeaky. 'Yes sir,' I said, standing rigidly at attention. There was no turning back now and further words would have been superfluous.

'Hmmph', said the Air Vice-Marshal, 'Hmmph', and then a long pause which I awaited with anguish to terminate. Then he looked out of the window at the sky and said, as if to himself, 'Commendable spirit really!' He looked directly at me for the first time. 'But you know you can't go around disobeying orders. I'm sending you out as a staff pilot at a gunnery school.'

And that was that. I never did receive official word as to the disposition of the charges, although I expect there was no doubt of my guilt. So also I was left with no doubt about the quality of British justice; I only wished they were not so eager to apply it. My step was lighter as I left the mansion, still under escort. I winked at Section Officer Thompson when leaving. She smiled and said not a word.

*   *   *

The next three weeks were fresh air to the spirit. I was sent to a place called Morpeth in Northumberland, near the Scottish border. I had no idea where my future lay but I was absolutely delighted; I would not be instructing and would remain flying while things were sorted out.

No. 4 Air Gunnery School had been forgotten by everyone in the RAF except the Air Vice-Marshal, who knew that it was on his chart somewhere. It consisted of three runways set in a sea of mud on the North East coast of England. On the side of the field, protected by vicious looking trees, was a round domed hut, the officers' mess of course. No hangars were in evidence. The flight

shack to which I reported was a newly erected tent. If
Solzhenitsyn's *Gulag Archipelago* existed in England, this was it.
The staff and ground crew greeted me in amazement, 'What could
a young officer possibly have done to be sent to join them?' Most
of the pilots were Polish sergeants and couldn't speak a word of
English. The Station Commander, a large Englishman of Wing
Commander rank greeted me with enthusiasm, as though I had
arrived at the head of a relief column. 'Do you play squash?' he
asked. I had never played the game but replied with some
confidence, 'Yes, a little'. – If he'd wanted to play tiddlywinks I'd
have played; I would need all the influence I could muster to get
out of there. He had commandeered one of the few available
buildings to make a squash court and had perhaps once been a good
player but he was now somewhat out of shape and slow of
movement. I frequently beat him but not by too high scores.

I was made Flight Commander of the Polish flight. The Poles
were wondrous young men – or boys really. There were four of
them in the flight, Medzibrowski, Jaworski, Garstecki and one
other plus a Scottish Flight Sergeant named Stewart and a
Canadian Flight Sergeant called Gebhard, all pilots.

Gebhard, big of frame, blond, with stooped shoulders was the
official instructor of 'B' Flight. 'Thank God you have come', he
said. 'If I have to teach one more bloody Pole to fly a Blackburn
Botha I'll give myself up to the Germans. They can't speak a word
of English you know and the last aircraft they flew were French –
you pulled back on the throttles instead of pushing forward. I always
take their officer along with me. He speaks a little English and I tell
him to explain to them what I am saying. Do you know that half the
time he doesn't know what the hell I'm saying, so can you imagine
what he's been telling them? I get sick just thinking of it.' As he was
saying this two Poles were walking on their hands on the board floor
of the tent to see who could stay upside down the longest. 'Look at
the crazy bastards', he said as keys, money and bottle openers fell
from their upside-down pockets. 'They've got more guts than a
slaughterhouse but we daren't keep any bombs around here, the mad
bastards would lug them over to Denmark or Germany and drop
them on the Germans. They're supposed to be flying gunners
around and once in a while I get one trained to do it.' He shook his
head, picked up a parachute and said, 'C'mon, I'll show you how to
fly one of these abortions.' So on October 10, 1942 Flight Sergeant

Gebhard gave me two hours and fifteen minutes instruction and said, 'OK I've taught you far more than I've ever taught a Pole. It's all yours.' So I happily did an hour's circuits by myself, glad to be flying again after a month on the ground.

The Botha was a twin-engined torpedo bomber powered by two 820 HP Perseus engines, so it was relatively large and had twice the power of the Oxford. It was regarded as too senile to take on the German navy and thus its gun turrets were used to train gunners. The pilot's job was to fly it within two hundred yards of a huge cotton stocking being towed by another, lighter aircraft while the gunners shot at the sock with a pair of Browning machine guns. The aim of novice gunners being what it was the pilot of the aircraft towing the 'drogue' was regarded as a hero. So it was not surprising that I was offered that job within a day or two. I respectfully declined until I'd become more confident on the Botha; this only took two or three days of up and down all day long and out to sea over the range with a fuselage full of gunners. The large air-cooled engines had a tendency to overheat which had to be remedied periodically by cranking open little baffles in the side of the engine cowling to let air flow over the fins of the cylinder pots; this seemed to do the job and I soon felt at home in the Botha. When on gunnery exercises I hoped that the interrupter gears in the turrets would work so that the gunners wouldn't blow off our wingtip or tailplane, and happily they worked. The guns sometimes jammed in the air and if they couldn't be cleared by the gunnery instructor we had to land and get an armourer to see to them. But most of the time they worked well and surprisingly, some of the gunners could put quite a number of bullet holes in a drogue at two hundred yards towed by a Lysander. I thought that if I ever got on operations in a bomber I'd be happy to have one or two of these keen eyed kids, for they were often two or three years younger than I, riding in the turrets.

In a squash game a few days later the Wing Commander mentioned that we should get in a few good games next week because he didn't expect I'd be at Morpeth long. 'I'll be sorry to see you go, old chap. ' I wondered what he knew that I didn't. I replied that in a way I'd be sorry to go too, for I liked the station, the aircraft and the staff, which was true.

When the weather was bad we played chess. Gebhard showed me the moves of the pieces but most often I played Garstecki and Jaworski. They were both experienced players, better and faster by far than I and playing with a good chess player is a humbling experience but I soon found that one's ability to play increased with one's determination to win. Soon too I was desperately reading books on the King's pawn gambit and the Sicilian defence, rather than endure the good natured suggestions that I must have been good at cutting trees or growing wheat.

The Poles hated the Germans and the Russians with equal passions. Garstecki eventually made known to me, as either I began to learn Polish or he English or both of us some form of sign language, that he had escaped from his village as a young boy. When the Germans attacked without warning, the Russians had also moved into Poland and his village was occupied by Russian infantry. When the soldiers unexpectedly pushed open the front door of his home he dived out the window and ran. Eventually he and many other Poles, he said, somehow got to North Africa; I was not clear how that happened; I imagine they travelled through Russia past Greece and Turkey and across the Mediterranean, where he ended up with the French. He learned to fly French aircraft and when France fell he somehow got to Britain. Had we been better able to communicate I could have learned greater detail. Even as we played chess a Polish squadron, later to become a wing, was operating Spitfires with the RAF and the Poles in the air, like those on the ground, were to become legendary for their courage. The Poles at Morpeth would have died happily just to take some Germans with them. Perhaps they did.

After a week I ventured across the field to 'A' Flight, a princely place with a wood frame building instead of a tent; this was the nerve centre of a complex, highly organised flight of four Lysanders. These big old single engined aircraft had fixed undercarriage covered by streamlined 'wheel pants'; they looked something like the 'Norseman', in service in Canada as a bush plane. The complex organisation consisted of four pieces of stiff paper, one for each aircraft, one stubby pencil, one gas truck and one Flight Lieutenant Houghton, a happy man with red hair and flaming red, handlebar moustache which would have excited the envy of a Bulgarian cavalry general. I liked the man on sight. About thirty years old he'd obviously served time in a lot of aeroplanes. Perhaps he'd been on those Lysanders which were attached to the army in France. He was still on Lysanders.

'Well, Thompson', he said, 'Come over to get checked out on

the Lizzie have you? Let's see what we can do. I'll show you
around.' That really hadn't been my intention in visiting the flight
but I thought, why not? So I climbed into the elevated cockpit of this
high-wing dragonfly while Houghton explained to me the knobs
and levers. I hadn't flown a single-engined aeroplane since the tiny
Tiger Moth and the engine on this one seemed huge. In the tail down
attitude the view ahead was obscured by the large round engine
cowling over the air-cooled cylinder pots. I only now realised that
there would be no dual instruction. Although it had two seats, one
for the winch operator when towing drogues and one for the pilot,
there was only one set of controls. Houghton finished his
explanation, I fastened the shoulder harness and he gave the cockpit
a slap and said, 'We can fill in the forms when you get down. It's
getting a bit windy, you may have trouble taxiing. Well, off you go.'

   'Trouble taxiing' was typical British understatement. I ground
looped twice before getting out to the take-off point. You may know
that in a single-engined aircraft, unless it has tricycle undercarriage
or otherwise has good forward visibility, one taxies by giving the
aircraft a short burst of throttle while steering with rudder and
brake from side to side in order to see the runway ahead and avoid
running into things. The air from the propeller flows back over the
tail and one can turn the aircraft by applying rudder – which moves
the tail to one side or the other. It is very important to swing the
nose from side to side to see ahead as one taxies, since people leave
gas trucks parked on the perimeter track and themselves walk on it.

   While taxiing out to the take-off point there appeared to be a
gale blowing from the left hand side. I applied full right rudder and
high revs on the engine, but with right brake on and stick back to
hold the tail down I still could not control the tendency of the large
wing to turn into wind like a weathercock. As I say, it did this
twice on the perimeter track, much to my embarrassment and each
time I was forced to keep it turning and complete the circle in
order to get straight again. I have never felt more helpless in an
aeroplane. After getting to the take-off point I noticed that I was
sweating, despite the coolness of the day. Flying the aircraft was
easy. It had a very short take-off run since it had been designed to
operate as an artillery spotter and thus to get in and out of small
fields. With a gale blowing to give added airflow over the wings it
seemed to be airborne as soon as I got it headed into wind and
fully opened the throttle. I climbed away, went crosswind to 1,000

feet, then turned onto the downwind leg. The airfield was streaking past. The wind gave fifty miles an hour extra ground speed. But I managed to get the thing around the circuit and down. Later, I thought of the story a duck hunter once told me, of hunting in a gale. He swore that when he swung his gun on the duck it was heading into the gale but was travelling backwards at twenty knots before his astonished eyes. The aircraft certainly didn't need flaps on landing. I managed to taxi back to Houghton's hut without further ground loops where he greeted me with a smile and a 'Bit breezy, eh? Have some tea?' He had a kettle and a hot plate so we had a nice cup of bulk Lapsang Souchong with sugar and powdered milk. 'Great stuff!', said Houghton sniffing the strong aroma, 'My wife scrounged it somewhere.'

While I'd been airborne he'd found a pen and a scrap of brown paper on which he'd written the date and, 'Certified that I understand the petrol, oil and ignition system and the automatic functioning of the slots and flaps of the Westland Lysander.' I signed it, as did he, and dated it 16 October, 1942.

So we pilots at Morpeth were the orphans and misfits of the Air Force. I never did find out how Gebhard came to be there; a thoroughly sound and competent pilot, I wondered of him, as of so many, where they afterwards went and whether or not they survived.

CHAPTER FOUR

Ready for War

MEANWHILE at Training Command someone looked at a calendar, noticed a file number to be brought forward, requisitioned the file of J 10506 W.R. Thompson and delivered it to the Air Vice-Marshal or to his aide. In any event a signal, no doubt decided upon when I walked from that office, went from Training Command to RAF Station Morpeth.

The Station Commander at Morpeth didn't tell me until after the squash game, 'By the way, Thompson', he said, 'You've been posted – to No. 19 Operational Training Unit, Kinloss.' I almost dropped my racquet from a sweaty hand, 'Where is that, sir? What kind of OTU is that?'

'It's in Scotland', he said. 'It's a good one too. A Bomber OTU'

I heard not another word as I thanked him. He knew my feelings. I thought of my classmates who by now had joined prestigious night fighter units, bomber squadrons and coastal squadrons. Whatever my destiny, it was to be with the British. At Canadian Air Force Headquarters, Lincoln's Inn Fields, London my name was on a large list labelled 'With the RAF'.

After the thousand bomber raids, changes were effected in Bomber Command. The Lancaster bomber now coming into service in increasing numbers was accompanied by a change in crew members. The second pilot who had been carried on all bombers was now considered superfluous, except as a position for training new pilots. He was replaced by a flight engineer, usually a trained engine mechanic. The Battle of the Atlantic was at a critical stage and bombers in 1942 were diverted in large numbers to assist in the sea war by mining German and French ports and by flying anti-submarine patrols.

The inaccuracy of bombing had resulted in the formation on August 15, 1942 of the Pathfinder Force, a group whose function was to locate and mark targets at night for the main force of bombers following after them. This group was comprised initially of four squadrons; No. 7 Squadron equipped with Stirlings, 35 Squadron with Halifaxes, 83 and 156 Squadrons with Lancasters, all of them four engined bombers and 109 Squadron equipped with the fast twin-engined Mosquito. The Pathfinder Force took time to get organised under Air Vice-Marshal D.C.T. Bennett and to acquire radar navigation and bombing aids and also to replace the Stirlings with Lancasters. But the Pathfinder policy soon began to have an effect. Coloured target indicator flares were developed and by late 1942 bombing accuracy began to improve. Strangely, Air Marshal Harris had opposed the formation of an elite target marking force but in this he was overruled by the Air Staff. Pathfinder crews, since it took time to develop their expertise, were asked to do two tours of operations without a rest between them. Their Squadron Commanders were of Group Captain rank rather than Wing Commander and their Flight Commanders were of Wing Commander rank rather than Squadron Leader. Their crew members after twenty operations were permitted temporarily to wear the Pathfinder badge, a small golden eagle on the flap of their left tunic pocket.

About one man in three on the average of all bomber aircrew survived thirty operational flights. If they did survive they were considered to have completed a tour and were taken off operations and assigned instructor or other non-operational duty for a period of six months to a year. About six to seven thousand bomber aircrew of all trades undertook a second tour, normally of twenty operations and some a third before the war ended. Generally, the same attrition rate applied to them. If they went straight on to a second tour after the first, as did Pathfinder aircrew, the second tour was considered complete after forty-five operations, at which time they were permanently awarded the right to wear the Pathfinder badge.

Bad weather restricted bombing activity in November and December of 1942. But even if the weather had been good Britain was not able at this time to launch a massive and sustained bombing assault on Germany, let alone to respond to the call made by Stalin in October for a second front.

In June of 1942 the tide had turned somewhat in the Pacific when the Japanese sustained heavy losses in the great air and sea Battle of Midway. In September the Australians halted the Japanese drive in New Guinea. In September also the Germans were halted at Stalingrad after having taken Rostov, Sevastopol and Kiev and having cut off the Crimea. But as winter came the Russians counter-attacked at Stalingrad. In the Atlantic the battle moved to its worst period of crisis; the Canadian patrol vessel *Raccoon* was sunk and the corvette *Charlottetown* was lost in the Gulf of St.

Lawrence. The Canadian steamship *Caribou* was lost in Cabot Strait with 136 lives. By October 700 lives had been lost in the Battle of the St. Lawrence. Freighters were being lost at a crippling rate in the Atlantic. Also in October the British Eighth Army under Montgomery, preceded by a 24-hour artillery barrage, launched an attack against Rommel at El Alamein which was to become the African turning point. I wondered where my friends of the 34th Armoured Brigade were now; pursuing the Africa Korps no doubt.

On October 20th I boarded the London Midland Scottish train for Edinburgh and thence North to Inverness and Kinloss. Here was a large, bustling air force station completely equipped with hangars, machine shops and all the necessary support buildings and staff for an operational station, which indeed it was on occasion for attacks upon the *Tirpitz*, lying in the Norwegian fjords, and German port installations.

As a bomber operational training unit Kinloss was supported by a satellite airfield a few miles east at Forres. The aircraft in use were the Armstrong-Whitworth Whitleys, powered with two of the early Rolls Royce Merlins of 1230 horsepower each. These elderly bombers had had their day in the early raids, dropping leaflets in 1940 and bombs in 1941 and were now removed from operations and used for training. Long and slim with twin tails they flew nosedown like hounds on the scent. We were to find that they handled easily and gently.

Arriving alone and a day or two after everyone else as a result of an administrative mix-up, I found myself in the midst of a group of eleven Australian pilots and sixty other crew members, mostly of British nationality. I quickly learned that the Australians, who were excellent pilots were about to launch a mutiny. They clearly and loudly despised the English station commander, one Group Captain Jarman, a stern disciplinarian. What he had done to arouse their anger was not clear to me but when I arrived they were in the process of asking permission to send a delegation of two to Australian headquarters in London to complain. Jarman wouldn't let them go. So they telephoned their Inspector-General in London who was soon on his way to Kinloss to see what the complaints were about. Part of it I know had to do with making them form up and march in a parade every morning. This they regarded as an indignity to fighting airmen. I didn't like Jarman either but wasn't going to let a stern commander interfere with the elation I felt at leaving Morpeth-in-the-Mud. Soon the incident ended and we all got to work.

A bomber crew at Kinloss was to consist of a pilot, navigator, flight engineer, bomb aimer, wireless operator and gunner. The pilot was the captain, or so he thought. Frequently major decisions were made by consensus but because the pilot was at the controls final decisions were ultimately his, irrespective of his rank. The navigator's duties were obvious but not always simple, he worked at a table keeping his air plot, completely surrounded by curtains so as not to let out even a portion of the tiny lights over the table. While over Britain he had ample radio navigational aids, one of which was a grid called 'Gee'; I suppose this represented the surprise most navigators felt when it showed them where they were. We were later to find over Europe that 'Gee' was useless because it was jammed by the Germans. Other crew members, chiefly the bomb aimer had to assist the navigator, if they could, by identifying coastlines and landmarks. The bomb aimer, in the final stages of a bombing run, guided the aircraft and told the pilot where to steer. On most bombers he also had to man the front turret with its two machine guns. The wireless operator received signals, though he seldom broke radio silence to send them. He had to obtain radio fixes and was a general handyman and look-out for fighters through the astro-dome. The air gunners were of course trained in air firing and aircraft recognition.

These diverse people met for the first time at an OTU to sort themselves out into crews. This was left to be done informally. I was assembled with everyone else in a briefing room where I was anxious first to secure a good navigator. The crewmen at first gathered themselves in groups according to their trades. I asked two likely looking sergeant navigators if they were yet crewed up, indicating that I didn't want a married man in my crew. You could tell what their trades were by their aircrew badges. One was married, so after my remark about married men he didn't want me either. The other one talked with something of an English plum in his mouth. I knew without being told that he'd been unable to become a pilot and had become a navigator as second choice. He turned out to be an excellent navigator, too good in fact. After our crew had existed a month they broke us up, saying, 'We need a strong navigator to build up another crew.' It remained to select a wireless operator and a bomb-aimer but a wireless operator from

Northumbria, or a 'Geordie' as they were called, somehow selected me; he was a sergeant and his name was Andy Wilkes. It remained for us to select a bomb aimer. Apparently Wilkes had already teamed up with a short redheaded sergeant with a small moustache and a frayed and sloppy uniform topped with nicotine stained fingers. I wasn't too certain of him and asked if I could see his logbook. I leafed through it, not seeing any proficiency assessments and asked him his name. 'Hanratty is my name', he said, belligerently avoiding the use of the word 'sir'. I said, 'Fine Hanratty, would you join my crew?' 'Just a moment he said in a strong Scottish accent, 'Let me see your log book.' He rolled the 'r' in 'your' and pronounced book 'bewk'. Taken a little aback I handed the book to him and watched him thumb through its pages with yellow fingers. The examination apparently satisfied his pride, if not his curiosity. He handed it back and said, 'All right, I'll come with you but only because you're not an Englishman', again rolling the 'r'. He looked and acted like 'Grumpy' in 'Snow White and the Seven Dwarfs'. I turned to Wilkes and asked, softly, 'What's he got against the English?' Wilkes said, 'Oh, he's just worried that he might have to salute an English pilot and call him sir. He swears he won't do it – and he's afraid he'll be put on charge for refusing to do it. He thinks it will be different with a Canadian.'

'Too bloody true', I said. 'If he doesn't do what I tell him I won't put him on charge. I'll take him out behind the hangar and beat the shit out of him. You can tell him that too.' I was safe in saying this. Hanratty, as I said, was a small man.

We then picked out a flight engineer and a gunner, Sergeant Tolman, a dark-haired, slim, young Londoner. The flight engineer was not with us long as I will later tell. Within a half hour crews had been formed of all those present and each pilot, or captain as he was now called, reported the names of his crew to Jarman. I was pleased that I would not have the additional responsibility of married men in my crew. I wanted no part of worrying about wives and children. As it turned out my crew had fooled me. Three of them, including Wilkes, were married. As the days went by, I and the members of the crew, got to know each other. The first task was for the pilots to learn something about the Whitley, so the pilots took separate lectures from the other crew members and did a few hours training on flying circuits until we could handle the machines. It took only three days to go solo and to learn the emergency procedures such as feathering a propeller and extinguishing an engine fire, single-engined landings, dinghy drill and parachute drill. An instructor, Flight Lieutenant Fenning, a young Englishman, took the Australian sergeant 'Pluto' Wilson and me up at the same time. One of us flew while the other observed.

When the pilots were competent a half dozen crews were sent to the satellite airfield at Forres where our training, now as crews, continued on a grass field. Here we did high level bombing and photography exercises, blind approaches to the airfield, beam flying, low level gunnery and combat exercises with fighters. This was all completed by December 12th. The weather was getting bad when we started night flying on December 13th but we continued unabated. At Forres I met my night flying instructor, Flight Lieutenant Molesworth, inevitably called 'Moley'. Here again was red hair and a moustache but this time the moustache was droopy, the hair thin and the eyes penetrating. A tall man, Moley wore a DFC recently earned on 'ops'. He was a caring man who did his job well. He checked out myself and the Australian Sergeant Desmond Sullivan on night circuits on a grass field. After Sullivan had completed a fine check I began flying, he in the right seat and Moley behind. The air was cold and the Merlins were functioning perfectly. I opened the throttles to the correct boost and revs, got the Whitley airborne, raised the flaps and undercarriage and climbed away precisely at the right boost and revs with trim set accurately and at a correct and steady airspeed. Keeping to the exact rate of climb, altitude, speed and rate of turn I came on to the crosswind leg and levelled off. The night was completely black but each of the luminous instrument hands in the blackened cockpit went to the unwavering and accurate position which it was supposed to assume. It seemed to me to be the best I had ever flown. Sullivan could not contain himself. He fairly exploded, 'You son-of-a-bitch, you can fly!' That was the greatest compliment I ever had in flying.

We now began four and five hour night trips with crew around Scotland and the North of England. The first of these was to Glasgow, east across Scotland to Aberdeen, out over the North Sea and back to Kinloss. Molesworth sat in the right seat, checking the navigation periodically. The night was clear and we could see the moon on the tranquil sea beneath bright stars. I could see from Moley's glances at his watch and at the gyro that he was keeping a mental air plot. On this trip we tried out oxygen equipment for the

first time. At the close of the trip we dropped practice bombs at a
bombing range, came in on a Morse homing approach and landed
in the early hours of the morning two days before Christmas.

*   *   *

On Christmas Eve there was an invitation for some officers to
attend Darnaway Castle, the home of the Earl of Moray, at the
nearby village of Forres. This hamlet with its stone cottages and
rock walls was supposed to have been the home of Macbeth.[1] Three
of us wasted no time in getting our uniforms pressed, buttons
shined and attending at the ancient Moray family seat. A party was
in progress. We were greeted by the 18th Earl and promptly handed
a glass of fine Scotch. We could see and hear the pipes playing in
the ballroom. Ladies in long dresses and some of the younger ones
in tartan skirts were accompanied by men, all of whom except the
Air Force officers were in kilts. Some Army officers wore the kilt
of their regiment with the dress tunic of the Army. Some wore lace
fronts and cuffs on their white shirts. All seemed to wear a sporran
dangling from the waist and a small, sharp dagger or dirk in their
stocking. They danced a wild mêlée called an eightsome reel and
enticed us into doing the same with the 'Gay Gordons'. We joined
in the hooting and yelling as at a square dance. Then we danced a
Sir Roger de Coverley and a Paul Jones, both of which seemed
equally wild and foreign to me. There followed champagne and
food such as must have been saved up in small quantities in war-
rationed Britain. And more dancing! When a young Scottish
woman wishes to dance with you she does nothing so brazen as to
ask you. As the music plays, she takes a station in front of and
facing you and dances a Highland Fling for your sole benefit. No
one, not even so inept a dancer as I, could refuse to dance with a
pretty maiden without injuring her reputation. So dance we did to
the wild music and the equally wild comments of the Scottish
dance critics of both sexes standing by.

In the small hours we arrived back at the station bawling ribald
songs at such volume and pitch as to wake the station. Silent Night
was anything but that but no matter, there was no flying on
Christmas Day even though the Scots did not celebrate it as we did.
They reserved their major celebration for a week later at New Year.

After Christmas, Sullivan and I had two days off and so on one

1. The home of the present Thane of Cawdor, built in the 14th Century, is not far
from the village.

of them it was to Inverness to see a Scottish town. We had a look round and a couple of drinks and started for home but missed the bus back and were forced to hitchhike. This was usually not difficult and we were quickly given a ride by a hospitable Scot who invited us to his home for tea. While sipping this ubiquitous brew and munching a biscuit in his living room I observed on the mantelpiece a photograph of a man who looked familiar. Looking closely I could see that the photographer was 'Stride Studio, New Westminster'. The man in the photo was Sandy Geddes, a relative of my host and a man I knew in New Westminster.

It was getting near the end of the course with only three more cross-country trips to fly. On New Year's Eve the weather looked bad again with the wind strong from the North. We had an evening meal in the mess and I dressed in warm battle dress and flying boots and walked by the officers' lounge. There in front of the fireplace was an Air Vice-Marshal with a tankard of ale in his hand. I was informed that he was a fellow Canadian, Air Vice-Marshal Collishaw, on an inspection tour of Kinloss. So this was the famous Raymond Collishaw of WWI, victor of sixty-two air battles. Since he was in the RAF rather than the RCAF he was not wearing 'Canada' badges. The blond hair was now grey and the face no longer thin but its angles were unmistakably his. He had been raised at Nanaimo on Vancouver Island where he'd become a teenage officer on coastal steamers. As I was leaving he pointed out the window. It was getting dark and he said. 'Watch out for snow. It doesn't look good.'

This was one cross-country upon which we embarked superbly. Take off and climb to altitude, oxygen on, all equipment functioning, we set course confidently for the Isle of Man in the Irish Sea. We arrived on schedule, circled a flashing Morse beacon and headed east to Edinburgh. It was very cold but we arrived on time skirting the known location of the protective balloons over the city. And now we set course north up the east coast of Scotland to Moray Firth. It started to snow at twelve thousand feet. The old Whitley, we were told, wouldn't go above 15,000 feet, although I'd never tried it. As we continued north we approached the large coastal indentation running east-west that leads inland to Kinloss. We headed inland a little and now were above the Scottish mountains. The snow became heavy; I began to let down and lose excess altitude. Glancing at the altimeter I saw that it was stuck, this was cause for alarm. Then the air speed indicator stopped functioning. For a second I was frightened but I knew the problem. Despite their heaters being fully on, the pitot head and the static head had clogged with moisture and had frozen. We would have to judge our forward speed by engine boost and revs. The artificial horizon and directional gyro were working however. I asked Wilkes the wireless operator, to contact Kinloss and get a course to steer to base. But the voice transmitter-receiver was not functioning. He tried in Morse code and sighed with relief as an answer came back. At Kinloss they took a bearing from our Morse transmission and gave us a course to steer. I told Wilkes to keep transmitting and get corrections to the course as frequently as he could. It was strange trying to fly blind without two of the most important flight instruments. I felt crippled. It was particularly bad without an altimeter. Oh well, we'd need sharp eyes as we let down. I asked everyone who could to look below. They could see nothing and I could see nothing. Then I noticed feverish activity from the flight engineer. He was getting at the back of the instrument panel with a small flashlight from underneath it; he had a knife in his hand and he yelled, 'I'm cutting away the tube at the back so the altimeter can get air.'

Now why hadn't I thought of that? 'Good man', I yelled. Almost immediately the altimeter started to function. The cockpit of course was not pressurised. I could do without an air speed indicator; I judged our forward speed by engine boost and revs and we let down. Wilkes said, 'Steer 270° now.' We had apparently reached Moray Firth so I swung from a northerly to a westerly course on the directional gyro. I said, 'Tell them to give us a course which will take us to the north side of the Firth. Then they can bring us in on a southerly heading to the airfield,' – which was on the south side of the Firth. They did this and I changed heading slightly north of west accordingly. Soon we were getting corrections to the heading at more frequent intervals as Kinloss kept taking our radio bearings and feeding courses back to us to steer; I periodically re-set the directional gyro. The base at Kinloss now estimated our distance as thirty miles and so informed us. All of this in Morse Code. All the while the snow was hitting us in big flakes. It was pitch black outside and still we could see nothing. Then the starboard engine, despite carburettor heat, stopped functioning. 'Goddamit, ice', I thought as I opened the throttle of the port engine fully to compensate; 'Probably should have run the engine at top speed in the snow – yet no one had said we should. Oh well, if one lives, one learns.' The engineer tried to free the right engine with throttle, and changes of pitch control. He tried feathering and unfeathering the propeller and shutting off the engine and trying to get it going with the windmilling propeller. No good, it refused to function.

The snow was still falling and despite glycol on the windshield, visibility was bad. I opened the side window a crack and was met by a monstrous blast of air – it seemed a necessary precaution in order to see. Wilkes said, 'They say we should be able to see the airfield.' Thank God for the altimeter. It said that we were now at 800 feet. We were over water; I hoped it was reliable. We couldn't see the sea. I swung on to a southerly heading – if we missed the airfield now we would almost certainly run into the mountains. The good port engine was roaring. We could see nothing. On and on we flew. Suddenly a film of blue lights appeared below, to starboard, barely visible through thin cloud. God, what a relief; it was the airfield. Because of the mountains I decided, contrary to the proper procedure, to do a turn to starboard on the good port engine. I knew I could do it if I was careful; I was glad Moley had taught us single-engine flying. The rest was easy. I could now see white lights as well – against the snow on the ground. We got the gear down and finally ourselves down with no further surprises.

Both Hanratty and Wilkes jumped out, kissed the ground and whooped like Indians when we rolled to a stop not far from the Control Tower. We couldn't taxi on one engine.

'That shows a hell of a lot of confidence in your pilot', I said. 'Kissing the ground like savages.' My remark had no effect at all. They were too happy. I was too of course and could have kissed Wilkes but thought better of it – we were now a crew and I was proud of them.

Upon landing I found that we were the only crew of five that took off who completed the trip. One had run into the Isle of Man and was lost with all crew; one had tangled with the balloon barrage at Edinburgh and was forced down with the crew being lost; two had landed away. Our casualties were worse than operations. On reaching the Mess I saw Air Vice-Marshal Collishaw, apparently unmoved from in front of the fireplace, still with the tankard in his hand. 'Well son, rough trip, eh?' he said. I knew that he was aware of the details of the homing assistance Kinloss had given us and of the difficulties we'd had. He had come to the lounge to greet me on our return but of course wouldn't say so.

* * *

This experience with the Whitley left me with a lasting affection for these old machines and with an abiding faith in one of every two Rolls Royce Merlin engines.

We quickly completed our remaining cross-country flights on January 1st, 2nd and 3rd, flying trips of approximately five hours duration on each of these nights. Each trip ended with a bombing exercise, simulating as nearly as possible actual operating conditions. On the last of these we carried for the first time live 250 lb bombs and watched them explode on the bombing range. I now had a grand total of 300 flying hours as a pilot and had been through at least two periods where I thought I knew most of what there was to know about flying.

After breakfast on January 4th I walked to the flight office at the edge of the field to enter up the flying of the previous five days in my log book. Much to my surprise Moley had done the entries for me, 'Had to get it finished Thompson and signed by the CO because you're leaving soon.' He handed the book to me. I said goodbye, shook his hand and left the office, not wanting to open the book in his presence. On reaching the outside however, I quickly opened it to see what assessment had been given to me. It said, 'Assessment of Ability as a Medium Bomber Pilot – Above average.' I was pleased; if we could embark upon the final stages of training with a good assessment we might get to a good squadron.

But the Air Force had other ideas. 'You have become soft and out of condition,' it said to us. 'We are sending you on a short course at an army combat school to toughen you up.' Would the training never end? We again traversed the length of England by train to a place called Barkstone in Kent, where there was an army commando training school. You undoubtedly know the sort of thing that was taught, every day useful things like bayoneting a dummy, running obstacle courses, jumping mud holes, road work, being shot at and missed by a skilled machine gunner, dummy bombs going off, crawling through pipes, soccer and calisthenics. After ten days of this I agreed with the Air Force. I was in atrocious condition and much to my chagrin Wilkes, who was a skilled soccer player, could run rings around me.

Then the value of all this physical activity was quickly lost; we got two weeks' leave. My crew raced to their respective homes in Britain, 'Goodbye, Skipper, see you soon. Have a good leave.' What did a Canadian do? Well, he certainly wasn't going home so he went where he felt most at home; I went to Bournemouth. I spent two days in London seeing the sights and rubbing elbows in bars with other servicemen, then to Bournemouth to see Jean Gaffikin. She meanwhile, perhaps on impulse, had joined the Women's Air Force; so that was that. I whiled away the time swimming in the large indoor pool and dancing at the afternoon tea-dances.

It wouldn't be long now. On January 29th, 1943 we reported to No. 1660 Lancaster Conversion Flight at Swinderby, Lincolnshire, near Newark. Here we picked up another gunner, Sgt. Kelly, a fair-haired, pink-cheeked English lad, to man the mid-upper turret. We were excited at the prospect of training on the Lancaster, the best and newest of the four-engined bombers. We were there about five weeks, first learning to fly the Manchester an earlier twin-engined version of the Lanc and then the Lancaster itself. I could see why the Manchester never went into full production. It was powered by two enormous engines, Rolls Royce Vultures, each of which was in fact two 12 cylinder Kestrel engines placed back to back to provide 24 cylinders; this was simply too many cylinders in one group to expect them to function smoothly and they seldom did. The aircraft could not be got above 15,000 feet; it was a failure. Not only that but if you lost part of the engine you lost it all and consequently you lost 50% of the power of the aircraft. I had a flat tyre in a Manchester one day and the fifteen foot, three bladed propeller on that side was so long it almost touched the ground. Spreading the power between four engines, as was done by the Lancaster, was much more efficient. So the Lancaster, a superb design, was conceived almost by accident.

The Conversion Flight was an extension of an operational squadron. In fact until just prior to this the squadrons had carried out their own conversion to type and their own crew training flights. The instructors here were only recently tour-expired operational pilots, anxious to teach Lancaster handling techniques to Squadron standards.

The first time one put a right hand upon four throttles rather than upon two, and opened them fully on take-off to feel the surge of power and the pronounced swing to port from the torque, then straightening this fine aircraft on its take-off run was a memorable experience. One knew as it started down the runway, its four Merlins snarling and tugging at the airframe, that this was an aircraft worthy of one's respect.

Only one incident of note occurred at the Conversion Unit. You have heard people say that they flew an aircraft on two of four engines or upon one of two engines. I became the first person I knew to fly a four engined Lancaster on one engine. I had been flying with an instructor who was showing me the flight characteristics of the aeroplane on two engines. One first throttled back the engine to be shut down and when its propeller was turning slowly, pressed a button which caused the propeller to 'feather', that is for its blades to be angled straight ahead along the line of flight of the aircraft. The flow of air equally over both sides of the blades caused them to stop turning. The engine was thus stopped and its propeller feathered. We carried out approaches with two engines, flew with wheels and flaps down on two and flew at high altitude, did climbing turns, gliding turns and steep turns, all on two engines. Sometimes we flew with one engine on each side, sometimes with two on one side then two on the other. We had about finished the exercises and were flying on the two port engines when the instructor said, 'OK, unfeather the other props'. With index finger I quickly pressed what I thought was the button for the starboard inner engine to unfeather that propeller. You guessed it, I pressed the wrong button. I feathered the good port inner propeller and it stopped. We had only one working. As you can imagine, before that engine was completely dead I was unfeathering both starboard engines and we soon had all four going. But the instructor said when I had finished 'I do not intend to demonstrate single-engine flying to every student.'

We completed the Lancaster conversion course on March 9th, 1943 and since I had been promoted automatically to Flying Officer (1st Lieutenant) some six months previously, I now regarded myself as experienced and ready to 'Smite the Hun'. Unknown to myself I wore from head to foot the armour of ignorance.

CHAPTER FIVE

Neophytes

IF the first seven months of 1942 had been disastrous in the Western Atlantic off the United States and Canada, the ten months from August, 1942 to May, 1943 were equally grim. The oil tankers along the coast of South America were constantly attacked. In the mid-Atlantic, where submarine wolf packs could hunt without fear of landbased aircraft, an estimated 110 U-boats were operating. Eighty-five ships were lost in the first twenty days of March alone. The Battle of the Atlantic was almost lost. But better radar, better anti-submarine weapons, including aircraft carriers that could cover the mid-Atlantic, and better tactics were on the way and would ultimately stem the tide.

Bomber Command in March of 1943 began the use of a new radio aid, code-named 'Oboe', for Mosquitoes of the Pathfinder Force. It gave an indication, by the intersection of two audial beams, of when to release flares and was a very precise target-marking device. Unfortunately its use was limited to short-range targets like the Ruhr. Long-range targets had to be marked by Lancasters of the Pathfinder Force using a ground search radar called H2S, which gave a picture on a tube of the terrain below through cloud. This was first used in January. Not as precise as Oboe, it was a vast improvement over purely visual efforts.

By early 1943 the Bomber situation was as follows:

1 Group was in the middle of changing over from Wellingtons to Lancasters.

2 Group, which did the short-range day bombing, flew Bostons, Venturas and Mosquitoes.

3 Group was operating Stirlings.

4 Group was almost fully equipped with Halifaxes.

5 Group, comprising ten squadrons, was now completely equipped with Lancasters.

6 Group, the Canadian Group, was formed on January 1st, 1943. Its eight squadrons were completing a changeover from Wellingtons to Halifaxes.

There was no *7 Group*.

8 Group, the Pathfinder Group, was now augmented by

a new squadron, No. 405, City of Vancouver Squadron, which came commanded by Johnny Fauquier from 6 Group.

By March 1943 Bomber Command comprised sixty-two squadrons and the full establishment for a squadron had become sixteen aircraft. There were most often two squadrons on one airfield.

*   *   *

As a result of the meeting of Roosevelt, Stalin and Churchill at Casablanca a directive was issued to Air Marshal Harris which instructed him to pursue 'the progressive destruction and dislocation of the German military, industrial and economic system, and the undermining of the morale of the German people to a point where their capacity for armed resistance is fatally weakened.' This of course is what Harris was fully intent upon doing in any event. Bomber Command was ready to commence an assault upon fortress Europe which Harris was later to describe as the 'Main Offensive'. It began with the Battle of the Ruhr which opened on March 5th, 1943 in an attack by 442 bombers upon the Krupp works at Essen. During the Battle of the Ruhr forty-three major attacks were made on German cities in thirty-nine nights. Although many of these were on targets far from the Ruhr the emphasis remained on Ruhr targets marked by Oboe. The Main Offensive lasted for a year until control of Bomber Command was passed to Eisenhower for support of the land assault upon Europe.

The attack on March 5th included 162 Lancasters, twenty-two of which were Pathfinders. But the first red target markers were dropped by Pathfinder Mosquitoes, flying the Oboe beam at 28,000 feet on an arc of almost north-south heading until the flare release point was reached. The release was triggered by the intersecting east-west beam. These beams were called 'cat' and 'mouse' and like television signals did not curve with the earth's surface. Consequently the farther one was away from the transmitters the higher one had to be to receive the signals. The operational ceiling of the Mosquito being about 32,000 feet placed a limit upon the range of the device. Although there were two sets of Oboe transmitters in England, each could carry only one aircraft at a time, thus only about one Mosquito every three minutes could mark a target. This they did with red flares and in the intervals between reds the Lancasters of the Pathfinder Force would keep the attack going by dropping back-up flares, coloured green to differentiate them, on top of the reds. The attack on Essen was the first use of Oboe in a major attack, it was a huge success. One might wonder why the Germans never stifled Oboe by jamming it. The fact is that because one had to be on a precise course in a precise location at a fixed time and height in order to receive it, the Germans never did detect it. And only one Mosquito was ever shot down in circumstances which might have betrayed its secret. Surprisingly, General Galland, Chief of the German fighter forces, in a book written after the war called *'The First and the Last'* was still not aware of Oboe. As will appear later, the writer's Squadron, flying Lancasters, shared an airfield with the Oboe Mosquito aircraft of 109 Squadron whose crews were sworn not to reveal to anyone, including ourselves, its secret; I only learned of it by deduction from remarks they made.

And so it happened that on the 11th day of March 1943 Flg. Off. Walter R. 'Punch' Thompson, RCAF, twenty-two years of age and freshly converted to Lancasters, arrived at RAF Station, Syerston in Nottinghamshire. I remember the young man with amusement and affection. Kit bags in hand I lumbered into the mess in the mid-afternoon of an overcast day. There were but two officers in the mess. The Wing Commander with the DSO, DFC and Bar must, I thought, be CO of 105 Squadron. The other, the flight lieutenant, must be his adjutant. He seemed the friendliest wing commander I ever met. Not a tall man but firmly and squarely made, his smile lit up the day.

'You must be Thompson', he said walking across the room and extending a strong hand. Before I could acknowledge he said, 'My name is Gibson, will you have a drink?' 'Thank you sir, a half of bitter would be fine.' The barman drew a glass as Gibson turned to the adjutant and I heard him say, 'Maybe he'll be another Joe McCarthy.' I had met McCarthy during my incarceration at Grantham, where he had landed one day. He was from New York. I forgave Gibson for blurring the distinction between Canadians and Americans. He said, 'You're just in time, you'll be flying tonight.' I hoped he hadn't seen me gulp as I asked, 'With my own crew, sir?'

'No you'll be coming with me, so get yourself settled in and I'll see you at briefing.' I had only a sip of the beer.

The target turned out to be Stuttgart. Gibson introduced me, in the Nissen hut which served as intelligence office and briefing room, to Scrivener his navigator and, strangely I thought, to a naval officer, Sub-Lieut. Jess, who was to be our bomb aimer. I also met the overgrown menace that was Gibson's dog. He was a huge black mutt with a white chest and appeared to be mostly Labrador retriever; he was reputed to deflate bicycle tyres with one bite and I was warned by one of the gunners to treat him with respect.

It occurred to me at briefing that notwithstanding the expensive training which His Majesty had lavished on me, no one had told me, or anyone else as far as I knew, the duties of a second pilot. I knew that they'd have very little to do with the success of the operation because there was but one set of controls in the Lanc. When I enquired what those duties were, Gibson too seemed a little puzzled. Fishing in a briefcase however he soon found a form called a fuel log. 'Here, you keep this', he said. It seemed to me that he'd written that job description on the spur of the moment. He went on, 'You keep a log of fuel consumption. Take readings from the gauges and write them down every half hour. And change the fuel tanks when I ask you to.' I put the form in the pocket of my battle dress.

We took off and climbed 'X-Ray' (ED649) into the night without event. The visibility was good above the cloud and I felt secure in the company of experts as we approached the French coast. For a few moments we witnessed a phenomenon which was new to me. Twinkling little lights were appearing some distance ahead on the starboard bow. I wondered what they were. Gibson, sensing my naïveté pointed to a long black shadow down off the nose on the starboard side. 'Enemy coast', he said. 'Flak – probably Cherbourg.' How could anything so deadly look so pretty I wondered? It was like Halloween. A few moments later we crossed the enemy coast and I saw one of those twinkles at closer range. It hit our starboard outer engine with a thump.

My immediate reaction as Gibson throttled the engine back was, 'Well, I suppose we'll be heading for home now. It does seem a pity but *c'est la guerre*.' But he didn't feather the engine and to my surprise said to the bomb aimer, 'We'll probably have to attack from below 15,000 feet, bomb aimer. Any problems?' 'No problem, sir', was the Royal Navy's answer.

'Well, let's have a course, Scriv', he asked the navigator.

The good visibility we had enjoyed changed abruptly as we lost altitude. I didn't have to ask Gibson, I knew that if we were going to be isolated we should seek cloud cover, even though it was pitch black outside.

This we did, gradually dropping to 12,000 feet and continuing to fly in cloud. We soon entered upon the bomb run over Stuttgart. It appeared a lively, well-lit but smoky place to this neophyte. I was intrigued at the sight of my first target. Vastly different from the old bombing range, I thought. Although we'd lost altitude we had managed to keep our speed. I could see Gibson applying left rudder as the starboard-outer was now virtually useless. The Navy, after some chit-chat, got the bombs away nicely. Or as I put it to myself, 'It's nice that he got the bombs away.'

I was examining the bombed area for remnants of target indicator flares when we were hit again. This time it was the starboard inner. Gibson asked me to feather the propeller which I quickly did, careful to select the correct one. By now I was convinced that if this sort of thing happened every time out I should have tried very much harder to be a night-fighter pilot.

Our load diminished by loss of the bombs we seemed to be making reasonable speed, though with only two engines, on the return journey. Gibson, even with full rudder trim, was working hard with left rudder to keep a straight course. He leaned over and said, 'Thompson, how much fuel do we have?' I looked at the gauges and blurted out, '400 gallons, sir'. 'Hm', he said, 'Barely enough to make the Channel. Are you sure? What does your log show?'

I was appalled. How could I tell him – 'I put the log in my pocket with a chocolate bar, sir. I can't read it. It's got chocolate all over it.'! I thought, 'My God, if we go down in the Channel it's all my fault. And if we don't I'll probably be shot.' I could hardly bring myself to look at him but when I did I could see the twinkle in his near eye. I quickly read the fuel gauges again. I'd only read the total shown on four gauges – 400 gallons. There were six fuel gauges in all, two below the other four and I had missed the lower two. Gibson knew what I'd done – in a four-engined aircraft one tends to look in fours. I thought to myself, 'Really, I'm not this incompetent, I won't do these stupid things when I am flying with my own crew', and with a few hair-raising exceptions this later turned out to be true.

Gibson by this time was having leg strain from holding on rudder with his left leg. Although the Lanc was designed to fly feet off with full rudder trim, on two engines, it never quite seemed to do so. He asked me to fly 'X-Ray' for a while. This I did as we changed seats and I bent my good left leg to the task of keeping her straight with rudder. We hared back over France at low level. Light was beginning to show in the east.

Gibson took control again over the Channel and we soon came in for the landing at Syerston. I noted somewhat smugly that even the squadron commander did not invariably land his aircraft like a feather. In fact our landing was more in the nature of a controlled crash. Gibson's grin was sheepish as he taxied to the dispersal area. His faithful black hound was there waiting impatiently for him to deplane. Intelligence officers were waiting for the rest of us to interrogate. I gathered, from listening to the crews and to the intelligence officers, that a large number of fires had been started in the southern part of the city and that these had eventually merged together into one large fire. This sounded exaggerated to me but I knew that the main industry of Stuttgart was precision engineering, with the Bosch plant making magnetos, spark plugs, fuel injection pumps and engine accessories and I hoped that it had been hit. It turned out later that the attack had not been successful and little damage was done.

The next day we had a 106 squadron photo taken and shortly thereafter Gibson let it be known that he had been asked to form a 'special duties' squadron. the details of which were still secret. He had at this time completed seventy-two bombing operations and 200 hours on night fighters. I understand that the Bar to his DSO was awarded to him for his efforts on the Stuttgart trip and his fine work on many others.

Some months later, when we had almost completed a tour of operations, we heard the great news of Gibson's 'Dam Busters' having breached the Möhne and Eder dams. We heard also with delight that he had been awarded the Victoria Cross. He was killed a year and a half later at the age of twenty-six.

When I saw them next day my crew were full of questions. 'What was it like? Where is Stuttgart? How was the weather? Did you hit the target? What kind of crew does Gibson have? What do target indicators look like?' I answered as best I could. 'It was quite interesting. The weather was so-so. I don't know what we hit. Gibson has a good crew. Not as good as you fellows though.' Big grins all around. 'The TI's are bright greens and reds – really spectacular! They explode in mid-air and cascade like a waterfall. But I didn't see any close up.'

*   *   *

Wilkes informed me that the crew were now settled comfortably in the sergeants quarters and Hanratty had been ticked off by the Station Warrant Officer for slovenly dress. I answered, 'For Christ's sake drag him over to stores and get him a new pair of pants. The bottoms of those are so frayed he's a disgrace'. Hanratty, his first name was Pete, heard what I said and let out a flourish of rolling 'r's. 'If eve-ry one wor-re their-r battle dr-ress as long as I the countr-ry would pr-rofit by a million poonds a year-r.'

I had heard of frugal Scots and had, like most people, passed off the remarks about their closeness of purse as prejudice. Hanratty was living proof that the stories were not always exaggerated. Wilkes said in his presence. 'Money is a one way street with him. When he opens his purse the moths fly out. He never carries paper money – only silver.' Tolman, the rear gunner, said, 'Yes and he hasn't bought much ruddy beer yet either.'

Hanratty changed the subject, 'Are you expecting another shipment soon of those Sweet Caporal cigarettes? I like them better than these crappy Woodbines. I swear they put saltpetre in them.' He was smoking, as always. Kelly the mid-upper said, 'I saw him the other day without a shirt on and he's got nicotine up to his elbow.' The London-born navigator said, 'Why don't we all have a beer now? You can be our guest in the Sergeants' Mess.'

Wilkes interrupted. 'They don't like it you know. It makes the senior sergeants and flight sergeants uncomfortable. Officers are not supposed to enter the Sergeants' Mess.' He looked worried. He was right. I thanked them and said, 'We'll all have a drink in a day or two in the local – after our first operation as a crew.' That was a promise.

In March of 1943 the air defence of Germany was based upon the well established and efficient Kammhuber line, a system of radar and radio surveillance and fighter control.

The first indication the Germans had of an impending bomber attack was from the *Nachtrichtentruppe*, the signal service under the control of the Luftwaffe. This service could detect transmissions from navigation equipment and from wireless operators testing their equipment on the Night Flying Test made by every bomber during the day preceding a night operation. Thus a warning could be obtained that a raid was pending, or at least possible.

In the evening, just before darkness, bombers would take off in great numbers for the night and would, on short-range trips, circle over their own bases to gain altitude before heading towards

Europe. If they took off and flew on a direct line to the European coast they would gain altitude as they approached Europe over the sea. In either event they were soon seen on the screens of the long-range radar stations positioned along the West Coast of Europe. These were the *Freya*. For example, there was one at Ostend in Belgium and north of that another at Texel, an island off the Dutch coast; there were others, south in France. When a stream of bombers was seen on these sets they could easily be tracked and their entry point to European air space forecast. Every approach to Germany was monitored by *Freya*.

In addition to the *Freya*, General Kammhuber had set up a chain of radar stations, each covering a smaller area, in a double line along and in from the coast, with a further group around Berlin. These each bore a code-name such as Lobster, Toad, Polar Bear, Bee, Oyster, Viper and many more. The Germans called the Kammhuber line the *Himmelbett* line, meaning heavenly bed or four poster. Each of these covered a box of air space. Each box had a *Freya* which could scan a hundred miles or so and which served to direct two narrow-beam radar sets, called *Würzburgs*, on to the approaching bomber stream. The *Würzburgs* had higher resolution but shorter range than the *Freya*. The fighter controller for the box could pick out a portion of the *Freya* stream, perhaps thirty bombers at about thirty miles, and on one of the *Würzburgs* concentrate on a single aircraft. Meanwhile his second *Würzburg* concentrated on his own night-fighter. The fighter-controller would co-ordinate the two *Würzburgs* and broadcast directions to his night-fighter by radio to bring the displays on the two sets together, much in the same way that a post-war airline flight controller could talk a pilot down to a landing on Ground Controlled Approach. With the interception almost complete the fighter would utilise his own airborne *Lichtenstein* radar set to make visual contact with the bomber. The *Lichtenstein* had a range of about two miles.

Directions to the pilot for an interception went somewhat as follows, with lengthy pauses between transmissions. The voice is that of the controller:

'*Antreten 170* (Steer 170 degrees) – *Kirchturm 43* (Height 4300 Metres) – *Fahren Sie express* (Full Speed) – *2 Lisa* (Turn 20° Port) – *Marie 9* (Range 9000) – *Kirchturm 42* (Height 4200)-*Marie 8* (Range 8000) – *1 Lisa* (10 degrees Port) – *Marie 5.5* (Range 5500) – *1 Lisa* (10 Degrees Port) – *Marie 4* (Range 4000) – *Marie 2*

(Range 2000) – *Halten* (Slower) – *2 Rolf* (20 Degrees Starboard) –
Noch mehr halten (More Slowly) – *Salto Lisa* (make a complete
circle to port) – *Antreten 150* (Steer 150 Degrees) – *Marie 4* (Range
4000) – *Marie 3* (Range 3000) – *Antreten 110* (Course 110) –
Marie 1 (Range 1000) – *Genau vor Ihnen* (Right in front of you) –
Sie sind dicht bei Kurier (You are close to contact).'

The radar operator or pilot of the aircraft would then say '*Wir
Beruhren. Bitte warten* (We are in contact, stand by).'[1]

In a minute or two if the controller heard, '*Pauka! Pauka!*' he
would know that there had been a burst of exploding cannon shells
and the bomber had been shot down. An interception of this kind
might cover a distance of fifty miles and take fifteen minutes to
complete, during which time, since only one interception at a time
could occur in each box, it was purely a matter of probability
which of the thirty bombers seen by the *Freya* was picked out by
the controller for interception on the *Würzburgs*. The remainder
got through unscathed. Obviously from the point of view of the
bombers it was best to put as many as possible through the box in
the shortest time. Those crews having the better navigational skills
had a better chance of getting through, for if one strayed off course
into an otherwise unused box he would be inviting the attention of
a controller with a night fighter at his disposal. There were
obvious limitations to this system; it depended entirely on radar
and didn't fully utilise the number of aircraft and crews available.
The system was to change adversely for the Germans in the
summer of 1943 when the *Würzburg* sets were rendered
ineffective by the jamming device 'window'.

The aircraft used for night fighters by the Luftwaffe were
primarily the Messerschmitt 110, twin engine fighter and the
Junkers 88, a converted twin engine bomber, although some Dornier
217 bombers had also been converted to the job. The Me 110 was
the faster with a speed of 350 MPH at 23,000 feet but the Junkers
88 had much longer range and larger load capacity and ultimately,
with modifications, became faster than the 110. Each of these types
shot down bombers by the hundreds. The armament varied but a
typical one was five 7.9 mm machine guns and two 20 mm cannon.

The German night fighter organisation was based upon the
Staffel, about nine aircraft. This was somewhat different from that

1. This is a transcript of a successful interception quoted by Martin Middlebrook
in his book The Battle of Hamburg, the translation and decoding are his and it is
quoted with his kind permission.

of the day fighters. The basic daytime unit was the *Rotte*, a fighter pilot and his wingman. Two of these pairs made up a s*chwarm* and three *schwarm* a *staffel*. Thus a day fighter *staffel* contained about 12 aircraft. A *Gruppe* contained three or four *Staffel* and there were usually three *Gruppen* in a *Geschwader*. So a night fighter *Geschwader* would contain about ninety aircraft. The Luftwaffe had five *Geschwadern* for night fighter operations at this time, each designated and numbered as a *Nachtjagdgeschwader* (NJG), followed by its identifying number.

Some night fighter pilots ran up impressive scores of British bombers. With heavy traffic through their boxes, both controllers and crews became adept at interception and attack. In March of 1943 the leading German night fighter pilot with a score of fifty was Werner Streib of NJG 1, 'the mother of German night fighter units', flying from airfields in Holland.

A glaring omission at this time on the part of the Germans was their failure to develop a strong force of intruder fighters. Such fighters flying stealthily over England at low level during congested landing conditions after a bombing operation would have created havoc among the returning bombers.

In the spring of 1943 another German fighter pilot was about to pass Streib in '*Abschuss*' or 'shot-down' aircraft. He was Heinz Wolfgang Schnaufer whose first 'shot-down' occurred in June, 1942. By August, 1943 Schnaufer's score was twenty. Stationed at Saint-Trond in Belgium his score by the end of the war numbered 121.[1] Helmut Lent with NJG I had a score of 110 before being killed in a flying accident in 1944. And there was Heinrich, *Prinz* von Wittgenstein, who flew Ju 88s in NJG 2. He was killed trying to land a Ju 88 after an operational flight in which it had been damaged, in January, 1944; he had shot down eighty-four bombers. These men of course flew out of the busy boxes; the less experienced pilots for whom there was no available box were permitted to freelance. Ultimately about twenty-five German night fighter crews shot down over fifty bombers each.[2]

The command upward from the *Geschwader* went to the Division and then to the *Korps*. There were seven Fighter Divisions

1. Schnaufer was killed in 1950 while driving his Mercedes on a French highway. Further information on this German night fighter pilot see the biography *Schnaufer*, published by Crécy, 1997.

2. See *Duel Under the Stars*, by Wilhelm Johnen, The *History of the German Night Fighter Forces*, by Gebhard Aders. Both published by Crécy.

in two *Korps* for the defence of Germany from the West, the 1st Division being Berlin, the 2nd Northwest Germany and Denmark, the 3rd Holland and West Germany and so on counter-clockwise through the 4th in Belgium and North France, the 5th and 6th in France and the 7th in South Eastern Germany back to Berlin.

The ground defences of the German cities were in the hands of the flak and searchlight units which were concentrated around the cities. These could put up an extraordinary display and always managed to account for some of the attacking force. There were at this time some 20,000 anti-aircraft guns and 6,000 searchlights deployed in the West. It was estimated that close to a million people were required to man them. The bulk of the effective fire was carried out by the all-purpose 88 mm gun batteries controlled by a *Würzburg* radar set but 105 mm and 128 mm guns controlled in the same way were used as well and there were always batteries of 20 mm cannon for low flying aircraft. The number of guns of a heavy calibre, i.e. 88 mm or greater, was placed by Albert Speer to be in excess of 10,000. This represented the total production of the German armament industry from 1941 to 1943, a production which otherwise would have been deployed in the East as anti-tank weapons.

The radar searchlight was a 2 metre 'master searchlight' which, when switched on, was usually directly on a bomber, blinding the crew temporarily by its intense blue light. It was soon joined by other 1.5 metre searchlights which would swing to the same point in the sky. Flak was then directed to the apex of the cone of searchlights. The blue appearance of the 'master searchlight' was due to its greater intensity. The radar controlled flak guns could of course fire without the help of searchlights and a six-gun battery could place an accurate box of shells around a bomber at 20,000 feet. But as the concentration of bombers increased in an attack the hundreds of guns around a city would fire a barrage of shells timed to explode at a pre-determined altitude. This static flak was augmented by 88 mm guns mounted on railway cars whose units were self-sustained and lived on the railways. They moved from one place to another as required to bolster local defences and of course there was competition between the cities for this flak from a common pool. It was not uncommon for a flak battery of six or more guns to account for two or three bombers a month. In the Ruhr valley the cities were close together and the concentration of flak and searchlights was awesome to behold. So also with Berlin and with the Frankfurt-Mainz-Mannheim area. Bomber crews for this reason called the Ruhr. 'Happy Valley' and Berlin, 'The Big City'. In addition to shooting aircraft down, flak compelled them to stay high above the German cities and of course was good for the morale of the civilian population. Flak ships offshore were a particular menace; I shall tell later of one that hit my aircraft.

CHAPTER SIX

The Dangerous Period

106 Squadron was in 5 Group. If you asked the air crews of Bomber Command to list the best groups in the command the greater number would list, after their own, 5 Group and 8 Group (PFF). 106 Squadron shared RAF Station Syerston with 61 Squadron, also of 5 Group. 106 had started with Manchesters but in May 1942 began equipping with Lancasters at Coningsby and in October had moved to Syerston.

The next night after Stuttgart, that is on March 12th, Gibson told me that I would be flying another second pilot trip, this time with Flight Lieutenant Edmonds, an experienced pilot and crew. Edmonds had fair hair and a small moustache and Gibson introduced me to him at briefing. He had completed about twenty operations with 106 Squadron and it was obvious that Gibson had confidence in him. It was characteristic of Gibson that he introduced him. Many Squadron Commanders seemed to have no time for such niceties and would simply have posted one's name on the operations board and left it to the crews to sort themselves out but Gibson, though young for the job of Squadron Commander, had a faint air of WWI about him; because there was a war on was no reason for lapses of courtesy, warmth and modest behaviour. Too, if the operation was to be a dangerous one, Gibson's name would head the flying list. He talked and acted easily and with confidence. Hemingway once described this quality as 'grace under pressure' but grace under pressure is a paltry quality; I have seen it in tomcats as well as in bullfighters. In Gibson's case the trait was more one of character than physique. Perhaps as his group commander said of him, Gibson was simply 'head prefect' wherever he went.

At briefing the target was announced by drawing a curtain from in front of a large map of western Europe. The ribbon on the map, showing the intended route, stretched straight from Syerston, east and a little south across the North Sea to the Ruhr. The target was Essen. An excited buzz went through the crews. Someone said 'Happy Valley'. Someone else groaned, 'Not again!'

I have so far said little about bombs. They are an unsavoury subject. I never failed to shudder at the name 'anti-personnel bomb'. Imagine someone sitting down at a drawing table and designing a bomb expressly for use against people. I imagined the task being delegated to the duller members of the armament design team, with its leaders saving for themselves the complexities of armour piercing bombs. Having suffered a court's judgement in getting to an operational squadron I was determined to drop bombs, as far as possible, upon obviously military targets.

Depending upon the target and the role the squadron was to play, the bomb load might vary from fourteen 250 pound or 500 pound bombs to a single 8,000 pounder. The Lancasters were all fitted to carry the 4,000 pound bomb and most of them could carry the 8,000 pounder. Later on they were fitted to carry special bombs of 12,000 and 22,000 pounds. The purpose of all these bombs was to smash and burn buildings even if their inhabitants were all in air raid shelters.

The smaller bombs were of various types, armour piercing, semi-armour piercing and general purpose and they were of low, medium or high capacity. Low Capacity bombs had a small charge to weight ratio and consequently penetrated before exploding. High Capacity bombs had a high charge to weight ratio and a light casing; these would explode on impact. A typical load was 1 – 4000 pound (HC) called a 'Cookie', 4 – 500 pound General Purpose bombs and 12 Small Bomb Containers. The latter each contained 8 – 30 pound, or 90 – 4 pound incendiaries.

Bombs were brought by tractor and trailer from the bomb dump, usually a shielded and underground installation, to the aircraft situated around the perimeter of the field at dispersal points. The bomb doors of the aircraft were opened and the bombs wheeled underneath; they were fitted to bomb-carriers which were lowered from the bomb cells of the aircraft and when securely fitted, the fuse setting control was adjusted and the bombs were winched up into the bomb cells. The armourers were careful that a special sequence of loading was maintained for a correct centre of gravity of the aircraft. Rigorous checks were made to ensure that each bomb was held securely and locked in position. The jaws of the bomb-carriers for the 4,000 pound or larger bombs were locked by a lever on the side of the bomb release. During the loading operation this got released once in a while and the bomb would drop on the ground or an electrical fault might cause a premature release. Fortunately when dropped straight down from a short distance the fuse was not activated and the impact was not sufficient to cause an explosion. But inevitably there were accidents and I shall describe in due course one which I observed.

* * *

The day had been fine and bright and the sun was still above the horizon as we took off. The target being a short-range one we had a good weight of bombs and less fuel than was customary. The take-off seemed easy and we climbed in circles over Syerston, examining the ground activity as we did so. An aircraft had burned on the ground that day for reasons unknown to me. Its scorched site was plainly visible. I didn't like sitting in a jump-seat on the right hand side, not nearly as comfortable as in the pilot's seat. At 10,000 feet we set course for the Ruhr, still climbing en route. The sun by now had set but about ten other Lancasters were visible in the gathering darkness, soon to be lost to sight. I watched the ground below before it became obscured. The barely discernible coast of England soon receded from view. As we approached the Dutch coast Edmonds began a series of rolling manoeuvres called 'corkscrewing'. This, in his case, entailed diving slightly, about 10° to one side of one's course, then pulling up an equivalent amount while steering 10° on the other side. Other pilots later described to me their own versions of this technique and no two of them were alike. In Edmonds' case it accomplished a rapid oscillation about a central axis but it would not have been difficult for a fighter to follow and would have had little effect in evading flak. I wished he would stop it as I was beginning to feel the signs of my old nemesis airsickness.[1] We flew this way unremittingly for an hour or so, by which time the nausea was powerful and the result predictable. I knew I was going to be sick. What do you do in order to be sick at 21,000 feet when wearing an oxygen mask? If you take off the mask you will pass out from lack of oxygen. The solution is a compromise; unfasten the mask and throw up in a sick container, breathing as best you can. This I did sheepishly and as unobtrusively as possible; then I was over it and we were approaching Essen on an easterly heading. There was a great deal of illumination from three or four cones of searchlights, each containing thirty to forty searchlights. The apexes of the cones were well ahead of us at about our own altitude. Bombs were now going off below – one could see the rippling shock waves from the

1. I had been airsick on my first 13 flights at Elementary Flying School, before finally conquering the malady by interminably practising tailspins.

explosion of 4,000 pounders across a smoky surface, like ripples from rocks on a pond. Small fires were blazing in the middle, getting larger as one approached. Flak was twinkling with some density ahead at our level. We flew through the smoke puffs left by the exploding shells in the sky; these appeared white at night against the black sky. Then the flickering flashes of the flak got larger. Red target indicators, dropped with an accuracy of 100 yards in clear skies by Oboe-equipped Mosquitoes were clearly visible far below and ahead. We were about to commence our bomb run when I noticed a single blue searchlight, closer than the others, it flicked back and forth across our view in front of our flight path. Then it appeared on my side of the aircraft and flicked across the cockpit, illuminating us as in a strobe light for a fraction of a second. It went by, then back again quickly and the illumination this time stayed in the cockpit; it came in from the sides and up from the bomb-aimer's compartment. There was light all around. We were coned! I watched Edmonds; despite the cold, his forehead glistened with sweat – he was breathing heavily from his oxygen mask and straining against his seat harness as he stared ahead and wrenched the Lancaster into a steep diving turn to starboard. No time to look for other aircraft, which were surely about somewhere. The danger of such a manoeuvre was one of collision but far worse was the danger from the cone of searchlights, for there was now more than one searchlight fastened upon us; I was half blinded. Edmonds continued to dive and to turn for what seemed an eternity. I knew that the flak would be feeling for us but it took a flak shell about 17 seconds from the time of its firing to reach our altitude. Undoubtedly several batteries would now be firing. The eternity stretched to perhaps three minutes of dazzling light and then blessed darkness swallowed us; the lights had slipped off and like a fish slipping away from the fisherman we were free of the hook. I saw the master searchlight flash past again but he missed. I looked at the gyro-compass; Edmonds was swinging round to the heading of the bomb run. Soon we were on the bombing run and in a minute or so I felt the bombs leaving their stations.

When we returned to Syerston we found that one aircraft from 106 Squadron had not returned. It was R5749 captained by F/Sgt. A.L. McDonald, an Australian. Out of an attacking force of 457 aircraft, twenty-three were missing and sixty-nine had been damaged. We had several shrapnel holes in the tail.

Apparently further severe damage to that inflicted on March 5th was done to the Krupp works. Two of the largest workshops which had escaped damage on the previous raid were destroyed. Large fires in the centre of the works were still burning the next afternoon when a reconnaissance aircraft took photographs. Bomber Command had been trying for months to strike a crippling blow to this strongly defended target but it was not until these two raids, marked by Oboe, that this was accomplished. Of some 600 acres of the Krupp works over half of the buildings had been seriously damaged.

We had been in the air 5 hours and 25 minutes, a short trip.

* * *

Between March 12th and March 22nd the weather was bad over Germany and no raids were carried out but I and my crew were not idle. We were told to become operationally ready as a crew as quickly as we could. On March 14th we practised bombing at a range called Whittlesey, near Peterborough. On March 16th we did two hours more practice bombing and a cross-country navigation trip of five and a half hours in daylight. The next day we did the same thing for 6 hours and 45 minutes. On March 20th we did a night navigation exercise of over five hours. We were ready to go on our own to Germany.

The weather was still bad but an operational list was posted on March 22nd. This was it. We would now see what kind of stuff we were made of! The briefing was conducted by my Flight Commander, John Searby, who had completed twenty-two trips and had now been promoted to Wing Commander and given command of the squadron. Gibson had gone to form the special duties squadrons No. 617. I had, of course, asked Gibson if I could go with him to his new squadron but he said that I hadn't yet acquired enough experience. 1 knew he was right but I was disappointed nevertheless.

When the curtain was pulled we saw the ribbon stretching across the map to our first operational target. It didn't get past the French coast. The target was the submarine pens at St. Nazaire. I knew that the submarines were protected by a roof of reinforced steel concrete, twelve feet thick and wondered what damage we could possibly do to them. In addition to the 4,000 pounder we had been loaded with 1,000 pound armour piercing bombs. I suppose the plan was to disrupt the submarine support operations because the 1,000 pounders had been equipped with time-delay fuses. The smaller bombs were to penetrate the support installations when these had been shattered by the blast of the larger bombs but they were not to explode for the various periods set on their time-delay fuses. The ones we were carrying had delays of six, eight and twelve hours and some were to go off on impact; these were going to surprise someone we reasoned. Little did we realise it would be ourselves.

What a pleasure it was to take off with one's own crew. I was confident as I checked the torque from swinging the loaded Lanc on its take-off run. We thundered down the runway; it was a year and ten months since I had entered the recruiting office in Vancouver. Many of my friends had stayed in Canada. Only two or three were in Bomber Command and they were in 6 Group. Out over the sea and down the coast we went. It was pitch black and we climbed through a fog layer to 10,000 feet. There was fog over the whole of the Channel and it seemed to be spreading to England. For most of the way to the target the visibility was poor but as we approached St. Nazaire from the north the sky and ground were clear of haze and the docks stood out clearly. The attack was not to be made as usual from 20,000 feet but from 15,000; it had started and we were about thirty miles away when I first noted the twinkling lights of the flak exploding. We crossed the French coast and I couldn't see very well from 15,000 feet so I brought the Lanc down to 12,000 feet. One should, I argued, obey the attack orders and bomb from 15,000 feet but I was finding out on my first operation that there were many decisions a bomber captain had to make that had not been foreseen in the battle plan. This was the first of many. You may wonder how, when one returned to base, anyone could possibly know the height or the heading one had bombed from or whether or not one had hit the target. The answer lay in a powerful camera situated in the nose of the bomber. When the bomb release mechanism was operated the camera was alerted. At the same time a small projectile, shaped like a bomb and called a photoflash was triggered to leave the fuselage. The photoflash fell at the same speed as the bombs. When it reached an altitude of 4,000 feet it exploded in a flash like a camera flash bulb. The shutter of the camera was timed in a setting made by the bomb-aimer to open at this instant. The exposed film recorded the ground picture just before the impact of the bombs. It was a simple matter for the intelligence staff to determine the position, height and course of the bomber at this point.

While still twenty miles from the flak I noticed a combat between an enemy aircraft and one of our own. Although the combatants were not visible their tracer shells were. First there was a burst of fire downward from our right, ahead about half a mile. This was answered by what appeared to be four or six machine guns upward from the target aircraft. I assumed that the first burst was downward from the fighter and was answered by upward fire from the bomber but it could have been the other way round; the range was too great to tell. The pattern was repeated twice more and if either object was hit I could not tell. It was not repeated again and there was no explosion. We were by this time reaching the target, which Hanratty could see ahead. He armed the bombs from a series of switches on a panel to his right and informed me that he was ready. He then asked for 'Bomb Doors Open'. I moved the bomb door handle with my left hand and felt the doors come open by the increased drag. Then followed the pattern of direction from bomb-aimer to pilot, culminating in his call 'Bombs Gone'. I closed the doors, made a turn to seaward and started back to England. Soon I dropped the Lanc. below 10,000 feet and it was a short run out to sea where we took off our oxygen masks. It was at this point that Hanratty's unmistakable voice called out. 'We've still got a bomb aboard!'

I said, 'How do you know?' and he answered, 'Well I just looked into the bomb bay – you can see it. It's a thousand pounder'.

I asked if he'd checked his release switch. He assured me that both it and the switch panel were in order. We had been drilled for this emergency. I said, 'Stand by; I'll open the bomb doors and we can dive and pull up. Make sure the bomb release switch is on.' I opened the doors and applied two or three extra G's to the aircraft as I pulled out of a steep dive. The bomb refused to budge.

'OK Pete', I said. 'What length of time delay did it have?' There was a pause then 'I know it had a delay but I don't know how long', he answered. 'You don't know? Why don't you know?' I asked. 'They didn't tell us', he said. I was amazed. Here we were carrying an armed bomb the fuse of which had been activated to explode at periods ranging from six to twelve hours from the time we were over St. Nazaire and we didn't know which. I said, 'Pete, can you tell by looking in the bomb-bay which bomb station it's on and get some help from that?' 'Not a chance, I can see which one it's on but that doesn't help,' was the pessimistic reply.

We tried without success to shake loose this reluctant bomb by pulling out from a dive twice more as we headed up the east coast to Syerston. I was wondering about our chances of a belly landing if for some unforeseen reason the landing gear wouldn't lower. But that was remote. I asked Wilkes to contact our base in Morse code and ask for instructions. The answer soon came back, 'Land at Wellesbourne'.

'Navigator', I said, 'Where the hell is Wellesbourne? And what is it?' The navigator located Wellesbourne on a map and gave me a course to steer but he didn't know its function. In two hours we were overhead and given permission to land. We landed without event to be met by a truck and a crew comprised of an armament sergeant and two armourers.

I explained what had happened and offered to open the bomb doors but the NCO said, 'No thanks. We'll handle it, sir'. And he did. I must mention that time-delay bombs were a dreaded thing to all armourers. They were fused with a pistol containing acetone; when the bomb was released an arming vane would rotate in the air and a crusher attached to it would break the acetone ampoules. This would eat through a small disc which in turn would allow a striker to move forward and fire the detonator. The time of the delay was governed by the strength of the acetone and the number of discs. If such bombs were brought back the armourers were much concerned as to whether or not any of the ampoules had broken. They had to look for discoloration of the blotting paper in the pistols, not the most pleasant of early morning pastimes.

We reported to the duty flying officer, the place was an Operational Training Unit and he arranged for a meal and a bed for us. We found while we were eating that an armament officer and the NCO had taken the bomb to a nearby quarry where either it detonated of its own accord or was detonated by them. They never did find out what time-delay it had.

Next morning we were surrounded by a crowd of eager students full of questions as to what it was like 'on ops'. An observer would have noticed that the information that this was our first operational trip was not volunteered to the students, either by myself or the crew. We had a short 50-minute flight back to Syerston.

There was no flying on March 23rd. The weather was poor over the whole of Europe. My crew decided upon a trip to nearby Nottingham. The town of Newark was closer but the aura of

Nottingham was more exciting. We travelled by bus and arrived first at a restaurant rumoured to have steaks on its menu. I knocked on the door, which was locked but by banging on the large brass knocker an attendant was summoned who opened a sliding panel, just like in the movies of a speakeasy. He stared down his nose at this aircrew. I hoped he couldn't see Hanratty. I stated our business and he opened the door and led us to a table.

There we partook of a fine steak meal with an egg on top. I hadn't seen a steak in a year and asked the waiter if they had their own herd of cattle. He said 'It's mammal all right sir but not bovine. It's whale meat.'

'Whale meat?' yelped my crew in unison, trying to adjust their minds to their stomachs. Hanratty was the first to say, 'It's not bad and the pr-rice is r-reasonable.' He took a swallow from his beer glass and cleaned his moustache with a napkin.

The meal completed we moved along the street and around a corner to a pub called 'The Trip to Jerusalem'. Here was a pub, we were told, that had been in continuous operation since the second Crusade. And it looked it. The ceiling was of varying heights not exceeding six feet six inches. The Crusaders were not large we deduced. The beams were blackened by tobacco smoke dating from the time of Raleigh but the beer had been made early that week. We didn't complain but drank a couple of glass mugs of it before heading down another street in search of the dance hall which, we had been told, contained hundreds upon hundreds of young women. We were a little early. There were nine.

But as the evening progressed the clientele increased. It seems that the Players cigarette factory was in Nottingham and a great many young ladies were involved in this vital war effort. Soon we had slipped out for another beer and were back again, happily dancing with pretty young women in bright dresses in a fine, dimly-lit ballroom, complete with a rotating, many-faceted glass ball at the centre reflecting coloured beams from three spotlights on the faces of the dancers. War was hell!

On March 26th the weather was foul. Eleven crews were briefed for a trip to Duisburg. This was an important target in the Rhine-Ruhr area, lying at the junction of the two rivers of those names. The Rhine-Herne canal connects Duisburg with Dortmund from where the Ems canal links it with Emden, the North Sea port. Duisburg has miles of docks and railway sidings, together with extensive heavy industry and chemical factories. The aircraft had been loaded with bombs and fuel and we went out by bus to the dispersal site of the Lancaster which we would be flying. We were standing on the pavement by the aircraft waiting for start-up time, parachutes in hand and smoking a cigarette when a mixture of rain and hail began to fall. Then a strong wind began to blow and it quickly clouded over. I couldn't see the end of the runway; the sky had been grey but was now black. One could almost reach the cloud base with one's hand. It began raining in sheets. I was just about to climb up the ladder on the starboard side of the fuselage when I saw a small van, headlights on, approaching out of the rain. I hesitated, knowing something was amiss and watched Wing Commander Searby and his driver get out of the van. Some of the neighbouring aircraft had started their engines. Searby walked over, 'Thompson', he said, 'You won't be going tonight. We've scrubbed your trip.' This was quite a shock. 'The weather is too bad', he continued. He meant that we hadn't enough experience. I didn't argue because I knew that he was concerned for our safety but I wondered at the reasoning which must have gone into this decision. I began then to have some understanding of the problems of a squadron commander. Frankly, I think that in Searby's place I would have sent us. I like to think that we could have done that trip easily. My crew was disappointed but they wouldn't argue.

* * *

Syerston was home to something over 2,500 people. Perhaps ten percent of these were aircrew. The station, like all bomber stations, had its own living quarters, canteens, hospital, food stores, generating plant, playing field and combined dance hall and cinema. Certainly not lush, most of this was housed in austere Nissen huts or wartime buildings. The buildings were heated by a round, coal burning stove which never seemed to be lit. The officers' quarters were like all the rest, a Nissen hut with a coal stove. I slept in a bunk in a hut shared with a half dozen junior officers. In the bunk next to me was a newly-trained English pilot called Brodrick who arrived a couple of days after I did, a replacement for the crew lost on Stuttgart. He was a fine, big, good-natured man and we immediately became friends. He always talked as though his words were something he'd thought of a few moments ago and his mind had passed on to another subject. The station had its own police, security staff and station maintenance personnel. The aircraft stores had parts enough to make up a half dozen aircraft. The fuel dump had 2,500 gallon fuel trucks, called bowsers, just enough to deliver a full load of 2,143 gallons to a Lancaster with some to spare and there were small trailers with oil tanks. It took half a day to fuel the station's aircraft. In the bomb dump crews brought out cases of incendiaries by hand to a section where these were packed into small bomb containers. Belts of ammunition were loaded and guns were sighted and cleaned. The larger bombs were taken out on trolleys and hauled to the aircraft. In the intelligence section maps and escape kits were collected and sorted for an operation. The kitchen staff prepared and packaged sandwiches, tea, coffee, gum, barley sugar and chocolate for the aircrew. The meteorological staff made up the latest weather maps and wind data and the parachute section was for ever airing parachutes in tall lofts and repacking them for use. The place abounded with mud and consequently wooden sidewalks laid on 2x4's led from one building to another.

The maintenance crews at the aircraft dispersals built themselves crew huts out of any lumber and corrugated tin they could scrounge. Here again was a round stove and a writing bench for the aircraft records.

On March 27th operations were again scheduled. The flight engineer said it looked to be a deep penetration of Germany judging from the fuel load. I had some concern about navigation on a very long trip. The only aid we had over enemy territory was 'Gee' from which one could read two co-ordinates fixing one's position. But the Germans were jamming it very effectively and it was useless over Europe. The only other aid, which couldn't of course be jammed, was astro navigation but the weather had been so bad of late that stars were seldom visible. Oh well, one could always go on dead-reckoning and look for flares at the target, dropped by the radar-equipped Pathfinders. So that is what we did.

At briefing the ribbon stretched north-east on the map from Syerston, across the coast north of The Wash, continuing in a straight line across the North Sea to Denmark, across Denmark and thence south east down the Kattegat into the Baltic and along the Baltic and across its coast on a line south-east to Berlin, 'The Big City'. So although Berlin lay about six hundred miles due east of Syerston the chosen route added a detour of about a hundred and fifty miles in order to avoid the heaviest fighter concentrations across Holland and North Germany.

We took off, one of over 400 aircraft and climbed en route. We were flying K for King and it was climbing easily. When about an hour outward bound, after we had cleared the coast and the gunners had test-fired their guns, I noticed that we would be entering cloud at about 16,000 feet. This we did, still climbing steadily and levelling off, still in cloud at 20,000 feet. We flew for just under another hour by which time we should have crossed the Danish coast. We saw not a thing but presumably in a few more minutes we had crossed the east coast of Denmark as well. It seemed strange flying in cloud over enemy territory. But safe from fighters I reflected. We would miss the 2nd and 3rd German Fighter Divisions and would pass through the territory of the 1st Division surrounding Berlin. We turned south-east, on the course fixed by the flight plan, having no way to tell whether or not we were on the correct track to Berlin. Nor did we know quite what to expect when and if we got there. The weather began to clear in the Western Baltic but I was unable to determine where we crossed the Baltic coast. We should now be somewhere north of Brunswick, approaching Berlin. I saw no sign of a bombing operation. On we flew. Almost four hours had elapsed from take-off time and nothing was yet visible. I had not seen a thing I could recognise. The navigator had no idea where we were. No stars were visible above. We kept heading eastward and I said to the navigator, 'We're overdue at the target now, aren't we navigator?' He readily admitted that we were. 'Christ, if we keep on at this rate', I said, 'we'll soon be in Poland.' I was getting worried. Still we headed east. Soon I would have to turn around if we expected to get back at all.

Then Tolman, the rear gunner, said, 'There's something funny going on way behind us on the starboard side.'

'Like what?' I asked. 'Well', he said, 'there are a lot of searchlights and a kind of orange glow on the ground.' 'Let's have a look', I said swinging the Lancaster 90° to starboard. There a long way away, perhaps fifty miles away, off the starboard beam was undoubtedly a target being attacked. 'My God', I said. 'That's got to be Berlin.' I turned a further sixty degrees to starboard. It took us fifteen minutes flying time to get back to the outskirts of Berlin; that is how far we had overshot. Tolman of course had never seen a large target before or he would have recognised it sooner. I was frankly delighted to see the place. At least now I knew where we were. I eagerly examined Berlin as we approached it from the east. 'They'll think we are the Russians', I mused, knowing full well the Russians had no strategic bomber force.

The searchlights were turning off in Berlin as we approached. I could see them shutting down one by one; the attack was over and the bomber force had departed. Then we crossed the eastern suburbs of Berlin at 19,500 feet. It took some six or seven minutes flying from there over the city before we could recognise anything. I strained against my harness, standing up to see the ground while trying to fly at the same time. 'Isn't that an airfield down off our port side, Pete?' I asked.

'I think it is', he said.

'Probably Templehof', I decided, swinging the Lancaster to the right. 'We should be near the Unter den Linden. Let's see if we can hit the Wehrmacht headquarters, Pete'. I was excited by the danger of being over this great city.

'Well, I can't see it but I know where it should be', he answered, giving me directions to steer. He too was excited. We plodded on. It seemed to take ages. Now some of the searchlights were being switched on again. They knew we were there but as yet no guns were firing.

'Pete, look for the River Spree or the Tiergarten or maybe a wide road', I said. 'I can see a wide road all right but it's dim – they've gone to bed', he said. We were still at 19,500 feet. We entered upon the bomb run, I opened the doors and after a minute or two of telling me where to fly Pete released the cookie and the thousand pounders; I felt them go. I don't know what we hit but it was near the nerve centre of Berlin. We were on a westerly heading which would have been exceedingly dangerous if the attack were still in progress because of the likelihood of several hundred bombers flying in the opposite direction. But with the attack over there was little danger of collision. Now some of the anti-aircraft guns began to fire and for the first time I felt the elation of battle. It was exhilarating. I wasn't worried about the guns, not when I could see the gun flashes. I changed altitude, dropping 1,000 feet and altering course as I saw the first battery fire. It then became a guessing game. Will the gunners expect one to turn to the right or to the left? Should one lose altitude or gain it? Probably they'll expect a left hand turn because it is easier for a pilot sitting on the left side to turn left. So we'll turn right instead and climb. Then there were rapid flashes from two or three other six gun batteries; I swerved again, feeling like a dancer, pleased with the response of the empty Lancaster. This went on for several minutes and then the guns fell silent as we were leaving the city. All we had to worry about now was getting home. The tail gunner said he could see large fires in the city and the searchlights had once again been turned off. I set course due west for base. At least we had a landmark to start from and the flight plan should get us home. Soon we ran into cloud again but this time it was a help, rather than a hindrance; visibility became zero. We maintained 20,000 feet and the cloud continued all the way to the North Sea. We had taken the direct route back and were well out over the North Sea, outside the range of German fighters, when I dropped the Lancaster to 10,000 feet and shut off the oxygen supply to myself and the crew. We could remove our masks and have a cup of coffee. The flight engineer lit me a cigarette. 'Turn on the IFF, Andy', I said to Wilkes. 'And make sure you've got the friendly recognition colours in your Very pistol'. I put on the automatic pilot and relaxed.

IFF was a transmitter called 'Identification, Friend or Foe'. It enabled the British fighter controllers to identify the aircraft approaching the coast of England as friendly or not. The Very pistol was for firing a signal code of coloured flares if one were fired upon by our own anti-aircraft guns.

The cloud cleared as we approached the coast. It was getting light. I saw a small convoy of freighters heading up the North Sea a few miles off Cromer and wondered idly where they were bound. Carrying coal to Newcastle perhaps? I was trying to identify the precise portion of the English coast we were approaching when two or three small lights twinkled on the ships below. I thought nothing of it for a few seconds and then noticed a puff of smoke at about our own altitude, two or three hundred yards off the starboard bow.

'The silly bastards are shooting at us', said Hanratty. 'Fire the Very pistol, Wilkes and tell them we're friendly'. I didn't watch to see the pistol fired or concern myself with where it was fired from. I quickly disengaged the automatic pilot, did a steep turn to port and dived two thousand feet before swinging back on course. They had fired again. I looked up and saw another two puffs of smoke. It was then that I remembered the motto of the British Merchant Navy as told to me by a seaman at Bournemouth. 'If it's got a single tail it's a Heinkel and you shoot at it; if it's got a double tail it's a Dornier and you shoot at it. That way there's little in the way of friendly aircraft that gets by either.' He was right. Soon we were back at Syerston, debriefed and eating a good breakfast after a flight of seven hours and forty-five minutes. 106 Squadron's eleven crews had bombed and returned safely. The next day Wilkes told me that our navigator had been sick all the way to and from the target. 'I suppose it didn't matter', I replied. 'There wasn't much he could see or do anyway, once we were in cloud.' But it was a troubling thought.

CHAPTER SEVEN

Young Warriors

I learned from the intelligence office that morning that my friend George Mabee and crew, who were on another 5 Group Squadron, hadn't returned from Berlin. 'Oh no!' George was a Canadian from Toronto whom I'd met at the Conversion Unit at Swinderby. I had finished the course there when he approached one evening in full flying gear.

'What are you up to?' I enquired. He was a youngish looking man to be losing hair at the rate he was. As a joke he and his crew had taken to wearing a badge containing a red hammer and sickle on the lapel of their battledress. The 'Russians' Revenge' they called themselves. 'Listen', he confided quietly, 'We are out on another bombing exercise tonight with a live bomb. We went out last night and couldn't find the bloody bombing range to drop it on. If we miss again tonight we're in trouble. How about lending a hand?'

'Sure, George, but what can I do?'

'Well, you've finished the exercise', he said. 'You must know where the damned range is.'

True, I did know where it was. So that night George's Lancaster had an extra Canadian aboard whose presence was not noted in either his log book or mine. The bombing range was easy to find when you knew what to look for. George was a good pilot and we carried out the exercise without event.

I thought of this when I heard the news that he was missing. And I felt a twinge of guilt. Perhaps if I hadn't helped him he would have been given a new bomb-aimer or a new navigator who was better at map reading. I wondered whether, like me, he had missed Berlin and then got lost and ran out of fuel. Or perhaps he was shot down as a stray. It could easily have been done, to get lost that is, particularly by a new crew. If he was now in the hands of the Germans they would not think the hammer and sickle badges very funny.

It was at about this time that my crew, who had been wracking their brains for some time for a logo to paint on the side of our aeroplane, came up with an idea. I had the veto power so they submitted it to me.

'We want to paint the head of a timber-wolf on the side of the aeroplane', said Wilkes.

This was academic until we got a plane of our own, so I said, 'Why a timber-wolf? You have never even seen one.' I hadn't seen one myself but didn't mention that fact.

'Well, you see, that's just it', said Wilkes. 'We think it would be symbolic of Canada. Wouldn't that be nice, to send a picture home? Your very own plane! With a Canadian timber-wolf on the side – and a few bombs painted on as well. I can just see it in the Vancouver newspaper.'

'It would be ver-ry Canadian', added Hanratty. I smelled a rat; these good souls were not usually so solicitous. 'Well, let's think about it', I said. 'We can talk about it again if we ever get our own aircraft.'

About a month later I learned that there was indeed a rat to smell. Do you know why they wanted to paint a timber-wolf on the aeroplane? Canadian be damned – they thought that I looked like a timber-wolf! They told me so. ' You have the same high cheekbones and slanty eyes – and you look as if you'd bite when provoked.'

By the time we got around to considering the question again a new factor had intervened. We had by that time done a number of trips without any symbol at all and perhaps, they said, timber-wolf or no, it would be bad luck to depart from the practice to date. So I gave up. We never did have a symbol, although I did manage ultimately to get a factory-new aeroplane for ourselves, and the ground crew painted the call letter T for Tommy on it. What more could a Thompson expect?

On March 28th we didn't fly. We had dinghy drill. Searby sent for me and asked if I wanted to volunteer myself and crew for a dunking in the River Trent. It had warmed a little but was not exactly beach weather.

'Nothing to it, Thompson', he said. 'Just have your crew there after lunch and we'll demonstrate what an inflated dinghy looks like to the other crews and, oh yes, wear some old clothes.'

I didn't mind; I liked swimming and my crew wouldn't object. I said without any doubt at all, 'Certainly sir, we'll do it.' But this was another instance of, 'Often wrong but seldom in doubt!' Hanratty refused absolutely. 'No sir-r. I'm not going in that water-r.' This, after we were all assembled at the river's edge and the big dinghy was being inflated. Searby was telling the other crews to watch carefully while Thompson's crew swam to the dinghy and got in.

I said quietly, 'Pete, for God's sake we're putting on life jackets.

Nothing can happen to you.'

'No sir-r, not on your-r life. I can't swim and I'm not going in the damned water-r. And you can't make me', he added for good measure. 'And I don't have to obey a stupid order-r like that', he concluded triumphantly.

'Wilkes', I said, 'See what you can do with him. Get a life jacket on him and get his shoes off and sit him at the water's edge.'

I swam to the dinghy and towed it towards shore. I was near to shore when a snake about eighteen inches long glided from a clump of grass at the water's edge. It was brownish-yellow with zigzag marks on its back and spots on its side. This was not alarming; I had often seen gartersnakes. Then Tolman saw it and backed off, 'You know snakes are often poisonous here.' No, I didn't know. Anyway we all got in the dinghy somehow, half frozen, and demonstrated to the other crews that it could be done. I had no doubt at all that they would easily accomplish it if they were down in the North Sea and their life depended on it. Even Hanratty would make it then.

*   *   *

On March 29th it was Berlin again. Twelve aircraft were detailed from our Squadron. One may wonder how it came about that with the Battle of the Ruhr having opened and with much of Essen flattened, we were going to Berlin, rather than to other parts of the Ruhr. The answer lay in the available Pathfinder techniques. The long-range targets could not be marked as accurately as those in the Ruhr; that was one reason why the Ruhr was chosen as the objective in the battle. We were to go many times to the Ruhr between March and July of 1943 and we would bomb the targets on the red target indicators dropped with great accuracy by the Oboe-equipped Mosquitoes, unarmed and travelling at speed at altitudes which made them immune to fighter interception. We had merely to find the brightly coloured flares burning through haze and smoke and bomb them carefully from 20,000 feet. But more distant targets had to be bombed also to keep the fighter defences from concentrating in the Ruhr. So Berlin it was. Searby said that the aiming point would be marked by Pathfinder Lancasters using H2S radar; Paramatta was the code name for this type of attack. The results from it were not as good as on those marked by Oboe but there was no other choice on a long trip. H2S gave good results on targets where distinctive land and sea features could be observed, for example on a coastal city where the set operator could distinguish water, showing as a dark area from the lighter land mass, and the built-up areas showing bright on the cathode ray tube. But on a large city like Berlin the display on the tube was uniformly bright with little of the contrast which would make for easy identification of a particular part of the target. Consequently Berlin attacks, while the bombs were usually all dropped on the city, tended to yield scattered results. This attack was to begin with five blind markers dropping yellow flares by radar. In the light of these, other Pathfinders would drop green target indicators, and these were to be bombed by ourselves of the Main Force. Every two minutes or so other Pathfinders would replenish the green markers until all aircraft had dropped their bombs on the target indicators. Sometimes after the blind markers had dropped their flares, it was possible for Pathfinders visually to mark the aiming point with red flares which were then backed up periodically with green ones. This visual marking attack was called a ' Newhaven'.

How could one, in these circumstances, be sure of bombing only military objectives? Clearly one could not. But, as was pointed out to us at briefing by the intelligence officer, if the housing of an industrial area and the physical plant are ruined, the industry is likely to be slowed considerably or halted or caused to disperse elsewhere – even if the workers were protected by shelters at the time of attack. I knew of course that as long as one was obliged to bomb target indicators one had little say in the target selection. Nevertheless, one could try to hit military objectives where they could be seen. You will be able to judge the success or failure of this philosophy as you follow the next few operations.

We went straight in over Holland at 20,000 feet. There was flak at the Dutch coast and route markers were dropped by the Pathfinders near Hanover. I felt no comfort from these; I thought I knew where we were without their assistance. Their only purpose it seemed to me might be to alert the German fighters, if they had not already been alerted, to our whereabouts. I flew a slight dog-leg around the markers. I watched an aircraft far to the south illuminated in searchlights; it was far off course; suddenly it was caught in a flak barrage and was fired upon steadily for about 30 seconds. Flak was bursting all around it. Then it blew up in a mushrooming, light-orange ball. We plodded on in the darkness, all hands alert and looking out for fighters. There were quite a number of eyes doing this in the aircraft – it was K for King again. The bomb-aimer looked out in front, the flight-engineer and myself out both sides and in front; the wireless operator observed to the rear and to the sides of the astrodome, a round plastic bubble in the roof of the crew compartment. The navigator was behind his curtains and like most navigators rarely came out for anything. He had come out for a few seconds over the city on our last trip to Berlin but had been so alarmed at what he saw that his illness got worse. I expected he was ill now, although I couldn't be sure. The mid-upper and rear gunners had good visibility to the rear and sides. The rear gunner had in fact removed the transparent plastic from the turret in front of him, preferring to suffer the cold rather than forfeit visibility. So the only place we couldn't see was just where we needed it most – underneath. I tried to remedy this by flying a constant and pronounced corkscrew path, asking the crew to look below as I alternately banked one way then the other. I did not fly straight and level until we reached Berlin, and then only on the bomb run. The city was visible this time dead ahead of us as we neared our Estimated Time of Arrival.

I was flying on a course slightly north of east when we entered upon the well-lit area of this large city. There was no cloud at all. I unfastened my shoulder harness and stood squatting on the pilot's seat, peering through the windshield, trying to see past the nose for a better view. Hanratty said, 'We must be getting well into the city.' He could see the panorama much better than I, but I knew that we were not. Berlin is a big city and we had been over it only three or four minutes. I looked ahead at searchlights fingering their way through the black sky. There was a red glow below, not of fire but red the colour of building bricks. Miles upon miles of streets were visible, minuscule ribbons from 20,000 feet, all showing light red in the haze and the searchlights. We continued on for what seemed a long time, carefully picking a path through the searchlights. Flak was exploding at our altitude. We were over the densely built up area of Berlin and the environment was hostile but where did one bomb? A searchlight flicked on us for a moment then shifted aft, fingering for someone behind. On and on we went, slowly it seemed, until Hanratty after a few moments saw some Green TI's. By this time I could not see below. I refastened my shoulder harness and opened the bomb doors at his request. As far as I could tell we were bombing Berlin but I did not know where. Hanratty gave directions for a much longer time than he ever had in practice. Finally he said, 'Left – left – steady – steady – bombs gone.' Then he added as an apparent afterthought, 'Rr-un for-r the shelter-rs you bastards.' Hanratty had been engaged to a girl from Plymouth who had been killed in a German air raid.

Analysis of bombing photographs after this raid showed that there had been poor concentration of bombs. I saw lines of burning incendiaries from many bombers over a widespread area but no large fires were started. Concentration of the attack, if accurate, was always desirable but it was not achieved this night. One might ask why, if accurate target marking and concentration of attack were the objectives, did the Pathfinders not go low enough to make visual identification possible and thus drop flares spot on the target. This was in fact tried with success on specific targets but on large cities it was generally not possible for two reasons, balloons and flak . German cities often had a dense network of captive balloons, the cables of which could tear a bomber to pieces. Generally these did not extend above 12,000 feet since there are limits to how high a tethered balloon, holding up a heavy cable, will rise – and flak at low altitudes could be murderously accurate. An ingenious method was devised for the bombers to cut the balloon cables; our Lancasters were equipped with a half dozen slots in the leading edges of the wing. Each slot contained a chisel backed by an explosive charge so situated that if a cable were struck in flight it would slide into the slot where the charge was triggered to fire the chisel and cut the cable. We later in our tour met a Squadron Leader who was awarded an Air Force Cross for testing these things and he assured us that they worked just fine but I was never tempted to verify his test results over German cities.

Flak and searchlights on the route out of Berlin were moderate and we saw no fighters. We returned to base without event, or so it seemed at the time. The next day the crew chief at the dispersal site of K for King showed me a small hole in the transparent plastic on the pilot's side of the cockpit. Strange, I thought, I hadn't heard any wind through the hole. Perhaps my helmet and the engine noise had obscured it. Then he pointed to a scratch on the armour plate behind my head and the flight engineer announced that his helmet had been cut. A piece of shrapnel had paid us a visit and had hit the armour plate behind my head, bounced off and cut the engineer's helmet. Three of our crews had returned early due to severe icing and we lost one aircraft, ED 596, captained by Squadron Leader Eric Hayward DFC who had needed only two more trips to complete his second tour. Hayward, a very tall man, left behind a large black Great Dane who appeared to mourn for several days before being adopted by a ground crew. It took a whole crew to feed him.

* * *

After the second Berlin raid we were given nine days' leave. It seemed half a lifetime ago that we had last been on leave. In future we were to receive nine days every six weeks. My crew looked forward to leave even more than I, since they all lived in the United Kingdom. I hastened to Bournemouth to see if any Canadians I knew had arrived. One had and I soon tracked down René Dupraz, who greeted me with delight. We decided to go to an afternoon tea-dance but it was jammed full and we were refused admittance. This was too much for Dupraz. He and I had been to Washington State University together where he had been senior to me, so he immediately took charge. 'Come with me', he announced grandly, clattering off down a marble hall in search of the Pavilion manager. This person when found clearly did not wish to see either of us but Dupraz would have none of that.

'They won't let us in', he bleated. 'They won't let this man in who has spent the last two nights over Berlin. Can you believe it?' I was embarrassed by this unexpected ploy. So was the manager; he examined me with great disinterest. Clearly, his manner seemed to say, this young officer possesses nothing to distinguish him from the dozens of other noisy, young Canadians who daily demand one privilege or another based upon just such false premises as these. Solely therefore to avoid further noise and clamouring from Dupraz he wrote a note on a ticket to admit us to the dance and in we stomped to partake of a few cakes, a cup of tea and a dance with the local young ladies. After a couple of days I tired of this, said goodbye to Dupraz and went to London where, based in an officers' club, I visited the sights and the pubs. I never saw Dupraz again. He was killed in action in a Spitfire.

Upon reaching Syerston on April 9th I was informed by Searby that my flight engineer was in jail in Nottingham. He had thrown a brick through a plate-glass shop window in order to get himself put in jail. It was obvious that he had had enough of operational flying. As one with experience of a Standing Court Martial I thought it an ingenious but purely temporary solution to his dilemma, for although he had not refused to obey a military order he would be asked to fly again upon his return and his reaction would then be tested. I never saw or heard of him again. But I felt a twinge of guilt when I thought of him. I had not made things easy for him. He was absent-minded and often didn't hear what I was telling him. I once saw him gazing into space when I told him to engage the supercharger, and when he failed to respond I hit him in the ribs with my elbow. This loss of temper had upset both of us and perhaps my conduct had something to do with his defection. So we were left with the problem of getting a new flight engineer at short notice. We acquired a splendid one in Flight Sergeant Bill Belton who had been biding his time as a link trainer instructor at Syerston, waiting for a crew such as ours to come along. I was never clear how Belton had become separated from his original crew; perhaps his pilot had failed to return from a second pilot operation. In any event he was a Geordie, like Wilkes who had informed me that he was available and willing to come with us. I found him to be a fine engineer and a strong addition to the crew. While we had been on leave the Squadron had lost Sgt. T.J. Ridd and crew in ED 542 on a flight to Essen and Sgt. J.L. Irvine and crew in W 4156 on a trip to Duisburg. I had come to know them both and was shocked by their loss.

On April 10th we were briefed for an attack on Frankfurt, lying about ninety miles south-east of the Ruhr and about 40 miles north of Mannheim. I felt as I was always to feel when returning from leave, anxious to become airborne and get an operation done, so as to hone one's expertise, get rid of accumulated stomach butterflies, and see what new tactical developments were occurring.

I didn't like the briefing for this attack. If the ground markers were not visible and it was expected they might not be, the attack was to be a 'Wanganui', that is a blind attack in which the Pathfinders dropped flares to hang in the sky by parachute. Each of these would be placed in a position so calculated that if they were aimed at by the bombsights of the heavy bombers above the cloud the resulting tonnage should hit the ground on target. I was sceptical, though we were assured that excellent concentration and accuracy had been obtained in test runs by this method. I was particularly concerned because I was to carry a single 8,000 pound bomb, together with some cans of incendiaries and I wanted them to hit the target. I hoped that the target could be seen, or at least that some ground markers would be visible. Despite the large bomb the take-off was normal but it became apparent while climbing that the weather would not be co-operative. Clouds towered to just below 20,000 feet over Belgium and their tops were not smooth. Upon arrival in the Frankfurt area the city, and any ground markers which had been dropped were obscured by the solid, thick cloud. But the Pathfinders were accurate I reasoned. We decided to bomb one of the sky markers which had been released and was hanging by its chute above the cloud layer. The bombs of most crews, it turned out, hit Frankfurt but they were widely scattered. My resolve to bomb only military targets was being tested. I have no idea what, if anything, I hit with that large bomb. Upon our return some crews reported night fighters above the cloud and intense flak over the target but I suppose one judged by one's own experience. I saw only moderate flak and no fighters.

Three days later, on April 13th, we were briefed to attack Spezia, a naval base in Northern Italy, about halfway between Genoa and Pisa. Here it seemed was a purely military target at last; I was pleased at the prospect. It was a long flight and the route would take us down the West of England near Reading. We were always routed so as to avoid flying over London. We would leave England at Selsey Bill, then across the Channel to the Cherbourg peninsula and south, down France, to the east of Paris. I noted as we passed Paris what an atrocious blackout it had. They were simply not worried about British bombers, which of course was as it should be. In southern France the blackout was even worse. Then came a climb over the Alps where we witnessed a strange phenomenon. Two of our bombers were shooting at each other. I could see four engine exhausts on each of them; one seemed to be a Stirling, the other a Halifax. But each was at a different angle to the other than I was for I could make them out fairly clearly. I gave them a wide berth.

Across the French Alps it was a quick descent to the North Italian plain and out to the coast, then along the coast east to Spezia. It appeared that we were going to be early and not wanting to tip-off the attack I did a dog-leg out over the Mediterranean near Turin, then back to the coast. Arriving at Spezia it seemed that we were still a few minutes early. No Pathfinder flares had been dropped. I later learned that the Pathfinders were eight minutes late in starting. This time I was determined to hit a military target. Assuming that the Pathfinders would now be running in on the target I headed in myself but to my dismay could see nothing but the coast. We were told to bomb from 10,000 feet but since nothing was visible I throttled back the four engines and quickly dropped to 7,500 feet. We had been warned in training that a Lancaster at 4,000 feet or below could get blown up by its own bombs. So 7,500 seemed about right. We ran in from seaward and when near the coastline could see the small city and the docks and ships. Too late! We went past the ships. I kept on far enough to make a 180° turn. We would attack on a run to seaward. As soon as we had turned around I dropped another thousand feet to 6,500 and opened the bomb doors. Hanratty was crouched over the bomb sight. I noticed no flak. We ran in towards the docks. There were three battleships there! We were not concerned about collision – most other aircraft would be higher than we and apparently there were no balloons. A smoke screen had been started by the ships off shore and was blowing a blanket of smoke towards the docks and over the battleships. Then the scene disappeared under the nose of the Lancaster and I could see only the black sky and the Mediterranean. Hanratty gave me directions to steer for a few seconds and then shouted 'Bombs gone'. I felt each thump as the bombs left their stations. At this time the Pathfinder flares came cascading down around us.

The trip home was uneventful and when our bombing photographs had been developed it was found that we had hit the aiming point. Each time a Lancaster of 5 Group was proved to have hit the aiming point every member of its crew received a small scroll containing a sketch of a Lancaster taking off and saying below the sketch, 'Aiming Point', with the name of the target and the names and ranks of the crew members on it. It was signed by the Air Officer Commanding, Air Vice-Marshal Ralph Cochrane. We were pleased with the results of the attack. Whether we hit the docks, the battleships or the arsenal I don't know but it should have been one of them, for all three were in the centre of our photo. Cochrane liked to keep up the morale of the crews and these scrolls were only one facet of his policy in that regard; where merited he was also liberal in recommending decorations. Most of the Victoria Crosses awarded to aircrew were from his group. He also liked to see precise bombing. He was the strongest of advocates of pin-point bombing and 5 Group under his command soon developed a reputation for attacking small but vital targets by a specialised force of squadron size with great accuracy and sometimes spectacular results.

The flight to Spezia and back had been a long one of eleven hours. I didn't care for trips of that duration with no relief at the controls. But one couldn't complain; we were far more fortunate than Flying Officer M.E. Chivers and crew of neighbouring 61 Squadron. They were three days late getting back. They had to ditch Lancaster ED 703 in the sea and take to their dinghy. Sixty-three hours later a Whitley on an anti-sub patrol spotted them and dropped down to fly a couple of circles around and let them know he had seen them. They were hauled aboard an RAF rescue launch and brought back to Syerston.

Next morning while examining the bombing photos outside the intelligence office Belton mentioned that the aircraft were being refuelled with a sizeable load of fuel. It looked like something was on. It was – we were briefed in the late afternoon for Stuttgart. By this time we knew that the previous attack on Stuttgart had been a failure because most of the main force had arrived late and had missed the target indicators before they were burned out. So we were to go again.

We were provided at briefing with a map of the target area of Stuttgart and I then began the practice, and asked the bomb-aimer to do the same, of committing the target map to memory. Stuttgart has a good-sized river running through it with two distinctive bends. The route in and across Germany brought us to a point north and a little east of the city. The night was clear and the visibility was excellent. I could see the river glinting in the moonlight as we approached. Then I saw some yellow and then some red target indicators dropped at the northerly of the two bends of the river. They were about thirty degrees to starboard of the course we were flying and they didn't look right to me. I dropped altitude from 20,000 feet to 14,000 where I could see better. We could still see the river ahead and the southerly bend of it near the aiming point, which was about six miles to the left of the target indicators. I asked Hanratty what he thought. 'I think the TI's are wrong and we are right' was his forthright reply.

'Good', I said, 'We'll bomb where we think it should be, OK?' We continued on our run-in, slightly west of south, altering course a little to port as we went. The bend in the river which we were approaching seemed to me exactly as it did on the target map. We ignored the target indicators and dropped our bombs where no other aircraft had bombed. I wondered briefly on the way back to England how we were going to explain this one. The intelligence officer shook his head when we told him at de-briefing. He called Searby over to our table to hear what had happened.

Searby said nothing. The next day's photos showed that the Pathfinders had marked the wrong bend in the river. Most of the bombs, while they had caused damage to Stuttgart, had gone down in the wrong place. Fortunately for us we had been right. This attack was the first illustration to me that unlike Oboe, H2S was far from infallible. One topographical feature on the cathode ray tube could be mistaken for another which it closely resembled and if the yellow H2S illuminators were wrongly dropped, those Pathfinders who followed and visually dropped reds or greens could be misled by the same similarity – such as two bends in a river which looked much alike. Bomber Command was learning.

Flight Lieutenant Brodrick in ED 752 did not return from Stuttgart. His empty bunk beside mine was hard to believe. I learned after the war that he had been taken prisoner.

* * *

There was no flying on April 15th but on the 16th a maximum fuel load of 2,154 gallons was pumped aboard each aircraft. We did our usual night-flying test and checked the operation of the aircraft and all its equipment. This took about half an hour. In the late afternoon we assembled in the round-roofed briefing room where on a stage the map of Europe was displayed as usual. The staff had obtained some extra red ribbon for this one. The target was the Skoda works at Pilsen in Czechoslovakia, a round trip of about 1,800 miles. Searby told us why we were going; it was a factory producing guns and tanks which had become more important with the devastation of Essen. We would go out of Syerston past Reading and down England to Selsey Bill, across the Channel, across France, across southern Germany and into Czechoslovakia. We would likely encounter fighter activity both ways. The intelligence officer described to us the delightful details of which *Geschwader* was based where and what flak we could expect if we didn't adhere strictly to the ribbon. The Met officer told us about the weather, which was expected to be reasonable; then we had our flying meal which was always a good one, donned our flying clothes and off we went. It was a long flight and as usual I didn't fly straight and level but constantly banked from side to side so that the gunners could see below. If the navigator gave me a course to steer I never actually steered it. I averaged it out, reasoning that the corkscrew path would ultimately yield the correct track. It did too; the only adverse effect of all this evasive activity was to reduce speed slightly. But the loss of speed was much less than I thought it would be. I always flew like a fast, migrating salmon in a boulder strewn stream.

When we got to Pilsen there was about 6/10ths cloud, some TI's were already down and the bombs were falling in a neat concentration. I brought the Lancaster down to 4,000 feet to have a good look. We were trying to find a built-up area at a bend in a small river. The Skoda works would be on the south-west side of the town, on its outskirts. I didn't see very much but Hanratty claimed that the target was between ourselves and the flares. This was unusual. The situation was usually the reverse. However, he could see better than I so I followed his directions as we dropped the bombs on our first run in.

Upon return to base everyone felt that the operation had been a success. But a few days later we found that while the attack had indeed been well concentrated it had been directed to a point near an insane asylum, while the Skoda works had received only one or two bomb loads. Once again the lesson had been demonstrated that accuracy on a small target with marking by H2S was difficult. The bend in the river near the asylum was similar to that near the Skoda works. And the fighters had exacted their toll. Out of 327 aircraft, thirty-six (11%) were missing and another fifty-seven had been damaged.

Two nights later on April 18th we were briefed for Spezia again. The second trip was easier to execute because we had an idea of what to expect. We were routed to fly low over France. As we were passing to the east of Paris it was still light enough to see well and I noticed a small German observation plane with its navigation lights on, flying ahead on the same course as we and at about the same height. We were not very high. I told the gunners not to fire at it for it was unarmed. It was a Fieseler Storch, a high wing single-engine monoplane with the German crosses plainly visible on its fuselage. We were faster than it so I pulled up alongside from its left side while the bomb-aimer trained the front guns on it; the mid-upper gunner swung his two Brownings on it and the tail gunner moved his four Browning, Fraser-Nash turret in its direction. Just then the German pilot looked out to his left and saw us. He probably was not a fighter pilot but he certainly acted like one. He flipped the Storch on its back in a diving turn away from us. I wondered what harrowing tale he would tell his friends when he landed, about having escaped an attacking Lancaster by sheer flying skill. This time as we crossed the French Alps the navigator said that we should soon be passing Mont Blanc, the highest peak in the Alps. Sure enough there it was, white in the moonlight, just below our altitude and ahead a little. I decided to have a good look at it and flew towards the peak. I dropped altitude and made a circle round it with our port wing towards the peak. Then I said I'd try to see how close I could come with our wing tip, though of course I didn't do so. Hanratty was not at all amused.

Proceeding on in the bright moonlight we dropped altitude and reached the coast. Then there was some excitement. An Italian single-engined fighter appeared off the starboard side and I thought we were in for a fight. But he didn't want to fight. With all of our gun turrets trained on him he showed us how he could fly aerobatics at night. He was a Macchi 200. First he did some steep turns, in and out, about 600 yards away. Then he climbed alongside, still out of range and demonstrated a fine slow roll, no mean feat at night. I thought that all of this fancy footwork might be the prelude to a slashing attack but it wasn't. It was hard to believe that a trained fighter pilot in a good aircraft was afraid to fight, but I don't think he was afraid. I believe that the war was over for this man and he would not fight unless attacked. This was his way of telling us that – even though we were on our way to bomb a target in his country, a fact of which he must certainly have been aware. When we reached Spezia I felt at ease in the familiar surroundings and this time we quickly found the target and bombed it from 8,000 feet.

We were coming back over the Alps when cloud seemed to be obscuring the whole of France. I had a feeling that the wind had shifted. It was important that we get a fix or two over France if we were to hit England. After a few minutes I began to speculate on the problems we could have if there was a significant shift in wind from the flight plan. We could get blown out over the Bay of Biscay or over a defended area in France. I asked the navigator what he thought of taking some astro shots with the sextant. He said 'Oh, we'll be back in Gee range in an hour or two. We can fix our position then.' I was not impressed with this reasoning and said, 'In an hour or two it may be too late. I think you should take some star shots.' I had never seen him use the sextant on an operational flight but he had done so in practice and I knew that he could do it easily.

He said, 'A star fix won't be accurate enough to tell us anything. We would need a couple of them.' I replied, 'Well let's get a couple of them then.'

'No', he said, 'It's not worthwhile.'

By this time I was getting annoyed. I habitually carried a loaded .38 Smith & Wesson revolver tucked in my battledress jacket in case we were shot down. What I would have done with it, I don't know. Probably I'd have hidden it in a culvert but I carried it anyway, deferring until the actual event any decision on that question. Now was an occasion when I thought it might be useful. I took it from my battledress jacket, turned around in my heavy pilot's seat and said, 'You get up there and take some star shots.' I was furious! I wonder what I would have done if he had refused. When I looked back in a few moments he was standing in the astrodome with a sextant in his hands pointed to the sky, so I didn't have to consider the problem. He did take some star shots and he did find that we were a long distance off track. And we certainly would have been blown out over the Atlantic if we had continued to fly on the flight plan.

After de-briefing I asked to see Searby. I explained to him what had happened with the navigator and added, 'This man is almost always airsick – and he's going to get us killed. It isn't fair to the rest of the crew.'

Searby agreed and the navigator flew only one trip more with us. I don't know what ultimately happened to him. To my surprise the rest of the crew thought this incident to be long overdue. I hadn't realised the depth of their feeling.

Once again, soon after our return, we received an aiming point scroll, signed by Air Vice-Marshal Cochrane.

CHAPTER EIGHT

Pathfinders

ON April 19th Searby said we would not be flying and that he was going to a place called Wyton to visit a Pathfinder Squadron. He asked if I would like to come along for a ride. Of course I would, I said. So I rode in the bomb-aimer's compartment while he flew a Lancaster south for a half hour to an airfield just outside Huntingdon, a few miles west of Cambridge. I was fascinated at my first sight of a permanently built peace-time operational station, complete with red-brick buildings, spacious hangars and permanent runways. It was from here that the first RAF operation of WWII took place, a reconnaissance of the German fleet. In addition to housing a Lancaster Pathfinder squadron it had a squadron of Pathfinder Mosquitoes. The headquarters of the Pathfinder force was about three miles away in nearby Huntingdon. Searby didn't tell me his business there and it didn't take him long to conclude it. On the flight back to Syerston he asked me how I would like to be on a Pathfinder squadron. I told him that I had already asked the adjutant to put my name down. I would like it just fine. 'Good show', said Searby and that was all that was said about that.

We got back to Syerston in the mid-afternoon and since there was no flying that night I and a couple of other officers went to Newark on a pub crawl, travelling to and from the town on a service bus with a contingent of airmen and their WAAF friends. It was great fun quaffing weak beer and singing bawdy songs, some of which seemed not at all appropriate for mixed company. But the young women seemed to know the words. They joined in and sang with good nature and without a trace of embarrassment. The British are a fun-loving, lusty people – great fun at parties – with little of the restraining self-consciousness of Canadians. Imagine a group of young women joining with a lot of young men singing, 'No balls at all – no balls at all, if your engine cuts out you'll have no balls at all.' I arrived back at Syerston having greatly enjoyed myself.

The next night, April 20th, it was Stettin, the largest and most important port on the Baltic and chief supply point for the German armies in North Russia. This too would be a round trip of about 1800 miles and while the main force was to go to Stettin, a small

number of Stirlings would attack the shorter range target of
Rostock, another Baltic port, and some Mosquitoes were to
celebrate Hitler's birthday by bombing Berlin.

We carried out the long trip at relatively low level in bright
moonlight. We were about three quarters of the way to Stettin and
climbing to bombing altitude when Tolman reported a fighter on
the port quarter, below, at about 600 yards. 'He looks like an Me
110, skipper,' said Tolman. 'And he's been sitting out there for a
little while. I guess he can't see me as well as I can see him. He's
coming in now – I'll tell you when to turn. He's getting into range
– Turn Port, Turn Port. Go!' At this I wheeled the machine into the
steepest, tightest turn that I, or it, could manage and skidded on
some left rudder for extra deflection. But if he followed this
manoeuvre he didn't open fire and neither did Tolman who said
afterwards, 'I couldn't bloody well fire. I was over on my arse from
the steep turn you were doing.'

'We've lost him', said Tolman, sounding almost disappointed.
Kelly, the mid-upper gunner had not seen him at all as the fighter
had been below his field of vision. We headed on again on the long
route to Stettin. I didn't envy the gunners, dependent as they were
upon their pilot for tactical decisions involving their safety.
Particularly the rear gunner; he sat alone, looking into blackness at
the rear; he had to be totally alert for long periods. Fighter attacks
most often came from the rear and he would be the first target. It
was lethally cold and he had to wear a leather suit equipped with
an electric heating apparatus. But even so one often saw gunners
with sores on their cheeks where the raw flesh had been seared by
the metal clasps of an oxygen mask at – 50°C.

We were one of 304 crews that attacked Stettin and the
operation seemed a success. It later transpired that it was in fact an
astonishing exhibition of accurate marking by H2S and accurate
bombing by the main force. On the camera evidence no fewer than
256 bombers dropped their bombs within 3 miles of the aiming
point. Nearly all the damage was concentrated in the centre of the
town where about a hundred acres of closely grouped industrial
buildings were devastated. This proved the worth of H2S on a
target of such topography as Stettin, a coastline with the town on a
bay. Ten hours later photo-reconnaissance aircraft found the whole
central portion of the port obscured by smoke from still-burning
fires. But the trip was not yet over.

Stettin lies on a southerly indentation of the Baltic into Prussia, north-east of Berlin and close to the Polish border. We were directed to fly back on a route north-west from Stettin across the Baltic to the town of Malmo on the southern tip of Sweden, thence west across the northern Baltic and Denmark and then across the North Sea. The planned route was a good one; we were to get away quickly from Stettin by dropping altitude as we went north. This I did, quickly dropping from our bombing height of 14,000 feet down to ground level. I could see the neat North German farmland only a few feet below as we raced across the open countryside to the nearby Baltic coast. We crossed the coast at a long sandy looking beach and raced over the water in bright moonlight. The path of the moon was on the right, ahead as we roared full speed for Malmo. I relaxed a little and breathed a sigh of relief. Too soon! Coming at us from the water on the port front quarter, on my side of the aircraft, were two lines of heavy tracer bullets. They moved out from their source like high speed streams of water from two fire hoses, neat regular spaces between each bar of light – vicious, unmistakable – coming straight for us. The question was, I had a fraction of a second to take action, should one move up or down? Down! I pushed the control column forward and turned to the right at the same time. The tracers whipped by, just above us, at enormous speed. Then a sudden glint of light on the starboard front quarter – God, it was the moon on the water – I pulled back hard on the control column, just in time – we almost hit the water with the starboard wing tip. I shuddered. But the tracer was still coming at us, swift and deadly, only now its source was on the beam, moving slightly to the port rear quarter. Again I saw the tracer shells moving to intercept us. I pulled up. Only this time the aim of the ship's gunners was inescapable. I heard two light flicks as explosive shells hit the fuselage and almost at the same instant a yell from Kelly on the intercom which I can only describe as a scream; I've never heard since such a cry from a human soul. But even while this was going on I couldn't help admiring the marksmanship of the ship's gunners. We would have to attend to them first. Looking over my shoulder I could see the black shape of the source of the exploding tracers. It was receding on our left, although they were still firing. There seemed no time for the rear gunner to return the fire but he did; I heard a long burst from his four Brownings as more tracers from the ship whipped by our left wing. The shells were coming from the rear now and were scattered across a larger piece of sky. Another few seconds and we would beat them. Several more streaked past the left wing tip. We did beat them – I looked back over the left wing and pulled up a few hundred feet. We were out of range. It all happened too quickly to be frightened but our adrenaline was certainly flowing.

Wilkes came on the intercom as we climbed. 'I'll get him on the rest bed', he said, referring to Kelly, the mid-upper gunner. I continued to climb while Wilkes slowly and carefully got Kelly out of his turret and on to the bed and hooked up his oxygen. We could climb quickly without a load and Wilkes was now moving about with a portable oxygen bottle strapped to his shoulder. Belton, similarly clad, went aft to help him. Soon they reported the situation.

'Two cannon shells came in the port side and exploded', Belton said. 'One of them exploded beneath Kelly's turret. He's been hit in the knees,' Wilkes added, 'I stopped up the blood and shot a morphine capsule in him. He's on the rest bed now – on oxygen.'

'Good lads', I said, unconsciously adopting the English term. 'Now let's see if we can get him home.' Soon we were at cruising altitude and could see the lights of Malmo in neutral Sweden as we turned westward.

I watched Polaris shining high on the starboard wingtip, confirming that we were travelling true west. The four Merlins purred as they pulled the unloaded aircraft, effortlessly it seemed, through the sky across Denmark, across the North Sea; then at last the welcome sight of the English coast loomed from the mist. When overhead at Syerston I asked for the ambulance and it met us at the dispersal site of F for Freddie. The trip had taken eight hours to fly and by now it was getting daylight. Kelly was taken first to the station hospital where his wounds were dressed. He was in great pain. Then he was transferred to the RAF hospital at Ely, a small town containing an ancient cathedral near Cambridge. We went as a crew to see him two days later, after the shrapnel had been removed from his legs. It was a fine hospital and he was being well cared for in a ward with many frostbite and burns patients. I noticed several aircrew, whose fingers and toes were exposed to the air; these digits were dark-looking, almost black, as if their owners were wearing wrinkled gloves on hands and feet. But the wrinkles were the useless flesh where blood circulation was no longer evident. Kelly was in good spirits but apologetic that he couldn't continue with us. I expect he'd been told that the war was over for him. Unquestionably he wanted to continue; he cried when we left and I too was upset. He seemed just a boy. I assured him that he had done well and could be proud of the nine operations we had flown as a crew. Had he done twice that number before being wounded he would probably have received a decoration but I didn't tell him so. We assured him that we would see him again, but I never did.

*   *   *

We had now flown six trips in the past ten days, fifty-three hours including our other flying, and no longer regarded ourselves as a novice crew. Neither, it seems, did the Air Force for Searby told me, 'Thompson, you've been posted to Pathfinders.' I was delighted.

He didn't tell me that he had himself been interviewed to take command of a Pathfinder squadron as soon as a vacancy occurred. I only learned that fact a few days later when to my surprise he arrived at Wyton after I did. So that's what his business had been about on the flight to Wyton that day!

We went by train from Syerston to Wyton and I learned at the station that the feelings of the crew about going to Pathfinders were mixed. Hanratty said, 'You had no right to volunteer me for the job as well as yourself.' I told him, 'You don't have to come if you don't want to. I can arrange for you to get into another crew who need a bomb-aimer.' He thought about that for a minute as he paced the station platform and lit a cigarette. I continued, 'I'm not twisting your arm – but I am going Pete, with you or without you.'

'It means two tour-rs', he said. 'Why should I do two tours when I need only do one. We'll be bloody lucky enough to complete one tour-r, let alone two.'

'You don't have to do two, unless you volunteer', I said. 'You can quit when you've done one'. I wasn't certain of this but threw it in anyway. Surely, I reasoned, they couldn't deny him the right to quit after one tour, if everyone else in Bomber Command had that right.

'All r-right, I'll come wi ye', he said. 'But I'll do only one tour-r'. He was the only one who made any remark about going to Pathfinders; the others, if they had misgivings, kept them to themselves.

What a difference there was between Syerston and Wyton! I even had a room of my own in the Officers' Mess. Not a large room to be sure but it had two beds, two small side tables, two

chests of drawers and two small closets. I thought it palatial. It was
intended for two junior officers but as I was soon to learn there
were not a great many junior officers on a Pathfinder squadron.
There were several sergeant pilots who had apparently done as
well or better than many officers on main force squadrons, and had
volunteered for Pathfinders. And there were many more senior
officers than a normal squadron had.

I was introduced for example to the Officer Commanding 'B'
Flight, Squadron Leader Walter Shaw DFC, a slim quiet balding
man in his thirties with dark hair and dark eyes, shortly after
promoted to Wing Commander. 'B' Flight also had on its roster two
other Squadron Leaders. These were ordinary pilots, like myself,
and since 'A' Flight had a similar complement, there were far more
senior officers than on a normal squadron. The officers' quarters
reflected this fact; there were more single rooms. After all, a
Squadron Leader or Wing Commander couldn't share a room with
a junior officer could he? Even if they were doing the same job!
Some of the senior officers had done a tour of operations early in
the war or had been in staff jobs at Bomber Command or at Coastal
Command. This type of operation was new to them as well and like
us they would not be marking targets until they appeared competent
enough to do so. 'You won't get a Victoria Cross in 8 Group,' it was
said. 'The AOC doesn't believe in them and has said so.' This
turned out to be true. No Pathfinder ever won a VC, though I can
think of a couple who should have. 'No', it was said, 'he wants
consistent, efficient performance and if you perform consistently
enough and efficiently enough for two tours, and still manage to
stay alive, you will be permanently awarded the right to wear the
little golden eagle, or 'shitehawk' above your left breast pocket'.
Well that was fine, at least we knew where we stood. Most
Pathfinders, like myself, felt that there was little likelihood of
surviving two tours anyway. So we might as well not think of
finishing anything. At least that was my attitude. I had accepted the
fact that I would probably not survive. Therefore I was not
concerned about being a junior officer amongst senior ones. Let me
explain this. After exposure a few times to bomber operations one
had to develop a philosophy with which to deal with the casualty
figures and the probability of one's death. This had to be different
from the attitude of a fighter pilot. Richthofen, for example, had
maintained that one must cultivate the unshaken conviction that the

enemy would fall; it had to be unthinkable that one should lose.[1] As I have mentioned, this attitude is helpful also in other kinds of head to head encounter, such as in chess, but although a certain amount of it was helpful to bomber aircrew it was not a complete philosophy. Something more was required. One had to learn to accept death and become used to the idea of it. One had to consider oneself as already dead. In that way one could live in honour, without fear of cowardice or death.

When I reported to the 'B' Flight Office where Shaw quietly held court, feet up on the desk, surrounded by other pilots, I noticed that he had a blackboard on the wall with the names of the 'B' Flight Captains printed on it in chalk and alongside each name was a red chalk square for each operation flown by that captain. Shaw's red squares traversed most of the board it seemed. I felt self-conscious when my eleven squares were filled in. On closer examination, however, there were several with not many more than I.

It was apparent also that, apart from Walter Shaw and 'Wimpey' Wellington, the two pilots who had done the most trips were only of Flight Lieutenant rank. These were F/Lt's Garvey and Wilmot. Garvey was a Canadian in the RAF, from Vancouver; Wilmot was English. I looked over the station personnel roster when I arrived and found that I was the only RCAF pilot there. As such I was paid £60 a month and with the pound at $5.00 I was receiving the same pay as the Station Commander, who was a Group Captain. A British officer of the same rank as I was paid only half as much. The crew informed me that they too had fine quarters compared to Syerston, and Belton said that the maintenance crew and the aircraft looked first-rate. We were well pleased.

1. About a year later, in June 1944, I finally met a pilot with whom I was able to discuss the differences between flying bombers and fighters. The meeting was a curious one; it occurred in the lobby of the Mount Royal Hotel in Montreal where, among a crowd of airmen, I was introduced to a tall, blond young man in civilian clothes. Struck by his piercing blue eyes I gleaned that he was a fighter pilot, but didn't catch his name. I asked him to join me in the bar for a drink. Strange, I thought, that a fighter pilot would drink only coke, while I was consuming coke with rum in it. I put it down to limited operational experience and began to explain what it was like flying bombers. The stranger listened politely for some moments, then remarked that flying bombers must be more dangerous and difficult than flying fighters. I agreed with that statement and there followed a silence which I finally thought to end by extending my hand. 'By the way,' I said, 'I should introduce myself. My name is Thompson'. The stranger stood, we shook hands and he said, 'Mine is Beurling'. And with that Canada's highest scoring fighter pilot of WWII walked away without another word.

We had arrived on April 28th, 1943, and did some local flying for a couple of days to inspect the nearby terrain and airfields. Construction was being completed by engineers at Alconbury and Polebrook for B-17 Flying Fortresses of the First Bombardment Wing, U.S. Eighth Air Force.

83 Squadron had the call sign OL painted on its aircraft. For example we flew OL-T on a local flight on April 28th. The squadron had been equipped with Lancasters a year earlier, in the spring of 1942, and had left 5 Group for 8 Group a couple of months later. I learned that it had lost three aircraft on the Essen raid of April 3rd, one on Stuttgart on April 14, one on Pilsen on April 16 and one on Stettin on April 20th, six in two and a half weeks. So we were the latest of the replacement crews.

*   *   *

On April 30, 1943, in a new and better equipped briefing room than at Syerston my crew and I assembled as strangers with the crews of our new squadron. On the map of Europe the ribbon led to a familiar place, Essen. A groan went up from many voices at thought of the most heavily defended target in Europe. Never mind, it was to be marked by the Mosquitoes with Oboe. They would release red TI's and our Lancasters would back them up with greens. I was to carry an ordinary bomb load without target indicators.

Procedure at Wyton seemed more organised. After an evening meal one could don flight clothes in one's room rather than in a barrack, then out to a bus in front of the brick, ivy-covered officers' mess. There was a spacious lawn in front. The rest of the officers got in the bus amid superstitious chattering, 'Oh wait, I forgot my scarf', or 'That is my seat – I always sit in that seat. Do you mind?' Then to the crew room, and vans to the aircraft. The crew had nav bags and flight bags and assorted junk. I asked Belton what he carried in his bag. 'Just a couple of spanners, a screwdriver and a sandwich', he said.

The most tense time for an operational crew seemed to be while standing on the round concrete dispersal site beside the aircraft. With the sun going down one tended to look at the freshness of the grass and the trees and at the nearby farm land while one smoked a last cigarette. There was always a wait for start-up time. This was when one felt butterflies. One would then get into the aircraft and start the engines and the butterflies would disappear. Once we had to wait for Hanratty. Unknown to me he always urinated on the tail wheel for luck and this night he couldn't do it. He was getting abuse from the rest of the crew for his poor performance when I finally discovered what was causing the delay.

We started the port inner engine first, for it ran the pneumatics and hydraulics. The ground crew were needed to get the engines started. They plugged in the 'trolley acc.', which was a battery cart, to the aircraft. Then a priming device was set for each engine in turn and they would prime each engine with fuel by a few pushes on a plunger. The engines were run up when the oil temperature reached about +15°C and coolant + 40°C. Each engine was run up in turn to about zero boost and the propeller pitch was checked for operation. The engine was then opened to a boost of + 4 pounds and the supercharger checked to ensure it was working. If the supercharger was put in 'S' (Supercharge) Ratio at ground level the revs would fall. This indicated that it was normal. It was then returned to M gear for use at low altitudes. 'S' gear would not be engaged again until about 12,000 feet had been reached on the climb. At this height the air had thinned to where the engine needed the 'blower' or supercharger to maintain its air supply to the fuel mixture. 'S' gear was then engaged.

One always checked the magnetos as well at about + 4 lb. boost. There were twin magnetos and twin spark plugs for the cylinders of each engine. When one magneto was switched off the RPM on that engine would drop a little. But if it dropped more than about 150 RPM it meant that the spark plugs were dirty or the gap on the contact breaker points needed resetting or the points were sticking. I complained one night to the 'chief' that there was an excessive mag drop on all four engines. Belton told me later that the crew had been required to work the rest of the night and half the next day to take out the spark plugs from each engine, clean them and put them back in. I hadn't realised it was such a job.

The weather on the ground on the 30th was bad and the operations of F/Sgt. Finding and F/Sgt. King were cancelled by the CO at the taxiing post because they were new to the Squadron and inexperienced.

We climbed through the cloud towards London on the first leg of the flight but before reaching the city turned to a heading slightly south of east. The sun had set, but a faint orange glow still remained above the horizon on the starboard rear quarter. We were

above a layer of cumulus cloud and five other Lancasters were
visible at slightly different altitudes, the nearest about a mile away,
all heading in the same direction. It was nice to have company. But
we lost sight of them as usual when the cloud and the darkness
closed in. We were now heading straight through the *Himmelbett*
line on a direct route to Essen. Sometimes Bomber Command
chose not to play games with a feint at one target and a thrust at
another. This was one of those times.

An hour after crossing the enemy coast I felt a strong jolt on
the controls and a thump on the wings as they took a sharply
increased load. We were approaching the target area but I could
see nothing near us. We had hit the slipstream of another aircraft.
It happened again a few minutes later. I could almost see the wings
bending upward from the stress. I don't know if it was the same
aircraft both times but this was not an uncommon event,
particularly now that efforts were being made to put up to ten
aircraft a minute over the targets.

It was cloudy and the attack became a 'Wanganui', that is six
Mosquitoes, each about three minutes apart, dropped sky markers
or parachute flares on Oboe. We were carrying an ordinary load of
11,500 pounds of bombs which we dropped on the sky-markers.
Lancasters of 83 and the other Pathfinder squadrons backed up the
skymarkers. I felt another thump as we were on the bomb run, but
this one was on the tail and didn't feel like a slipstream. 'Jesus',
said Tolman, the tail gunner, 'What was that?' We could not see
where the bombs were falling. We were at 18,000 feet when we
dropped ours. It turned out that most were accurately placed. Two
of the eight Mosquitoes failed for one reason or another to drop
their skymarkers so that there were times when none were visible.
Some crews reported watching the markers go out while they were
running in and so they could only estimate the position of bomb
release. Crews also reported that for the first time dummy flares
were shot up from the ground, away from the bomb release point.
But this caused only slight confusion because the dummies were
not as bright as our own flares. 305 aircraft attacked Essen that
night. Fifty-one turned back for one reason or another, twelve
were lost and forty-five were damaged. Ours was one of the
damaged. We had four large shell holes in the tail plane and
bursting fragments had perforated the two stabilisers and rudders
so that they looked like colanders, but Tolman in the rear turret had

not been hit and his turret had continued to function. The round trip required only four hours forty minutes flying time.

On May 4th it was fourteen of our squadron to mark and bomb in a large attack on Dortmund, an industrial and transport centre in the Ruhr. I blush to admit it but our stupidity almost got us into trouble. The route in was straight from England and we were to climb and reach full height by the Dutch coast. I found with some alarm that our rate of climb had fallen off. Even with extra throttle settings we couldn't get enough boost. We were levelling off at 15 thousand feet, rather than the expected twenty. Belton and I felt equally stupid when we simultaneously noticed that we had forgotten to engage the superchargers. The carburettors were starved for air above 12,000 feet. When engaged the engines surged with power and we rapidly gained most of the shortage of altitude. Dortmund's importance had increased by reason of the damage to Essen, and its industries had been working to replace gaps left by wrecked factories in that city. Large fires were started. Thirty aircraft were lost including our R 5629 piloted by Sgt. J.R. Leigh, with the Squadron Commander, W/C J.R. Gillman, aboard as an observer. They were both killed. Gillman had adopted the commendable practice of flying with new crews to give them confidence.

On return to base it was fog-bound and many crews reported difficulty in landing, while some were told to land elsewhere. Next day they trickled back to Wyton.

On May 9th, to my surprise, Searby arrived to take command of the Squadron and on May 12th it was 572 aircraft to Duisburg, on the Rhine, fourteen of these from our Squadron. This time nine Oboe Mosquitoes marked the target. Eighty percent of their red markers, on the photographic evidence, fell within two miles of the aiming point. They, and the back-up flares dropped by PFF Lancasters showed where to put the bombs and 410 bombers did so, most of them within three miles of the aiming point. This took one hour and was a remarkable result. Forty-eight acres had been smashed and much industrial damage done, including four factories in the August Thyssen steel works group. We lost one aircraft from 83 Squadron, W 4955, piloted by Flight Lieutenant L.A. Rickinson, DFC, which crashed near Emnes. Two others of our aircraft were coned in searchlights and received minor damage. The following will give some idea of the assessment of the ground photos from each aircraft. 420 prints were examined. 166 of them could not be plotted either by the ground detail or by the fires shown in them. nineteen were plotted by fires to be 3 miles or more outside the aiming point and eighteen were plotted by ground detail also to be outside 3 miles, but 126 were plotted by fires to be within 3 miles and eighty-eight were plotted by ground detail to be within the same 3 miles of the aiming point. This confirmed the conclusion that the Oboe ground-marking technique, if not accurate enough for very precise attacks against small targets, was nevertheless a reliable means of carrying out effective area bombing. This was proved time and again in the continuing Battle of the Ruhr.

The same could not be said for H2S with which our aircraft were fitted. H2S was still in short supply. The Pathfinder squadrons were not all equipped with it until the following September and of course none of the main force squadrons had it. We went on a second attack on Pilsen on May 13th and the marking this time achieved an excellent concentration of bombs but they were in open fields about two miles to the north of the Skoda works. At the time I thought it a much better attack than the first. But although the result was fruitless, the marking was not that bad. If the target had been larger the damage would have been great. A small target on the edge of a small town, without distinctive topographical features, was simply not a profitable objective for H2S. Some lessons had to be learned twice! On the way back we were followed for some time by a Ju 88 but its pilot must have been inexperienced. Despite several opportunities in the clear, dark skies he did not attack. It is conceivable that we were one of the earlier of the bomber stream and he was tracking us as a guide to other fighters for the following bomber stream but that seemed unlikely to me. If it were so he would ultimately have attacked. We lost another aircraft from 83 when W 4981 piloted by Sgt. A.S. Renshaw failed to return; he was killed. F/O Mappin had been forced back early with an oxygen failure in his mid-upper turret.

There was another attack on Dortmund on May 23rd which I missed. I mention it only because my Yorkton friend Phil Weedon had his aircraft damaged that night by flak and his gas tanks were holed. He got the aircraft home to 6 Group but when over his base two of his engines ran out of fuel and cut out. He made a crash landing and fortunately neither he nor his crew were injured. I should mention too another incident which occurred the same night to Sgt. S.N. Sloan, the Canadian bomb-aimer of a 6 Group aircraft. After bombing Dortmund his aircraft was coned by searchlights and badly damaged by flak. His pilot put the aircraft into a steep dive but couldn't shake the searchlights and of course received more flak while coned. The pilot and three of the crew baled out but Sloan did not. He took control of the aircraft, flew it clear of the defences and headed for home. A gale was blowing from front to back of the fuselage because the front hatch was gone where the pilot had baled out and the rear turret door was left open by the exit of the rear gunner. The navigator managed to give Sloan a course to steer, although his nav. lights were out. Sgt. Parslow and F/O Bailey, who had stayed with Sloan, helped him land. Sloan was immediately commissioned and awarded the rare Conspicuous Gallantry Medal. Bailey was awarded the DFC and Parslow the DFM.

There followed a thirteen day lull in operations for Bomber Command. Persistent early morning sea-mist and fog over British airfields made landing conditions impossible for returning bombers.

During the lull we were not idle. There were constant training exercises to be done and one day we were sent up to take photographs of our airfield. We did simulated and actual bombing exercises from 20,000 feet on ranges to improve our accuracy and we did fighter affiliation exercises with P-47 Thunderbolt fighters of the U.S.A.F. These were powerful, heavy machines. One afternoon after one such exercise, I had a pleasant lunch at his airfield with a Lieutenant from Tacoma, Washington who was flying Thunderbolts. It was like meeting someone from home. When I asked how the Thunderbolts were to handle he said, 'They have the gliding angle of a streamlined crowbar.' But he seemed pleased with them and in our exercise had come screaming down upon us like a falcon from great altitude. There seemed little doubt in his mind that he could easily have shot us down; there was equally little doubt in mine.

*   *   *

If I have given the impression that all was operational flying I have erred. We had now been on a squadron for two months and during that time I had flown fifteen operations. Excluding the time spent on leave this averaged out at one every 3-4 days. So on the nights when we were not flying we were usually out to a movie or to the 'Jolly Butchers', the 'Ferryboat' or the 'Pike and Eel'. So it was either a movie, a pub, a dance or all three. Also, there was the

nearby town of Huntingdon with two cinemas and several pubs; the
other way was the village of St. Ives where Oliver Cromwell had
lived. The large red brick barn in which he had trained his troops
was still standing, within walking distance of Wyton. We
occasionally had the use of a swimming pool at a nearby mansion.
There were squash courts and a combined cinema and dance hall
on the station and of course there was female company. I must tell
you about the WAAFs who did a wide variety of the necessary and
difficult jobs at an airfield. They were everywhere, except in
aircrew, and one of them in the intelligence section had already
addressed herself to that male bastion. She was Section Officer
Jocelyn McLean and she had persuaded Garvey to take her up on
both day and night flights. We heard via the grapevine that she
intended stowing away with him on an operation as well. Searby
however heard of it also and warned her that she was not to do so.
I doubted that Jocelyn would be stopped permanently by such an
ultimatum but it did slow her down for a while.

Most of the young women however were not officers. They
worked in the parachute section and in armaments; they drove
trucks and tractors, they staffed the control tower, the radios and the
met office. They were sometimes aircraft fitters and riggers and
they staffed the kitchens, the canteens, the hospital and the
administration section. One day while scrambling up the narrow
fuselage and over the main wing spar of a Lanc to get to the pilot's
seat, my way was blocked by a round rear end. The head and
shoulders attached to it were stuffed inside the H2S set. I gave the
rear end a friendly slap to warn it that I was coming by when
around turned the prettiest face and brightest blue eyes I had seen
in a long time. I was startled; I asked her what she was doing there.
She said, 'I'm the RDF bloke,' meaning radio direction finding, but
'bloke' she most assuredly was not. These women were all very
good at their jobs and worked with intelligence and dedication.
Being healthy and young they liked to play with equal vigour. And
this is where the RAF and I once more did not see eye to eye.
Officers were not allowed to fraternise with 'Other Ranks'. Most
officers obeyed this rule and I too found it easy not to fraternise
with males of other ranks but with young women the rule was
impossible. When one saw a pretty face and a snugly fitting blue
skirt wrapped around shapely hips, below which was a pair of grey
stockings encasing beautiful legs, how could one mistake these

creatures for 'Other Ranks'? I for one could not be so blind.

One such young woman joined me for a drink at the 'Jolly Butchers' one night and after closing time we were walking home in the bright moonlight. My spirits had been enlivened by alcohol and by this beautiful female's presence, so I took hold of the gas mask which we were required to carry in a shoulder bag and, swinging it round in an arc, tried to see if I could fling it in the air and get it stuck on the telephone wires. Not a very brilliant idea, because a large black limousine appeared at this time and I missed the telephone wires anyway. The car passed by and the 'Other Rank' agreed that it would be fun to tarry a while in a haystack near the road. After a pleasant hour's kissing and dalliance in the hay we both could happily have thrown our gas masks away. But I had not heard the last of gas masks, even though the rule to carry them was soon rescinded. The next day was a Sunday and all officers were asked to appear in the officers' lounge by order of Group Captain Graham, the Station Commander. It transpired that Graham had been driving to base at Wyton the night before when, of all things, he saw an officer whose identity he couldn't ascertain, (although he now was looking directly at me) drunkenly swinging his gas mask in the air and shouting at the top of his voice while he had his free arm around the waist of a WAAF. He could not have mistaken me for anyone else; no other pilot then at Wyton had 'Canada' sewn on his shoulders. I felt like clucking my disapproval of the loathsome display he described, but hadn't the nerve. In future, continued the Station Commander, there was to be no more of this fraternising with other ranks. Two nights later the same young lady and I were occupying another and larger haystack when I told her of the CO's attitude and warned her sternly about fraternising with officers. She assured me that she had never fraternised with an officer because officers were gentlemen and she certainly had not been out with any gentlemen.

CHAPTER NINE

Attrition and Hamburg

ON May 27th I was not feeling well when I got up. I had a headache and felt feverish, but I would have to forget it – operations were on, and so I flew a night flying test of 35 minutes. We went to briefing and learned that the target was Essen again. I was by this time feeling quite ill. Some would say that Essen was enough to make anyone ill, but I had to decide; should I go on the operation and risk myself and the crew in the hands of a sick pilot or should I tell Searby how I felt? I decided to tell him. He said, 'Why didn't you mention it at briefing Thompson?' To which I replied, 'At briefing sir, I thought I'd be able to go. But I don't feel well enough.'

'Well, you'd better get over to the hospital', he said. He appeared concerned that the squadron might be one aircraft short of a maximum effort, which the attack was to be. I went to the hospital where the doctor took my temperature and put me in bed. Searby came in and I heard him muttering with the doctor who was saying, 'He's got a temperature of 103.' I wondered then what the case would have been had I felt as bad as I did but with no temperature. I would probably have been whisked off the squadron and labelled 'L.M.F.' – lack of moral fibre. There was indeed such a classification; it was applied to the flight engineer whom I mentioned earlier. I was always curious about what happened to such people. In the case of a pilot, probably he'd be sent to Morpeth to relieve one of the Poles. As it happened, the operations of five aircraft from our Squadron whose crews had been briefed that night as markers, were cancelled.

Many men lost the battle with fear and suffered a breakdown of nerves during their first operational tour, although I knew of no instance of it happening on a second. It is difficult to say how many men were removed from a squadron for this reason but everyone knew of crews who had lost one or more members, if they had not themselves lost one, because of uncharacteristic petty crimes, air sickness, ear trouble, reckless flying, nightmares, insomnia, bed wetting, waking screaming or other causes. It was rare that fear manifested itself in a flat refusal to fly, although there were cases of that as well. I learned from some who knew, that the Air Force dealt harshly with these people, first stripping them of the rank which had come with their aircrew status and then posting them to unpleasant ground duties. Marginal cases were sent to 'Aircrew Refresher Centres' where they spent a few weeks doing PT and attending lectures but this rarely did any good. Most of the L.M.F. cases, if British, were offered a choice of working in the coal mines or going to the Army. I don't know what happened if they were Canadian. I expect they were simply sent back to Canada, perhaps to join the conscripts. There was one case of a bomb-aimer on 76 Squadron who, while on a practice exercise, fell through the forward hatch of his aircraft. It was only after several minutes that the crew realised he was still desperately hanging on underneath. They finally got a rope around him and dragged him in. When he got on the ground he flatly refused to fly again. The poor man was pronounced L.M.F.[1] At the opposite end of the scale was the flagrant case of three members of a crew who left their aircraft as it taxied out for take-off on operations. They were summarily court-martialled. But I don't know how much good all of this discipline did. I knew of squadron commanders who were afraid to fly and, having some choice in the matter, picked only the easy operations. It was my conviction that no amount of discipline was any good if the person was not motivated.

My crew were overjoyed at the unexpected good fortune of my illness. 'Thompson's sick and can't fly, so they've given us ten days leave. Goodbye Punch, have a good leave.' How one was expected to have a good leave lying in a hospital bed was a mystery to me but I said, 'You too. Have a good leave.' I was up and about in a couple of days and the fever, whatever it was, receded as quickly as it had come on. While I was ill however, Wilkes, before he went on leave, managed to get a couple of extra trips with another crew. At that rate he would finish before I would. I took advantage of the leave to visit Jean Gaffikin who by now was a teleprinter operator in the WAAFs at an RAF Group Headquarters at Gillingham, Kent. After a day there we had a quarrel and I was intending to leave but we patched up our differences and I stayed at a nearby club for a couple of days more and took her dancing. We dined and had our portrait taken together and went for walks. Does that sound mundane? But then we quarrelled again. I should have realised that some twosomes are not ordained to be but one's pride and ego get in the way and prolong a relationship which, if both parties could

1. This incident is mentioned in the book Bomber Command, by Max Hastings. See page 217 of that book for a more detailed discussion of L.M.F.

be objective, they would quickly end. We were reluctant to end it, partly I think because it never really got started, and each of us felt that it should have. In retrospect it seems stupid and masochistic to torture oneself in this manner. I never understood until then the passage in the Bible which says, '...if thy hand or thy foot offend thee, cut them off ...if thine eye offend thee, pluck it out...' I was learning however that emotional surgery cannot be anaesthetised for it must be performed by the surgeon upon himself.

After being on leave a few times I found that I was learning more about England than the English; but this is always true. Strangers quickly see more of one's own country or city than one does oneself. I returned early from this leave on June 11th. Operations were on and the squadron went to Munster, losing Squadron Leader Swift, DFC and crew aboard R 5686. Swift survived.

When I reached the station that evening there was some entertainment going on in the airmen's canteen. A dance orchestra, some professional female dancers and Vera Lynn, the famous wartime singer, had come to Wyton. I later asked one of the attractive young women in the company to dance and we became friends. We spent a pleasant sunny Sunday afternoon in Cambridge, walking the grassy backs of Trinity, Kings and St. John's College. She was a delight to be with. She danced at the Windmill Theatre in London. Her name was Marion Lind but although I tried to turn our relationship into something other than a platonic one we remained just friends. I later saw her in London a couple of times. My ego suggested, though she didn't say so, that she had a boy-friend somewhere in the forces.

*   *   *

But this is a flying narrative! On June 12th we did the usual night flying test and were briefed for Bochum, slightly east of the geographic centre of the Ruhr. It was a centre for transport and heavy industry including iron and coal and had chemical plants and branches of the Krupp concern.

It was impossible to get at Bochum from any direction without being shot at for thirty miles each way but probably the best approach was from the south-east. In preparation for running this gauntlet I decided *en route* that I should first go to the toilet. I would have no other opportunity to do so once the fun and games commenced. The Air Force had thought of this problem and its designers had developed a hot-water-like bottle equipped with a snap-shut lid. This was for the pilot who couldn't leave the pilot's seat to use the more commodious facilities in the after section of the aircraft. Imagine the mechanics of this when the user was wearing thermal underwear, heavy clothes, a pair of zippered flying gauntlets and silk flying gloves. I had solved these problems successfully and we were well past the enemy coast when the mid-upper gunner called out, 'There's a bandit low on the starboard quarter.'

I immediately snapped shut the lid of the urinal device and grabbed the control column to make a steep turn to starboard. Unfortunately the lid snapped shut on the nearest portion of my adjacent anatomy and hung on like an enraged lobster, while I required the strength of both hands to execute a manoeuvre which by now was becoming habitual – a very steep and very diving turn towards the fighter, before he attacked – not during his attack. And then pulling out in the opposite direction, followed by a continuing turn back on track – not caring if we toppled our gyros. Whether this was an intelligent thing to do or not I had no way of knowing but if I could topple his goddam gyros I would. Whether by luck or not, it worked. We didn't see the fighter again and the gunners were once more annoyed that they hadn't fired a shot. I unfastened the lobster from between my legs and resumed the route to Bochum, climbing at full power to regain four thousand feet of lost altitude. I had told the gunners that they should tell me immediately they saw a fighter and I would take evasive action. Only if we couldn't shake him off in the dark were they to fire their guns. They of course hadn't much choice in this because they couldn't fire from an almost upside down position. Besides, firing .303s would be no match for the fighter's cannon.

We were able to reach eighteen thousand feet before Bochum, high enough to attack, if not high enough to feel comfortable. I squeezed another few feet from the four Merlins before we reached the city. Then in the usual display of flak above some scattered strato-cumulus cloud we dropped our bombs. We had not as yet carried target indicators.

The aircraft were well concentrated, moving over the target at the rate of five a minute. The defences had recently been strengthened and since all the attacking aircraft were bombing upon flares placed by Oboe it was a case of each side attempting to saturate the other. All the flak guns had to aim at the same relatively small box of air space and all the aircraft had to fly through that box, so how many shells per minute could be put into the box and how many aircraft per minute could be run through it, without running into each other? Also, how many would likely be shot down? Survival or 'shot-down' in these circumstances was a nice statistical problem for someone with a mind of that bent. We lost one aircraft, ED 603, piloted by Flying Officer E.A. Tilbury.

One fact which continued to surprise me on these raids was the number of aircraft which could pass over one spot at the same time as oneself without seeing each other. I was seldom tempted however, to turn around and fly in the opposite direction. I will tell you later of one occasion when this became necessary.

During the following week I did several hours of Beam Approach practice. The instructor for these exercises was a New Zealander, Flight Lieutenant Val Moore, DSO, DFM. Val's normal duties were as one of the pilots of the Bomber Command meteorological flight at Oakington near Cambridge; he used to take off every two or three days in a high-performance Mosquito from which everything but a camera had been stripped. It contained no armament or armour plate and no bombs. He would reach an altitude of close to 40,000 feet and fly over selected targets in Germany, relying upon his speed and altitude to avoid interception. He would observe the weather systems as they moved over the continent and would report back; then he would depress the nose of the Mosquito and streak for home. In this respect we had an advantage over the Germans. The weather came to Europe from the Atlantic, moving on the prevailing winds from west to east, so the British weather forecasters had an easier job predicting weather over Western Europe than did their German counterparts. They knew what the weather was and what it had been over Britain, whereas the Germans had to guess, based upon what they could see, and upon scattered information received in hasty radio transmissions from German submarines which had surfaced in the Atlantic.

Val was a happy chain-smoking man who had completed two distinguished tours of operations with 83 Squadron, starting as an NCO. I wondered later whether he would have been quite so happy in his souped-up Mosquito if he'd known that the Germans had a Me 262 jet, easily capable of intercepting him and only prevented from doing so by Hitler's order to turn it into a 'blitz bomber'. This splendid aircraft, the first jet aircraft in service, did not see general service until 1944. With a top speed of 540 mph it was far more deadly than any allied fighter, particularly when firing rockets, and undoubtedly would have changed the course of the war had it been used earlier as a fighter. Only 200 of them saw action out of 1400 built. But even without pursuit by 262s, the met flight of nine aircraft would lose about one aircraft a month. One of Val's additional duties was to come to Wyton periodically and to supervise pilots in practising beam procedures, in an Oxford. We always looked forward, like farm youngsters to a travelling salesman, to Val's visits; he invariably had news or gossip of something new in the air, either in Britain or Germany. We believed that Air Marshal Harris wouldn't make a move without first consulting Val.

We also had a visit that week from the representative of Gieves, men's tailors of London. This poor man, who appeared every month or so with an assistant, carried out his ancient trade in the same way it had been done in the Boer War. He would carefully measure one for a uniform, return to London to have a preliminary fitting made up, and a month later bring it back rough-stitched, with loose threads hanging, and padding showing at the shoulders. He would have the officer put it on for a final fitting before taking it back again to London and having it finally sewn with stitched lapels, pockets, badges, buttons and rank. In this way a uniform took about six weeks to make up. The only problem was that many of the officers at Wyton didn't last six weeks. So there was a brisk trade in brand new, second-hand uniforms. 'Did you know Flying Officer so and so? Well, we have a fine uniform here which he ordered but I am told he is no longer at Wyton. Would you care to try it on?' After a while this gentleman learned why his final sales continued to be less than his initial fittings. He bore this loss with equanimity and soon learned to say, instead of it having been ordered by Flying Officer so and so, that Gieves had had it made up in standard size for final alteration and fitting to one's individual size and taste. Yes, those were his words! A uniform made to one's taste. I had been under the impression that it was the Air Force's taste which governed such matters. But he was not dismayed by such suggestion from me. After all he had made uniforms for Lord Kitchener and Emperor Haile Selassie; he wasn't about to be upset by one flippant, flying Canadian.

I was a little larger of frame and bulk than most of his customers so I never did succeed in getting a new second-hand uniform. But to my amazement he extended credit so I had two uniforms made up on the never, never plan. Here was someone who had a lot more confidence than I that six weeks from now I would be there to accept the finished product.

*   *   *

It was in June of 1943 that for the first time Fighter Command made an effort to assist Bomber Command in the night offensive against Germany. It seems incredible that for three years after the Battle of Britain, Fighter Command had kept up to 1,000 day fighters sitting around England without rendering any assistance whatever to Bomber Command. Yet such was the case. If they did not possess the technology and equipment to fight at night one might have expected them to donate their cannon to those who did. But Bomber Command continued to fly its aircraft with no belly turrets and with only the small calibre .303 machine guns, similar to those used in WWI. Finally, in response to the pressure upon Bomber Command the Air Staff allocated a single squadron of Beaufighter IV's to the task of engaging the German night fighters over their own territory. Not the far superior Mosquitoes, not an aircraft equipped with the latest night fighter radar, not several squadrons but a single squadron whose elderly aircraft would not be able to keep up with the German fighters, let alone shoot them down. What, you may ask were the reasons for this apparent blunder? And of course there were reasons; they were good ones too. The best night fighters, several excellent Mosquito squadrons, were in existence, but they must be kept for the defence of Britain. That was one reason, although clearly the Germans were in no position to launch another Blitz against Britain. But the very best and latest of airborne interception radar must not be used; it might get shot down and then the Germans would have it wouldn't they? This timorous philosophy could not have been developed by people who knew that if you have an edge in war, you use it because you won't have it long. As if the Germans weren't doing very well with what they had! That was another reason. However, the main reason was that, unlike the Germans, who kept both fighters and bombers in each of their *Luftflotten* under one operational control, the

British had split their Air Forces in two. There was Fighter Command and there was Bomber Command and, as you might expect, 'never the twain shall meet'.

Whatever had happened, one wondered, to the cry of the founder of the RAF, Lord Trenchard, who in World War I had said, 'You are asking me to fight the battle this year with the same machines I fought it last year. We shall be hopelessly outclassed, and something must be done...' No doubt this quotation was prominently displayed in the offices of those who decided upon a single squadron of Beaufighters. The task was given to Wing Commander Bob Braham and 141 Squadron, an effective and aggressive leader and a fine squadron. The squadron was equipped with 'Serrate' an airborne radar which enabled their aircraft to home on the airborne interception radar transmissions of the German fighters. The range of this equipment was about ninety miles but it indicated only the bearing and not the distance of the enemy, and this was a serious limitation for the slow moving Beaufighters. Serrate was displayed on an ordinary airborne interception (A.I.) radar tube so that in the final stages of intercept the set could be switched over from Serrate to A.I. The A.I. would then be used to bring the enemy within visual range. The set operator also had to navigate the aircraft, so he was equipped with a Gee set as well and was given a swivel chair to get from the A.I. to the navigation equipment. 141 Squadron first operated on June 14, 1943 but by September their results had clearly not been spectacular. Serrate, in this period, made 1,180 contacts with enemy fighters but only twenty of these resulted in combats. The Beaufighter was clearly inadequate to match the speed of the German night fighters.[1] The Me 110s and Ju 88s immunity from attack and the Bomber Command casualties were reflecting this fact. The cover of darkness for Bomber Command was rapidly being lifted.

Statistics of the 141 Squadron experience for the period 14 June – 7 September, 1943 are as follows:

Sorties despatched: 233

Sorties completing patrols: 179

Casualties: 3 lost

1. This conclusion was reached by the authors of The Strategic Air Offensive Against Germany, p.110, but it was well known at the time to the crews of both Bombers and the Beaufighters.

3 damaged

Serrate contacts: 1180 (approx.)

Too brief or distant to follow: 520 (approx.)

Held and followed: 490 (approx.)

Converted to AI: 108

Resulting visuals: 33

Resulting combats: 20

Claims: 13 destroyed

1 probable

4 damaged

Fifty-four contacts, none of which resulted in combats, were obtained by A.I. without the prior use of Serrate. Ten of these were on friendly aircraft. Four fortuitous sightings of enemy aircraft also occurred. These resulted in the claim of one enemy aircraft being damaged. O.R.S. (F.C.) Report, 10th Sept. 1943.

On June 16th fourteen of our Squadron's aircraft went to Cologne, a trip I missed because of some extra beam approach training which I had undertaken. We lost Pilot Officer Murray, an experienced captain and crew. Three of our aircraft suffered flak damage and another was badly mauled by a fighter. Next day I and my crew, with cameramen and senior officers aboard as passengers, put on a demonstration on a bombing range of coloured pathfinder pyrotechnics.

On June 18th we lost a newly-arrived crew captained by Flight Sergeant Cummings when he was caught by bad weather on return from an exercise. With cloud at 400 feet he was seen on fire coming below the cloud when he hit a farm building and ploughed into some trees near Grantham. All were killed and no one knew the cause of the fire.

On June 21st we went to Krefeld, a city about five miles west of the Rhine, between Duisburg and Dusseldorf. Now that I was on a Pathfinder squadron I realised that we would have to carry out the precise role allotted to us and would be unable to freelance visually in search of military objectives of our own. We were using H2S every night in preparation for the roles we would soon carry out. The first of these would probably be to drop green back-up flares for the red Oboe markers on short range targets, or green back-ups for the red visual markers on long range targets. Possibly however we would open the long range attacks by dropping yellow markers blind on H2S, or we might mark the targets visually with reds after the yellows had been dropped. But on Krefeld it was routine bombing on the Oboe flares. Two thousand tons of bombs were dropped. We carried a typical load and flew a typical flight in heavy flak to the Ruhr. The losses were untypical in that forty-four of the 705 aircraft taking part were lost. This was above the average but the target was well defended and the attack took place in bright moonlight, ideal for the fighters, so the loss was predictable. The target was a solid mass of fires, glowing orange and giving off huge clouds of thick smoke to 15,000 feet. 83 Squadron sent out fourteen of the total and lost two aircraft, ED 907 piloted by Flight Sergeant D.W.C. Fletcher, and EE 121 piloted by Pilot Officer H. Mappin, both of whom were killed. Two nights later nine crews from our Squadron went to Mulheim, losing one, Sgt. Rust and crew. The Squadron Operations Record Book states that my crew was one of the nine, but my log book does not show this and I accept my log book as the more accurate.

An interesting sidelight to this raid was provided by Wing Commander 'Doc' MacGown, a London ophthalmologist who, in World War I, had been shot down as a fighter pilot. Doc was a tall, lean, hawk nosed man in his mid-fifties. In good physical condition he several times scrounged a ride on operations, ostensibly to test some infra red binoculars which he had developed, although most of us thought this only an excuse to fly on operations. He reported at interrogation after the raid that he had seen the target quite clearly without the glasses.

*   *   *

We marked our first target on July 3rd. It was my 18th trip, an attack by 600 aircraft on Cologne. 83 Squadron provided nine of these. We carried the usual 4,000 pounder, four 1,000 pounders, two 500s and in addition, five Target Indicators. Our function was to back up or reinforce the aiming point by dropping green flares on top of the reds which had already been dropped on Oboe. We now had a new aircraft of our own, equipped with H2S. It was ED 601 and although it was not exclusively ours we flew it frequently and its call letters were OL-T. On the route in we observed two aircraft blow up with bombs on board, in bright shattering explosions. It was easy to tell whether or not an exploding aircraft had bombs on board.

The Luftwaffe conducted a test this night of a new idea put forward by *Major* Hajo Hermann; this was to send up freelancing day fighters over the target at night, piloted by night-bomber pilots. The idea was to exploit the light from the searchlights, fires and flares to find the bombers. Typically the searchlights alone would illuminate a hundred or more aircraft for brief periods during an attack. Hermann had difficulty in obtaining aircraft but did manage to scrounge five Fw 190's and seven Me 109's to test the idea. It worked. He reported three days later to *Generalfeldmarschall* Erhard Milch, 'I opened fire on one bomber which began to burn at once but carried on flying for about four minutes although it was on fire. So I let him have it again from the side, right in the cockpit, and then it went down like a stone – the crew must have been hit'[1] his pilots accounted for ten bombers that night. Milch was delighted.

As for ourselves, we carefully dropped our target indicators not far from the railway station. We knew that the Cologne cathedral was close to the station and of course we had no desire to hit it; neither however did we take any special pains to miss it. We were concerned only to drop the target indicators as back-up flares to the Oboe Mosquitoes' ground markers. Large fires were started in the Kalk, Dentz and Mulheim area, three congested industrial districts on the east bank of the Rhine comprising an area of some five square miles which contained the Humboldt-Deutz Works, Germany's largest producer of U-boat diesel engines, and the Gottfried Hagen Works, a major producer of batteries. Upon the return journey I was awed at the apparent damage; there were immense fires and a cloud of smoke reaching to 12,000 feet which I could still see from a distance of 90 miles, on the journey home. On landing we found that one of our crews had been forced to return early with a sick navigator.

It was now clear to all in Bomber Command that if we had not developed a rapier-like ability to attack Germany, we were, despite the increasing losses being inflicted upon us, a formidable bludgeon. With the attack upon Cologne the Battle of the Ruhr drew to a close. There would be no attacks on Germany for a week because of a full moon but the main offensive would then continue.

Our next operation happened in R 5868 Q for Queenie. This Mark I Lancaster alone of some twenty-three which I flew, survived

1. Hermann is quoted to this effect by David Irving in *The Rise and Fall of the Luftwaffe*, p.225

the war intact, having completed 137 operations. It is now on display in the Royal Air Force Museum at Hendon. But first a word about the man who regularly flew Queenie; he was Flight Lieutenant Frederick Garvey, known to us as 'Rickie'. He was a Canadian in the RAF, the son of Art Garvey, a sports editor on the Vancouver Province. Rickie was himself a reporter for that paper. He worked his way to England on a freighter in 1940 and became the first pilot in Bomber Command to complete sixty trips, straight through without a break. He was awarded first a DFC, then a DSO on completion of his second tour, but was killed on a training flight in an Oxford a few weeks after completing the sixty trips. Garvey flew Queenie more than any other pilot. He flew her to Hamburg on July 27th with Brigadier General Fred Anderson as a passenger, observing the operation. Anderson was commander of the 8th Bomber Command, U.S. 8th Air Force. I flew Queenie to Turin on July 12th and was not at all impressed with the way she handled. She tended to keep the right wing low and I couldn't trim out this fault. When Garvey returned from leave I told him what a dunker he had for an aircraft.

We took off at 10.46, an all-Lancaster force, fourteen of them from Wyton, intended to hasten the surrender of Italy now that the Allied armies were starting the advance up the Italian boot. This raid followed immediately upon Mussolini being deposed. After crossing France above the cloud and over the Alps, which were covered with cloud, we reduced altitude to about 5,000 feet on the run up to and over Turin. This is a good-sized city and it was clearly discernible. I could see apartment buildings and tenements, even commercial areas in its northern half. We ran up towards the huge factories of the Fiat Works with Queenie's bomb doors open. I clearly saw the factories but we were a few seconds late in dropping and although I think we hit the target, we did not hit its centre.

Soon we were flying over southern France *en route* back. There was not as much darkness, due to the season, as the planners would have liked so they had routed us home on a detour, flying west from Italy across France near Bordeaux, and well out over the Bay of Biscay before turning North for England. An hour later the sun had risen and we were heading up the Bay of Biscay when I saw a U-boat sitting calmly on the surface, charging his batteries in the early morning sun. Damn! We had no bombs and without them were not keen to exchange machine gun bullets for exploding cannon shells. Admiral Dönitz had temporarily withdrawn most of the U-boats from the Atlantic in May, and the Allies now dominated it, but that was no reason to allow this blatant stranger to sun himself with impunity; I asked Wilkes to report the sighting and its position, which he did, and I understand that a Beaufighter came out shortly thereafter and sank the sub. The detour over the Atlantic gave us extra flying time. We took 9 hours 30 minutes on the flight and it was fully daylight when we brought Queenie down at Wyton.

I learned on our return that Maurice Chick, my English roommate, had seen two submarines surfaced on this trip and, being either braver or more foolhardy than I, machine-gunned them without receiving any return fire. For a couple of days after this we did gunnery exercises and engaged in mock battles with fighters at Debden.

Bomber Command losses in the four months between mid-March and mid-July 1943 amounted to 1056 aircraft and crews. The maximum strength of the Command's aircraft during the same period had been 826 aircraft (sent to Dortmund on May 23rd). So the Command had suffered a loss in excess of its maximum strength over a period of four months.

We had been forced to use spare navigators since our trip to Stettin but a new navigator finally arrived for us on July 23rd. He was fair-haired Flying Officer Jack Bedell, and what a navigator he was! We flew a couple of cross-country trips around Britain while he and the crew got used to each other. I couldn't believe the difference; a torrent of information came to me in calm cultured language from the navigator's compartment; courses to steer, wind changes, E.T.A.'s, safety altitudes, prohibited areas, balloons, weather reports, airfield facilities, set your watch; whatever a pilot wanted to know, Bedell had it ready and waiting. He had already done some operations, not many, and had volunteered for Pathfinders. Now he was operating the H2S set like a veteran, he was swearing at it. I would be greatly surprised if we got off track with this man aboard.

With a navigator training programme to be carried out we missed the opening night of the Battle of Hamburg on July 24th. Books have been written about these attacks and I do not wish to add to what has been said except to give the impressions of myself and crew.

The battle consisted of four raids by the RAF on July 24th, 27th and 29th and August 2nd, together with two raids on July 25th and 26th by the U.S. 8th Air Force.

The total number of aircraft sorties flown by Bomber Command in the four raids, was as follows:

1 Group – 5 Lancaster Squadrons, 3 Wellington Squadrons, 564 sorties bombed

3 Group – 7 Stirling Squadrons, 1 Lanc II Squadron, 2 Halifax Squadrons (Special Operations), 407 sorties bombed.

4 Group – 7 Halifax Squadrons, 1 Wellington Squadron, 578 sorties bombed.

5 Group – 11 Lancaster Squadrons, 518 sorties bombed.

6 Group – (Canadian) – 5 Halifax Squadrons, 2 Wellington Squadrons and 2 Wellington Squadrons converting to Halifaxes, 250 sorties bombed.

8 Group – (Pathfinders)-3 Lancaster Squadrons, 2 Halifax Squadrons, 1 Stirling Squadron converting to Lancasters, 2 'Oboe' Mosquito Squadrons, 1 Mosquito Squadron, 386 sorties bombed.

Fighter Command flew Intruder Operations by 7 Mosquito Squadrons, 1 Beaufighter Squadron.

20% of the aircrew involved in the total of 2,703 sorties were Canadian.

The Order of Battle of American Heavy Bombers, U.S. 8th Bomber Command, Eighth Air Force at that time was as follows:

1st Bombardment Wing – 9 Bomb Groups – Boeing B17's

4th Bombardment Wing – 6 Bomb Groups – Boeing B17's

Of the fifteen American Bomb Groups, six took part in the attacks on Hamburg. These were the 91st at Bassingbourn, 303rd at Molesworth, 351st at Polebrook, 379th at Kimbohon, 381st at Ridgewell and the 384th at Grafton-Underwood. Between them 161 sorties bombed Hamburg. A greater effort than this by the other nine groups of the U.S.A.A.F. was devoted at the same time to other German targets.[1]

The most significant tactical fact of these raids was the use for

1. For greater detail of British, American and Luftwaffe battle orders see *The Battle of Hamburg*, by Martin Middlebrook, Appendices 4,5 and 6.

the first time on July 24th of strips of silver paper dropped in bundles from each aircraft, usually by the bomb-aimer, which rendered the *Würzburg* radar sets virtually useless.[1] To the set operators the scattered strips looked like thousands of aircraft which could not be distinguished one from the other. To the aircrew observing the effects of this it appeared magical. Our attack on the 27th, for example, was from the north-east. We crossed the base of the Danish peninsula north of Heide towards Kiel, thence southeast towards Lubeck, finally approaching Hamburg on a line from Lubeck to Bremerhaven. The initial stages looked like a strong force heading for Berlin which swung back and attacked Hamburg. The route home was between Cuxhaven and Bremerhaven. Approaching the city one could see the usual display of searchlights stabbing the blackness, but as one got into them it was evident that they were impotent. They flicked aimlessly back and forth across the sky; some turned off and then on again. Wilkes tuned his powerful radio to the German night fighter frequency and treated us to the sound of chaos, the barking of frustrated German controllers. While we couldn't understand the language, we could easily tell that all was not efficiency and discipline. The flak was a mess, fired indiscriminately in the wild hope of hitting something. We were surprised and delighted.

The Pathfinder marking technique was unusual for an H2S attack. Yellow markers were to open the attack as usual, dropped blind on H2S. But there would be no visual markers to follow. Probably it was felt that with smoke still over the city from the first attack, visual markers would see nothing. The backers-up were to aim with a two second overshoot at the centre of the yellows. The topography of Hamburg was such that H2S had put up an excellent performance on the first raid, better than the visual markers had. So H2S was to be relied upon exclusively in this, the second raid. The confidence was not misplaced. Zero hour for the main force was 1.00 a.m. and 787 aircraft were to attack within 43 minutes of that time. The weather was clear, except for smoke haze left from the fires. The attack started with fifteen salvoes of yellow target indicators dropped blind on H2S at five minutes before zero hour. They were exceptionally well concentrated, between a half mile and three miles south east of the aiming point. This seemed no problem since the main force attacks usually dragged back somewhat from

1. The Freya long range sets were not effected by 'window'.

the markers. In this case however the main force quickly put a massive concentration of bombs directly on the flares and although there was some drift of the attack eastwards there was no pronounced 'creep back' as there usually was. This was no doubt due to the dropping of window and the resulting ineffectiveness of the flak and the lack of controlled fighter attacks. Just under half the crews bombed within three miles of the aiming point. This was the second round in the disaster which was happening to Hamburg. The German fighter controllers switched to a new technique which, although not effective at the outset, later produced results. They gave their fighters a running commentary of the course and height of the bomber stream ignoring individual aircraft. They shot down only seventeen bombers this night with such methods, but they were already getting round the effect of 'window'. I was awed at the damage we had wrought upon Hamburg. Flames and smoke from the firestorm rose in a conical column to a towering 20,000 feet. I could see the city burning furiously from over 100 miles away on the return journey.

Although 83 Squadron suffered no losses, Searby and another Lanc from neighbouring Warboys had a mid-air collision over Wyton on the 24th. Fortunately, they only sliced protruding pieces, like Searby's top turret and starboard fin, off each other and both landed safely.

On July 29 it was a beautiful evening with high cloud showing orange against the setting sun. We were not surprised to be going to Hamburg again because we had been told that we were to continue going until we had smashed the city and the will of its people to continue the war. The route was the same as the previous night without the feint towards Berlin. This night we were carrying one 4,000 pounder, 10 – 500s and five Target Indicators. We were one of the early backers-up. Route markers were being dropped by 156 Squadron from Warboys. One of their aircraft piloted by F/O Crampton, an experienced captain and crew, was the first to be shot down at the head of the bomber stream crossing the coast. His yellow TI's blew up as he crashed into a river estuary. Another aircraft was shot down near the route markers.

The Germans this night used their new tactic of 'Wild Boar' fighters on a full scale for the first time. These were again the single-engined Me 109s and Fw 190s, day fighters pressed into use over the target as night fighters. And they were effective. As regards our own work, if I thought the previous night had been fire-filled, this one repeated the performance on a larger scale. There was smoke at my flying altitude and the fires were enormous.

Window was not as effective to screen the first few aircraft in the stream as it was the later ones, nor did it protect the highest aircraft from night fighters because the large number of single blips on the radar caused by the tinfoil strips could be traced to a common source early in the raid. Further, the Wild Boar day fighters, together with the now free-lancing twin-engined night fighters, were allotted priority over the flak in the competition for air space above the city. Jack Finding was caught in searchlights and shot up by a fighter and I saw one Wild Boar attacking a bomber over the southern part of the city after we had bombed but before we turned north-west for home. Our Pilot Officer King, an Australian, returned in a damaged aircraft and crashed at Sibson but he survived. We all liked King; he repeatedly threatened that if he were shot down he would fight his way out of Germany. He was married while on the Squadron, a rash act many of us thought at the time. Squadron Leader Manton loaned his Mayfair flat to the blissful couple for a honeymoon. King was later shot down but was taken prisoner.

On July 31st another attack on Hamburg was cancelled due to bad weather. The final attack occurred on August 2nd and you cannot imagine how one's confidence could increase with a fine navigator aboard, as we had in Bedell. I felt in command of the aircraft rather than being along for a fortuitous ride. I now had some direction as to where we went and where we dropped our bomb load and, by virtue of the target indicators, we could give direction to many other bombers. I realised how lucky we had been on our previous operations when we had reached the targets almost by accident. The weather forecast predicted appalling weather, including high cumulo-nimbus clouds and ice, but there was a good chance such weather would not be over Hamburg itself. The forecast was right about the appalling weather and wrong about it not being over Hamburg. I never saw a thing until we broke through the cloud at about 15,000 feet over the North Sea prior to our rendezvous point. Then as we passed between Cuxhaven and Bremerhaven at about 20,000 feet on the route in to the target, we entered the worst storm I have ever flown in. Towering cumulo-nimbus clouds were all around us. One wouldn't have seen them in the dark, except for

Walter R Thompson
DFC & BAR, MA, LLB, QC

Flight Cadets at Medicine Hat, Alberta, June, 1941

Author two weeks after enlistment – May 1941

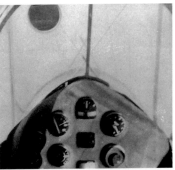

Bill Snow and author at Elementary
Flying School in Regina,
Saskatchewan October 1941

De Haviland Tiger Moth
instrument panel

Leading Aircraftsman Thompson, age 20 with D.H. Tiger Moth

Cessna Crane – Yorkton, Saskatchewan

Cessna Crane instrument panel

W/C Guy Gibson and crews of 106 Squadron – ready for take-off

Sept 1943

Officers of 106 Squadron, Syerston, March, 1943

Officers of 83 Squadron, Wyton September, 1943

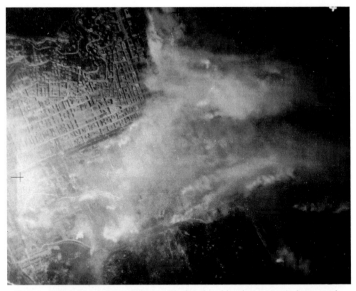

This target photograph was taken just before bombing began, a smokescreen is blowing offshore to hide battleships – Naval base at La Spezia, Italy, April 1943

The author reunited with an old friend, Ottawa, 1951

the massive and violent lightning strikes. St. Elmo's fire shot blue sparks across the windscreen and instrument panel and blue flames circled around the four whirling propellers and off the gun barrels. Lightning struck our aircraft twice. At one point huge blue balls of static electricity, two feet in diameter, headed down the fuselage beside me, presumably to run out of the trailing aerials. When approaching Hamburg a dazzling display of lightning lit up two clouds directly ahead of us and between them a Lancaster was flying. I saw a flash of what appeared to be lightning across the gap between the two clouds and then was shocked to see the Lancaster blow up in an orange and black ball of flame. Whether it was hit by flak or whether the lightning had caused a fire I was not sure, because a white flash preceded the orange ball.

On this night entire *Gruppen* of NJG 3's night fighters were sent up to work free from ground control. The controller's running commentary, giving details of course and height of the bomber stream, was repeated over and over again. Several combats had occurred before the bomber stream reached the German coast. Many bombers jettisoned their bombs and returned home. We managed a run-in on H2S with Bedell confident that we were on track and we dropped our TI's, supposedly to re-centre the attack but there was nothing visible to re-centre. The flight back across the North Sea was uneventful and the weather was clear over the UK when we returned. Thirty-three aircraft were missing but due to the weather no serious additional damage was done to Hamburg. The Battle of Hamburg was over with 45,000 German dead, almost as many as the Germans had killed in Britain during the blitz. It was not until many years later, after I had learned this figure, that I came to regard our three operations, because of the casualties at Hamburg, as in any way different from the many other operations we had carried out. Historically however, these attacks are regarded, along with the attack on Tokyo of 9th March, 1945 when twice as many people were killed, as illustrating the power of strategic bombing without use of atomic weapons.

People have expressed the view that the use of window in the Hamburg attacks was a significant tactical advantage achieved over the German defences. In the long run this probably was not so. Window forced the German night fighters to scrap the boxes of the *Himmelbett* line and to adopt instead a command control centre giving a running commentary of the bomber force, albeit one which was based on the ground. At the time of writing air fighting tactics still make use of command control centres, only such centres now are sometimes airborne.

The Americans fought splendidly in their daylight attacks on Hamburg. They lost seventeen aircraft in their two days of attack but their defences had remained intact and it was the stragglers, who had first been hit by flak, who were most frequently shot down by the fighters. Only five of their losses were due solely to fighters. So the American theory of bombers protecting themselves if given adequate fighter support was beginning to bear fruit. Ultimately of course this theory would win air supremacy for the Allies in Europe. But this would not be for another year when the long range single-engine P-51 fighter was able to escort and protect Fortresses on flights across Germany.

*   *   *

It will now be apparent to the reader that one's choices in war are limited. One starts with the decision whether or not to fight at all. That is the last clear choice one has. One then chooses the service and the trade, if lucky enough to be able to make that choice. You have seen the events which befell me; they were in no way untypical. One wants to be a fighter pilot? Oh well, if the block required this week is for multi-engine pilots then any pilot's job will do, so long as it is fighting. Fighting you say? How would you like to be a navigation instructor instead? No? – Then let's see if you can run the air force your way. Not easy, is it? Well, a bomber pilot can attack military objectives, can't he? Certainly he can, if that's where the target indicators happen to be, or if he decides that he will bomb somewhere other than on target indicators. But you don't wish to kill women and children? How quaint and old fashioned you are young man. Strategic air policy was made before you were born by people who had fought in a conflagration in which millions of men were killed in static warfare. What difference is there that those millions include the civil populations of the combatants? The best way to put an industry out of action is to kill everyone who works in it – Ghengis Khan knew that! And so one is carried on the tide. One sometimes swims against it, sometimes with it but it is the tide which moves, and even exceptional individuals who ride the crest of that tide are as much a part of it as are the rest of us. There was no longer any feeling in

Bomber Command that we were attacking industrial targets. We were desperately trying to win a war with air power alone.

The Germans meanwhile had things figured out in their own inimitable way. They were justified in seizing territories for themselves they argued, by the harsh treatment of the Treaty of Versailles, which took away their colonies and in their view caused the economic depression which followed. After all Germany, in her own eyes, had done nothing in her attacks upon Poland, France, Holland, Belgium, Denmark, Norway, Yugoslavia, Greece and Russia to merit the harsh treatment of area bombing; she had merely wanted to subjugate Europe and rid it of Jews. And if Germans had killed civilians in Warsaw, Rotterdam, Belgrade, Coventry, London and Liverpool, that had been necessary. Why, the Luftwaffe attacks on three of these, Warsaw, Rotterdam and Belgrade, had been part of the tactical support of the German armies. And what business was it of Canada's? Joseph Goebbels, the German propaganda minister, was aware that RAF aircrews were 20% Canadian, if Canadians were not. He of course was more appalled by Hamburg than I was and wrote in his diary, 'It drives one mad to think that any old Canadian boor, who probably can't even find Europe on the globe, flies here from his super-rich country, which his people don't know how to exploit, and bombards a continent with a crowded population.'

Well, some of us boors managed to find Europe on the globe. Yet throughout my operations I never hated a single German, and had no hatred for them as a people. Even I found that to be strange.

It should not be forgotten that there was real doubt in all of this; firstly, doubt that one would survive long enough to see the outcome of the war and secondly, doubt as to what that outcome would be. Oh yes, one had faith that one's side would win just as some religious people had faith that God was on their side, but the narrow field that the individual was capable of viewing left both those doubts unanswered. I am astonished now, as I write this, at the magnificent panorama and the feeling of omnipotence one has, looking back through the eyes of history at a view which, when it happened, extended only to the next few hours. Hitler was very much alive and in control of Germany in 1943. It was our job to smash him, and if we had to smash his people to effect his destruction we would do that too.

CHAPTER TEN

Tame Boars and Schrage Musik

THE day of the last Hamburg raid I received a short letter, signed by Bennett, saying that I could now wear the Pathfinder badge but adding that the authority was only temporary and one had to have a further written authority from him to wear it after leaving the Force. I took offence at this and refused for some time to wear the badge at all. Bennett I knew had flown operations himself as commander of a Halifax Squadron in 4 Group in 1942 before being shot down in an attack on the *Tirpitz* in Norway. He managed to get into Sweden and was brought back from there to England in an aircraft. Late in 1942 he was selected to head the Pathfinder Force, because of his expertise in navigation. In the mid nineteen-thirties, then a pilot of Imperial Airways, Bennett had participated in the long range experimental 'piggy back' flights across the Atlantic. In these it was decided to establish a freight service across the Atlantic by getting a small flying boat 'Mercury' aloft, piloted by Bennett, on the back of a large flying-boat, then to take it out over the Atlantic and let it fly the remainder of the way on its own. Great savings in fuel were possible and the Mercury's range could be increased in this way. Bennett, an Australian by birth, was already the holder of a first class navigator's licence, as well as a pilot.

Churchill in 1940 had named the Canadian-born Lord Beaverbrook as Minister of Aircraft Production and Beaverbrook appointed Morris Wilson, president of the Royal Bank of Canada, as his North American representative and asked him to organise an Atlantic Air Ferry. Edward Beatty of the CPR was asked by Wilson to assist and in July 1940 CPR Air Services was set up to take delivery of fifty Lockheed Hudson aircraft from Burbank, California. Beaverbrook sent for the then Capt. Don Bennett and another Imperial Airways pilot, Capt. R.H. Page, who both went to Burbank in August 1940 to take over the first two Hudsons. Because of the U.S. Neutrality Act these aircraft could not be flown to Canada. So they were flown to Pembina, North Dakota, and hauled across the border into Canada by horses. Bennett and Page flew them to Montreal where Bennett planned and organised the first Atlantic Ferry crossing. There were then no radio aids across the Atlantic. As other Hudsons and other pilots arrived to man them at Montreal it became clear that they would have to fly formation with Bennett in the lead, navigating. Some of the pilots had no expertise at all in navigation, having simply 'ridden the range' throughout their airline careers. Bennett therefore made a flight plan and handed it to seven crews, chosen to be the first group to leave Gander. He gave a card to each crew, giving courses to be steered and times for alterations of course and told them that if they were forced to separate they would know what to do. They had many problems and the formation became dispersed. They encountered storms mechanical difficulties and oxygen problems but all seven of them made it. Bennett was first to land, at Aldergrove, near Belfast.[1] This was the man, now in the RAF, chosen to form the Pathfinder Force. As a Group Commander Bennett would have as an ally in the policy differences which inevitably developed within Bomber Command his old group commander from 4 Group, Air Vice-Marshal Carr, and would find his chief rival in Air Vice-Marshal Cochrane.

Notwithstanding their undoubted talents Cochrane, the brilliant 5 Group Commander, and Saundby, the Deputy Chief at Bomber Command, displayed in 1943 an astonishing attitude to the defensive armament of heavy bombers. Consider the following: Air Vice-Marshal Cochrane, in a letter to Saundby dated 2nd July 1943, contended that a greater willingness on the part of the Bomber Command gunners to open fire might 'convert the German night fighter trade from one of the safest in the German Air Force to one of some peril' and concluded, 'In the process, we shall, no doubt, put a number of .303 bullets into our aircraft, but I doubt whether that would matter very much.' Saundby supported this contention in a Bomber Command Tactical note of 1 August, 1943.[2]

I ask the reader to consider what damage we, for example, would have sustained from the flak ship I referred to if it had been firing .303's-none whatever! Cochrane's reference to .303 bullets is precisely the point. Can you imagine a high speed gun-fight at a range of 100 yards with one gunfighter, the German, having 20 mm and 30 mm cannon which fired explosive shells and the other, the British, with .303 machine guns? A .303 is about 7.7 mm, the size

1. These facts about Bennet, though well known to most Pathfinder crews, are set out more fully in The *Canadians at War,* vol. 1, pp 114-21. Bennett is the author of *Pathfinder,* also published by Goodall.

2. *The Strategic Air Offensive Against Germany,* p 139

of a hunting rifle! Fighter Command had long ago given up reliance upon .303's in favour of 20 mm cannon which possessed far greater range and hitting power. Were bomber crews expected to believe that Fighter Command was wrong? Yet in the Bomber Command view Heinz Wolfgang Schnaufer and his colleagues (German night-fighter crews) had to get within 100 yards at night to use their cannon effectively and at this point, it was thought, one could literally shred them with the .303's. The trouble was that no one had told the German fighter pilots of this. They often began firing their cannon as soon as they could see the bomber well enough to do so and when they got close enough for the bomber's gunners to use .303 machine guns the bomber's gas tanks or its bomb load had already been hit, or its gunners had been torn to bits and so couldn't carry out Cochrane's suggestion. And this was particularly true because the commanders had not seen fit to put any of the .303's where they might do some good, in the belly of the bomber.[1] In a belly attack the fighters had no need to fire at long range; they usually got quite close enough without being seen.[2] Bennett in an answering minute to Bomber Command dated 3rd September, 1943, perhaps because he had operational experience himself, objected to Cochrane's idea and suggested that the great readiness on the trigger which this theory encouraged, would merely help the German fighters to find their quarries. Bennett was right of course, but even a policy of 'Don't fire boys, the enemy may see you', was no substitute for the bombers having something sensible with which they too could fire.

German night fighter pilots never lost their astonishment at our suffering the loss of 7,000 heavy bombers, virtually every one of which was without a belly turret[3] when each of them had two machine guns in a front turret. I venture to say that not a front gun in one of those 7,000 front turrets ever shot down a fighter making a frontal attack. And for good reason, no fighter pilot could see well enough at night to attack from the front; he had to attack from the rear or from below. There are of course rare recorded instances of

1. None of the group commanders, except Bennett, had any substantial personal experience of bombing operations in World War II.

2. The development of upward firing guns by the Luftwaffe was one of those rare instances of a major change in weapons design made specifically to exploit an enemy's continuing weakness of design.

3. In the last year of the war 6 Group equipped some of its bombers with a 'belly' turret.

front gunners shooting down night fighters but these appear to have been where the fighter overshot while attacking from the rear, or where the bomber stumbled, unseen, across the fighter. I suggest therefore that even if cannon were not available (and they could have been stripped with impunity from 1,000 vegetating fighters), the turrets and the .303's to put in the bellies of the bombers were all available right there as surplus in the noses of all those Lancasters, Halifaxes and Stirlings.

Bennett was later to say of the bomber force in the Battle of Berlin that they had 'baulked at the jump' and that those who had bombed short were 'fringe merchants'.[1] These are harsh judgements upon courageous men who would happily have slugged it out with German fighters had they been given anything in the way of slugs. I saw the 'fringe merchants', dropping far short of the aiming point on the bombing run. I also saw aircraft dropping 4,000 pounders *en route* so as to lighten their load and gain more altitude, and I do not for a moment support those who did these things, but I know too that they would not so readily have done them if they had possessed the armament they deserved.

The difficulty lay, I think, partly in the unofficial motto of Bomber Command, 'Press on Regardless'. In this is contained an echo of Tennyson's 'Charge of the Light Brigade', and if one's chief concern is a Kipling-like keeping of a stiff upper lip, while all about one are being shot to pieces, then 'Press on' is a fine motto, but if one wishes to fight intelligently and to create an atmosphere in which air supremacy and victory can be achieved then one doesn't press on regardless – one arms oneself and gets assistance from professional gunfighters and then presses on. I am not unique in holding these views; many bomber aircrew held them but did not express them lest they be regarded as being afraid.

So if it be thought that I have exaggerated the menace of fighters or complained too loudly of the lack of proper armament, consider the casualty figures for 1939-1945 aircrew. If 100 aircrew reached a bomber OTU and then began their two-tour cycle of service with Bomber Command the following shows what happened to them:[2]

---

1. Memo from Bennett to Bomber Command, 3 November 1944.

2. These figures, summarised by Martin Middlebrook in his book *The Nuremberg Raid*, are for the whole war and have little meaning for any particular period. For the month by month periods of loss see the percentage table, Appendix 'A'.

Killed on operations	51
Killed in crashes in Britain	9
Seriously injured in crashes	3
Prisoners of war	12
Shot down and evaded capture	1
Survived unharmed	24
	100

* * *

Let us now shift our attention to Southern Europe. The situation in Italy was critical. On July 25th Marshal Badoglio took over the Italian government. By August 17th Sicily had been captured, and on September 3rd British and Canadian troops landed on the Italian mainland. In the first half of August Bomber Command contributed to the confusion. On August 7th we attacked two North Italian cities, our Squadron sending fourteen.

I suppose the purpose was to show the Italians that they were vulnerable. Our crew took a small load of six 500 pound medium capacity bombs and eight green target indicators. We dropped the bombs and four of the TI's on Milan, circled around a little and then flew to Genoa where we dropped the other four. Separate forces of bombers bombed each set of TI's and there was a resulting suggestion from Hanratty that he should get credit for two operations, rather than one.

On August 10th the target was Nuremberg in eastern Germany, not a great distance from the Czech border. I was not enthused about bombing these old cities but the rationale appeared to be, 'Let them evacuate their cities of all but essential workers. Then no innocent people will be killed. After all Britain evacuated London during the blitz'. This would have seriously disrupted the German economy and that, of course, is what we were seeking to do.

Our intelligence officer at briefing, of whom we were all fond, was a Squadron Leader whose face had been badly burned. He spoke fluent German and listened to their broadcasts frequently. This night he presented defence data with his customary clarity. The trip was to be a low level operation, and since it was important to avoid the flak concentrations we should be careful to fly through the gap in the defences between Karlsruhe and Mannheim. We took off and headed south, across the water and across France and then as we approached the gap between Karlsruhe and Mannheim at about six thousand feet we found that the gap had disappeared. The flak was horrendous; the Germans had placed railway wagons with heavy and light flak guns along the thirty mile space between the cities. So much for low level flying! I climbed immediately and proceeded due east at a higher altitude to bomb this ancient city. The cloud was not heavy and began to clear near the target. The bombing appeared to be accurate and some large fires were started. I hoped the Germans would soon get smart and evacuate their cities, but I could not convince them; they stubbornly refused.

The flight home presented a problem since the route went again between Karlsruhe and Mannheim and the instructions were to 'fly low and avoid the flak'. I decided to fly high and avoid the flak, but I knew that there was a risk in doing so. We would be alone, since most of the aircraft would obey the order. It followed that if we were going to be high and alone, we should be very high. The controllers would undoubtedly see us. The question was, would they send a night fighter up after one aircraft. I reasoned that they would not and so climbed the Lancaster to its limit, which turned out to be 29,500 feet; I couldn't get any higher. At this altitude the Lancaster was inefficient; we wallowed about the sky like a drunken hippopotamus but eventually made our way back through the gap. Looking down from our superior height I noticed that, sure enough, the returning aircraft were taking another pasting through 'the gap'. One of our new pilots, Pilot Officer Allcroft, had his aircraft hit over the target by pieces of an exploding bomber. These put his radios and front turret out of action but he got back safely. It was at about this time that Flight Lieutenant Tommy Wilmot finished his second tour of operations. This was a rare event. The only completion's I ever actually witnessed were Garvey's, Wilmot's, 'Wimpy' Wellington's and my own. So there was a tremendous thrash in the mess. All the games of glory were played, like 'Are you there Moriarty?' This was an ancient game, the words of which were derived from Sherlock Holmes' famous duels with his Nietzschean nemesis Professor Moriarty. Two contestants, usually unfortunate junior officers, were blindfolded and directed to lie on the floor, facing each other and clasping each other's left hand. In the right hand of each was a rolled up newspaper or magazine. The first contestant had to ask, 'Are you there Moriarty?' and the other had to answer, 'Here'. Then, from the sound of the answer, the first contestant was allowed one whack of the newspaper at his opponent to see if he could hit the sound. The roles were then reversed. One was permitted to roll in either direction after answering 'here', so long as the hands remained clasped. After a few exchanges the contestants became surprisingly efficient at whacking each other over the head with their paper bundles, notwithstanding that their heads, like that of Moriarty, were 'forever oscillating from side to side in a curiously reptilian fashion.'

Then there were races by three or four contestants on hands and knees under the large carpet in the lounge. People emerged from these panting, red-faced and dirty.

And when the party was well established, there was the usual steeplechase over the chairs and tables around the circumference of the lounge, with bets on the contestants. If no serious casualties were sustained it was time for 'foot prints on the ceiling'. This was performed by blacking one's feet in the fireplace, climbing atop the piled up oak tables, chesterfields and chairs and lying down on the topmost one to place one's footprints on the ceiling. Only at Wyton and we were Pathfinders, weren't we? It was necessary to find a new path. It was suggested that Wilmot be the first to place a buttocks print on the ceiling. A quick vote showed this decision to be unanimous with the exception of Wilmot's 'nay'. This presented problems, but they were not insurmountable. Willing volunteers assisted Wilmot to lower his pants and to back him into the sooty fireplace where a supply of pigment was spread on each *gluteus maximus*. Then, assisted by strong attendants including a pilot of the RCAF, Wilmot was handed to the top of the pile of furniture where his backside achieved immortality. Unfortunately he then fell off the pile of furniture and broke his arm, thus receiving the only injury he sustained in two tours of operations.

On August 14th fourteen aircraft from 83 were to participate in the attack on Milan but two were not able to take off. We went in JA 940 which I had managed to have coded OL-T for 'Tommy'. This was a new aircraft, just delivered to the squadron and a pleasure to fly. I rather enjoyed saying on return from an operation, 'This is Foxglove 'T Tommy' and listening to the clearly discernible female voice in reply. We were ultimately to do eighteen operations in JA 940 before switching to another aircraft for a more specialised role.

South into Vichy France we went and, crossing the Rhone between Lyon and Geneva, turned eastward. Keeping Mont Blanc on our left we crossed into Italy south of Switzerland. The Italian flak and searchlights at Milan seemed ferocious as we approached the city but they could not have been guided by radar, or if they were, it was by a radar not as good as the *Würzburg*, for it was soon apparent that the searchlights remained almost stationary and the flak was fired at random; together they amounted to no defence at all.

On this night we marked Milan visually I saw the city but as usual could not see what we were aiming at because of the intervening nose of the aircraft. This was frustrating; I maintained that the designers should have been able to mount a periscope or telescope downward from the pilot so that he could make tactical decisions on bombing. It seemed absurd to me, and I used to tell this to Hanratty, that in the final stages of an operation complete control of the aircraft was handed over to a bomb-aimer who had probably failed as a pilot because he couldn't read a map. This produced the anticipated reaction, 'You just steer-r this machine as I dir-rect you to and this oper-ration will be a success.' That was no way to speak to an officer I said, particularly one of Flight Lieutenant rank. Like Christmas presents by mail, my promotion to Flight Lieutenant had arrived late. I suppose these lists had to make the rounds in Ottawa and at Lincoln's Inn Fields, London, before the news was passed on to the RAF.

Next day we were up again in the early afternoon, did a night flying test in T for Tommy, were briefed, and went to Milan again as visual markers. Because of the shortage of darkness, the route back across France required that we fly for a half hour in daylight before reaching the Channel. This was risky so we were told to fly low level from about Le Mans, south-west of Paris, to Beachy Head. This was great fun since we didn't often get the chance to see the countryside. I was thoroughly enjoying the sight of the beautiful French farms in the pre-dawn light near Argentan. Hanratty didn't like being in the bomb-aimer's position when low flying so he had moved up to the front turret and was enjoying himself moving it from side to side and elevating and depressing its two machine guns. Some distance ahead, near Caen, I could see what had to be a group of German barracks. I called to Hanratty, 'German barracks on the starboard bow', and he swung his guns slightly to the right and depressed them. Then from a door in the end of one of the barracks, still some distance away, a sleepy soldier emerged. He was wearing German field boots and pants and his suspenders were down from the shoulders of his underwear, he had no tunic on. As we came abreast of him at an altitude of a hundred feet he heard our motors for the first time and looked up in surprise. At that moment I heard a long burst of machine gun fire belching from the front Brownings and realised with shock that Hanratty was firing. I saw his turret turn to the side, still firing but could not see whether or not he had hit the soldier. I was about to bawl him out for firing without permission when he said, 'Take that you bastard.' He thought he had hit him. My stomach felt uneasy. Yet, I asked myself, 'Why do you shrink from killing? You do enough of it every night. Why will you not fire upon the pilot of a Fieseler Storch or at a German soldier when you will bomb their grandparents?' The familiar rationalisation quickly came to mind – we had jumped into a game the rules of which we had no part in framing. But this was a sad thought to carry at high speed, low across France. Soon my heart lifted at the welcome sight of dawn and the south coast of England.

The attacks on Italy were politically motivated and Italy surrendered on September 8th. Two days later the Germans seized Rome and the Italians turned their fleet over to the Allies.

The next operation we flew was destined to become the most important of the European War, although at the time we thought of it as routine. There was, in retrospect, one aspect which was unusual. We were told at briefing that the target, although not large, was very important and if we didn't succeed in wiping it out on the first attempt we would have to continue going back until we did. The operation was to Peenemunde, the German experimental rocket installation on the Baltic, north of Berlin. It was my 27th trip. However, we were not told at the time the true nature of the target; only that it was manufacturing electronic parts. I was a 'blind marker'. In books written about this operation my role and that of others performing the same function is described as a 'shifter', meaning we were to shift the aiming point of the main force from the point at which the attack opened to a second aiming point. This is true; we were indeed to drop markers so as to shift the attack, but the term 'shifter' was not used in squadron parlance because an aiming point, once established, was rarely shifted. So I use the description contained in my log book, that of 'blind marker', albeit not on the original aiming point.

At briefing Searby introduced us to a man in civilian clothes who said he had been to Peenemunde. We assumed he was an intelligence agent and were more interested in how he had got away from there than in his description of the place. He told us nothing about Peenemunde's true function which, as we later learned, involved Germany's rocket missile programme. Nor did he mention that such new weapons might soon be used against Britain. Instead, he pointed with a stick to a map of the installation and said, 'This is the main building for manufacturing valve components' (radio tubes). It was obvious that there was more to Peenemunde than we were being told. But we didn't care; as I say the operation was just another flight. Then he mentioned that part of the place had been disguised as a Nazi 'Strength Through Joy' camp. My room-mate, Maurice Chick, himself a slim, dark, handsome man, nodded wisely at this remark and winked a large brown eye to indicate that he knew all about those SS breeding establishments to propagate the master race.

There were about 600 aircraft on the attack and three aiming points were established to destroy a number of buildings. Searby in fact directed the main force by radio on this, the first time that a master bomber was used in a major attack.[1] I do not recall Searby, by this time a Group Captain, telling us that it would be he who would be doing this, although I knew that there would be a master bomber. Perhaps I was not paying close attention or perhaps I was indifferent because the master bomber would be directing the backers-up and the main force, but not the blind markers. We were instructed to do a timed run from a promontory on Rugen Island, near the Baltic Coast, to the aiming point, as a guide to the flare release point, and we did. There was low cloud as we approached the target but Peenemunde itself seemed clear. We ran in at a lower level than usual, about 12,000 feet, still high enough for good radar coverage, and Hanratty was muttering with delight at the bombs and markers he could see. He claimed to have a good view of the aiming point. I don't know if he was right because I couldn't see the second aiming point, but I could see the exploding bombs, and the flares and smoke of the first aiming point as we ran in, and I had confidence in Bedell's navigation and in Hanratty's ability to hit a target if he could see it. I listened as Hanratty and Bedell did a count down. Then the flares and bombs went down. We and four other aircraft dropped red flares on the second aiming point at 00.26; it then became well covered with bombs. I saw no flak.

1. See Appendix 'E' for the 83 Squadron Operations Record Book, 14 August - 31 August 1943, which is reproduced verbatim. Searby's report is included.

On the way out of the target the fighter attacks began. Every fighter between the Baltic and Bavaria had been expecting an attack on Berlin but were soon vectored northward to Peenemunde. They were slow at first to realise that we were not at our usual altitude; some of their pilots in fact refused to believe it when told by their controller that the main force was at 6,000 feet. But I saw the first orange ball of an exploding bomber as we were leaving the target area. Someone had quickly found the height. Soon, every few minutes, an orange ball lit up the otherwise black sky. Then two of them occurred together, quite close to us. Relieved of our heavy load, we quickly climbed to 20,000 feet, expecting that most of the fighters would lose altitude down to the bombing height, and no doubt many of them did, but the explosions were now occurring at all levels. I climbed higher and watched as the flaming balls continued to burst. I felt slightly ill; it seemed hard to believe that seven of our men were in each of those burning spheres. As we headed west for base the explosions continued, getting farther behind on the starboard quarter until, after seventeen of them, I could see no more. But these were not all of our losses; forty-one of our aircraft did not return.

It was learned later that two hundred fighters had at first been assembled over Berlin where that city's flak opened fire on them by mistake because of orders issued by General Jeschonnek, Chief of the German Air Staff. This was the last straw for Jeschonnek – his position had become intolerable. By-passed by Goering, who had set up a staff to get round him, berated by Hitler for an hour after the American attack on Wiener Neustadt's aircraft factories on August 13th, then fiercely upbraided by Hitler again after four hundred Messerschmitt workers had been killed four days later in an attack on Regensburg, Jeschonnek's body was found next day with a bullet in the head and a suicide note saying that it was impossible to work with Goering any longer. Albert Speer states that Goering nevertheless attended the funeral and laid a wreath from Hitler.

The attack was considered at the time to be a huge success, and this was borne out the next day when Bennett invited Searby, Shipway, Slade and myself and a couple of others to his home on the base at Wyton. He gave us a glass of sherry and asked us to look at the reconnaissance photos through a small stereoscopic viewing tripod.[1] We were told later, when the rocket attacks against London had commenced, that the raid on Peenemunde had set back the schedule of these attacks by six months.[2] We were pleased. This was the kind of thing we had joined up to do. Searby was awarded his DSO after this effort, and it was well earned. He had steadily proven himself to be a fine Squadron Commander, and by agreement of those in a position to know did a first rate job on Peenemunde.

* * *

The Distinguished Service Order is normally awarded to officers of Squadron Leader rank and above for services such as its name implies. For example a squadron commander on completion of a tour would usually get a DSO. Occasionally however it was awarded to a Flight Lieutenant or even to a Flying Officer. Val Moore received one as a Flying Officer, as did Buzz Beurling, and in one extraordinary case it was awarded to four junior officers, including one whom I knew, Sub-Lieutenant Lee of the Royal Navy, who had been a bomb-aimer attached to 106 Squadron. Lee was the only person to escape unscathed from his entire squadron of torpedo-carrying Swordfish who were shot down attacking the German cruisers *Gneisenau* and *Scharnhorst*. He was fished out of the Channel.

We hadn't long to bask in the glory of Peenemunde. The crew and I were given extensive H2S training exercises two hours a day for the next three days including significantly, a specially arranged solo run over London in daylight to see what a large built up area looked like on the tube, and to see if the operator could distinguish topographical features within a big city on it. One needn't have been clairvoyant to predict that the next target was Berlin, or as Chick loved to call it, 'The Big City'. He said to me after briefing, 'Tommy, can you believe all those beautiful blonde Aryan popsies going for the chop? My God what a waste!' I realise how callous

1. Martin Middlebrook, in his book *The Peenemunde Raid*, criticises some of the target markings by Pathfinders and suggests that 5 Group crews should have been permitted to bomb freely at the end of their time and distance run: but I doubt that this would have improved matters. The time and distance method was routinely used, both visually and with radar, by Peenemunde crews, and was in fact used by them on Peenemunde. An improved accuracy would more likely have been achieved had some of the blind markers flown an intersecting course to that of the first blind markers.

2. Six months was an overestimate; two months would probably be more accurate. Perhaps the greatest loss to Germany was that of 750 scientists and workers, including two of her top propulsion experts, killed in the raid.

that sounds but Chick was not then and is not now a callous man. It was his way of expressing regret at the carnage that was going on. He, even more than I, found it difficult not to fraternise with WAAFs; in fact he was on a campaign to fraternise with one of each rank of WAAF on the station, and was already courting a senior NCO. On two occasions he had jumped on my bed when he came in late and found me asleep, to wake me up and give me a blow-by-blow description of the night's activities. He liked having a Canadian for a room-mate. Since I made twice as much money as he, although we were both Flight Lieutenants, he felt duty bound to borrow half the difference between my earnings and his. It got so that I was telling him to be careful – I didn't want him going missing when he owed me 20 pounds.

So six days after Peenemunde we went to Berlin where T for Tommy's job was to re-centre the attack. We crossed the Dutch coast just south of Friesland, then flew eastward, south of Bremen and across the old Duchy of Brunswick-Luneberg into Prussia. By 23.45 we had reached a point about 30 miles south-east of Berlin where we turned on to a course of magnetic north for the target.

By this time an increasing number of Pathfinder aircraft had been equipped with H2S; its serviceability was better and its operators were more experienced. 727 aircraft were dispatched. ninety-four carried H2S. Ten of these failed to return and ten more made abortive sorties but sixty-four of the remaining seventy-four H2S crews, including mine, found that the equipment functioned well throughout. However, the technique which worked on Hamburg was no good on Berlin. The target was so large that all that could be seen by the H2S operators was a blaze of light indicating solid built-up area and the searchlights were so dangerous that one simply could not map-read properly. This, combined with sometimes intense flak, made it almost impossible for a crew to say that they had visually identified the aiming point. Nevertheless Berlin was well and truly bombed.

We came in after the blind markers on this occasion and dropped four Green TI's in addition to a four thousand pounder and three one-thousand pounders. Our drop time was 00.03 hrs; altitude was 19,500 feet; we were flying a course of 359° magnetic and the speed was 155 knots indicated. I know this because the Operations Record Book says so. The first greens seemed well placed around the reds and all of them were well concentrated. We saw many fires starting up and observed two large explosions, one at 23.57 as we were running in and the other at 00.03 hours. Some of the red flares only burned red for a few seconds then became yellowish, which caused a little confusion. Some crews thought them to be dummies, but this seemed unlikely. Probably a batch of inferior flares. There seemed to be no shortage of flak or fighters in the Berlin area. As we headed north-west from Berlin to the Baltic I saw a Lancaster on fire close by, on our port quarter. We crossed the Baltic coast near Rostock and then flew on a track of about 295° true south of the large Danish islands and crossed Denmark near the border of Germany. Nearby, to the south at Flensburg, the usual display of fierce flak blossomed in anger, then at last we were out over the North Sea, north of the Frisian Islands and, keeping well away from Sylt and its flak, we headed for home. We landed at Wyton at 03.42, having been in the air seven hours and 12 minutes.

We lost two aircraft, ED 984 A for Apple piloted by Flight Lieutenant Brian Slade, DFC and JA 927 piloted by Pilot Officer J.A. Reid, both of whom were killed. Brian was a good friend and I felt his loss keenly; I did not know Reid very well. We called Brian 'The Boy Slade' because he was our youngest pilot, having just turned twenty-one. He had set himself the goal of completing sixty trips but was killed on his 59th. On several occasions he and Chick and I had taken the bus to Cambridge for an evening's pub crawl. On one of these we found Clark Gable, a gunner with a nearby Fortress Squadron, with his foot up on the brass rail of a pub near King's Parade, his hat bent correctly at the peak and olive green trenchcoat turned up at the collar; we were impressed to find a movie star who actually flew on operations. He flew about five of them and of course was not alone; Jimmy Stewart was a pilot and commanded one of the Fortress Squadrons near Wyton.

Slade, a voluble Londoner, always sang the loudest, drank the most, and told the funniest jokes on these nights out. I think too that he was loved by the most WAAFs for he was another who refused to obey the non-fraternisation rule. It was probably Slade whom we saw hit as we entered Berlin because we saw an aircraft far to the north of us, coned in searchlights; it blew up in a shower of red Target Indicators. This, after the long flight across North Germany, and after we had passed Brandenburg but before we reached the bomb-run. I couldn't understand what this aircraft was doing so far north of track. He should have seen Brandenburg on his H2S, but perhaps it was not working. Slade, having once attacked Berlin on three engines, would have gone on without an H2S.

We went to Nuremberg on August 27th but I will defer mention of this to discuss two more Berlin raids which we made in the next few days. These were on August 31st and September 3rd, the latter being Hanratty's last trip. True to his word he quit after thirty trips. The procedure on each of these Berlin raids was the same. The attacks were opened by blind markers, of which we were one. There was no attempt to have visual markers establish an aiming point; the main force dropped their bombs on the blind markers.

On September 3rd, although there was considerable cloud *en route*, Berlin was clear when we got there. The blind marking in particular seemed quite remarkable to me. As our own yellow target indicators exploded in a pyrotechnic shower far below I saw four other sets of yellows burst and fall within an interval of three seconds. How could five aircraft take off from England, fly in complete darkness and radio silence for three hours or more without seeing each other and, independently of each other, drop their flares in a space of three seconds?

And the dropping had to be independent because the flares fell for longer than three seconds before they exploded. This may have been a fluke but if it was, some rather remarkable navigation was required to produce such a fluke.[1] The total loss on the three raids was 123 bombers, 7.2% of the force sent out. Undershooting by the blind markers, the backers-up and the main force was a problem and there was a creep-back in these attacks. Whether or not T for Tommy contributed to this I do not know but Bedell seemed to be doing well on the H2S. As for myself I certainly knew that we were over Berlin on each occasion but I was never quite sure where. The route home this time was north across the Baltic to the southern tip of Sweden thence on a track north-west up the Kattegat and south-west down the Skagerrak. Before reaching the latitude of 57° North the aurora borealis had turned night into day with nature's flashing green, white and mauve searchlights illuminating the northern half of the sky. I had never before seen the northern lights so beautiful, or if fighters were about, so dangerous.

The following passage from Webster and Frankland's *The*

1. Field Marshal Milch and Hermann Georing were both grudging admirers of Bomber Command's night navigation. Each had commented that their enemy could unerringly find his way to Berlin across hundreds of miles of darkened Europe while the Luftwaffe often could not find London at night from 120 miles away.

Strategic Air Offensive Against Germany describes better than I can the fighter activity.

'The German night fighter force, rallying after the initial chaos caused by Window and assisted by the depth of the penetrations which Bomber Command had to make, operated under the running commentary system with great effectiveness and was responsible for the bulk of the British losses. In the first attack on the night of 23rd August, the zero hour was 23:45 hours, but already at 22:38 hours the German running commentary suggested that Berlin was the probable target. At 23:04 hours all night fighters were ordered to Berlin. Returning Bomber Command crews reported seventy-nine interceptions, thirty-one of which had led to combats with night fighters. Twenty-three of these combats occurred within a hundred miles of Berlin and fifteen of them took place over the target itself. Of the thirty-one bombers which were damaged by enemy action it was evident that twenty had sustained their injuries from night fighters. Of the fifty-six bombers which failed to return it was likely that at least thirty-three had been shot down by night fighters. At least twenty of these were probably destroyed over Berlin, but three of them were shot down in the vicinity of route markers laid by Mosquitoes as a guide to the main force, and therefore, also to the German fighters. Flak at the target was not intense and searchlights were used to assist the night fighters more than the anti-aircraft guns. Only eleven of the returning bombers had been hit by flak, which on this night, therefore, did less damage than accidents not due to enemy action. Of the fourteen bombers 'damaged' by these so called 'other causes' four were in fact completely destroyed. Two of them collided over England, the third crashed on take-off and the fourth crashed on landing. The German night fighters achieved their successes in spite of the fact that their effort was drastically curtailed in the later stages of the operation by the prevalence of fog at their bases.

In the second attack on the night of 31st August they came even more effectively into action. Flying from bases as widely separated as Grove in northern Denmark and Dijon in central France, they probably accounted for nearly all the forty-seven Bomber Command aircraft which failed to return. An even higher proportion of these kills than before occurred over Berlin itself and it seemed probable that about thirty bombers were destroyed by fighters while they were over the target. Returning Bomber Command crews reported ninety-eight interceptions which included forty-two combats in the target area, eighteen on the outward route and fifteen on the homeward route. The casualties would probably have been much higher if, as the Germans clearly expected, Bomber Command had returned, as it had done eight nights earlier, by the 'north about' route. The 'south about' return undoubtedly achieved its object on this occasion.

This second attack, like the first, showed that the Germans were relying predominantly upon their fighters. Though thirty of the returning bombers bore flak marks, the barrage at Berlin had been of only moderate intensity and the searchlights had once more been mainly used to help the fighters. Brilliant fighter flares, which were soon to become a familiar and disquieting sight to Bomber Command crews, were also used to assist the 'cat's eye' interceptions.

The success of the night fighters against the all-Lancaster attack on the night of 3rd September was more limited. Even so it seemed likely that ten of the twenty missing bombers had been destroyed by fighters.

Thus, of the 123 bombers which failed to return from these attacks on Berlin, at least eighty or perhaps more, had fallen to night fighters. Though there could be little doubt that the losses and the incidence of damage would have been even higher in the absence of Window and that bombing would have been even more inaccurate and dispersed in the absence of H2S, it was also apparent that these devices had not solved the Berlin problem, any more than in 1942, Gee had solved that of Essen. Moreover, the withdrawal of the Halifaxes and Stirlings and the use of the Lancasters alone in the last attack had failed to reduce the casualties below a level which was higher than Bomber Command could afford on a sustained basis. All these issues were about to be put to a further and much more drastic test in the great Battle of

Berlin which was now impending, but a consideration of the evidence arising from the three attacks in August and September scarcely provided the grounds for an optimistic expectation as to the outcome.'[1]

Let me amplify these remarks a little. As I have mentioned, the German night fighters were aware, early in the evening of an operation, that a raid was pending. When we switched on our radio transmitters and H2S sets to warm up, while the aircraft were still on the dispersal sites, the monitoring service knew it. Each fighter division made its own decision to send up aircraft based on its assessment of the whereabouts of the bomber stream and its likely target. The fighters in the two classifications, the Wild Boars in the single-engined machines and the Tame Boars in the twin-engined A.I. machines, navigated by means of beacons, radio beacons for the twin-engined aircraft and flashing light beacons for the singles. These were the fighter assembly positions, and although their location was known to us it was impossible to fly a route more than fifty miles from a beacon. Even more ominously, however, the first SN2 radar sets had been installed in early August in a few Ju 88's to implement an idea of a bomber pilot, Colonel Victor von Lossberg. The idea was for a 'shadower' aircraft transmitting a signal to a ground controller to be directed to the vanguard of the approaching bomber stream by the controller and for it then to home on the H2S transmissions of the Pathfinders leading the bomber stream. The main body of two to three hundred fighters which had assembled nearby would then follow the shadower's radio beacon until they too found themselves in the bomber stream, in this way the complete force of twin and single-engined fighters could be brought into action. The running commentary and the shadower method soon replaced entirely the Kammhuber system. Meanwhile *Major* Hermann's Wild Boar force was expanded and in the three months prior to September 30th the German fighter force in the West, to the surprise of British Intelligence, increased from 1,288 to 1,646 fighters.

Many of the junior German pilots were corporals or sergeants with a *Gruppe* Commander of 40 aircraft being a *Hauptmann* (Captain). Losses suffered by these pilots were greater from accidents or crashes than from casualties inflicted by the RAF. Schnaufer's *Gruppe* at Saint Trond, Belgium, for example, didn't

1. *The Strategic Air Offensive Against Germany,* reproduced with permission of the Controller of HMSO.

lose an aircraft from RAF action in 17 months.

The conventional method of attack in use by the night fighters was the *von unten hinten*, literally 'from-under-and-behind'. This was a long approach on radar, ending in a visual sighting. The fighter then approached from a little below and astern in a slightly nose-up attitude, aiming and firing its fixed forward guns at the bomber's fuselage and bomb bays. Since the bombers usually carried a 4,000 lb. thin-skinned 'cookie' in addition to several smaller bombs, a strike here would often cause a massive explosion. In the from-under-and-behind, the attack usually cut down the defence of the bomber first; the pilot aimed at the fuselage and crew and if their resistance ended he aimed at the gas tanks. This approach however was not without risk to the fighter from the four tail guns and two mid-upper guns of the bomber. Accordingly, in the winter of 1943-1944 the Tame Boars developed a new form of attack, the *schrage musik* attack, in which the fighter approached on the controller's running commentary of the bomber stream and finally on its own radar to make visual contact. To this point it was the same as the from-under-and-behind and it is important to note that the gunners of the bomber usually had not seen the fighter. The fighter then dropped altitude a little, keeping the bomber in sight above him and accelerated to come up slightly ahead of the bomber, still well beneath him. The bomber of course had no under-turrets and the fighter, by staying low enough and by watching the bomber and its four engine exhausts silhouetted above him, could invariably reach this position unobserved. [1]From there it was a simple matter to pull up in a slant and fire. In fact, however, a more deadly variant was evolved. The fighter crews found that firing at a heavily laden bomber from a climb was unhealthy to the fighter also. When the bombs blew up, some fighter crews were lost with the bomber in the explosion. So, upward-firing guns were developed, pointing up vertically from the nose of the fighter. These were mounted right on the squadron by its own personnel in a demonstration of that remarkable adaptability which was characteristic of the Luftwaffe. The pilot, with a sight in the roof of his cockpit, aimed his upward firing cannon from below, with plenty of time for accuracy, usually at a point between the two port engines of the bomber. When he fired,

1. This was by no means a novel method of attack. Billy Bishop had perfected its details in daylight in World War I while stalking his favourite targets, the German two-seaters.

the exploding cannon shells would set the bomber's fuel tanks on fire and the fighter pilot, knowing that an explosion would quickly follow, could pull away immediately without himself being blown up. If the bomber crew baled out quickly enough they might escape alive from a *schrage musik*, or Jazz Music attack, but that probability was remote. These upward firing guns were successfully used on their first trial at Peenemunde, and by March of the following year factory-produced *schrage musik* fighters were reaching German fighter squadrons.

Needless to say few bombers returned from such an attack so as to describe it and those who did were not aware that they had been attacked from out of the darkness by cannon which did not use tracer bullets.[1] Having seen many bombers blow up in flames from exploding fuel tanks, both before and after having dropped their bombs, and in most cases not having seen a single tracer shell fired by either the fighter or the bomber, we suspected that they had been hit from belly attacks without tracers. Some crews, because they had seen no tracers, thought these orange mushrooming explosions to be 'scarecrows', fired aloft by the Germans to affect aircrew morale. I never believed that theory for an instant.

Months passed before, early in 1944, bomber crews actually saw the *schrage musik* attacks. Bomber Command and its leaders should have been aware before a single bomber was lost that any fighter pilot in his right mind would use just such a method of attack on a bomber which possessed no defensive armament underneath it, particularly when it was armed elsewhere with short range .303 machine guns. Like others, I was very conscious of the vulnerability of a bomber to belly attack, with or without upward firing guns, and as I have said, could not understand why the front turret of each bomber, which was virtually useless on night operations, was not moved to the belly, or rotated 90° to shoot downward and backward.[2]

I cannot leave the discussion of fighters over Berlin without mention that in the attack of August 23rd I had a close-up view of

1. Our aircraft were equipped with a sensing device which warned us if other aircraft were in the general area, but since it could not distinguish between 'friend' or 'foe', and our own aircraft were always nearby, it became a nuisance and so we invariably turned it off!

2. I have heard the opinion expressed that a 'belly' turret (or 'ball' turret) was of no use at night, due to the limited visibility therefrom, but I was never convinced of this.

a Wild Boar. What a sight he was! We were over the target and I was looking ahead and down to my right at the city appearing dark red from the glow of searchlights and incendiaries. We were still some distance from the release point for the TI's when I saw the outline of a single-engined fighter climbing steeply towards us at an angle from my right. I made known to the gunners that he was coming and kept my eyes on him. He still seemed on a collision course but suddenly it was apparent that he would pass by ahead of us, and he did, a Focke Wulf 190; he was heading like a rocket for something above and to the left of me. He was so close I could see the shape of the pilot in plain view in the cockpit. The distinctive black crosses on his wings seemed large and square. He was then directly in front of us and climbing steeply, but there was no time to shoot him down because the bomb aimer wasn't in the front turret; he was hunched over the bomb sight. On September 3rd however our Pilot Officer Davies and crew did shoot down a Wild Boar Me 109 over Berlin. It was the rear gunner's first operation.

One observation on the attack of August 31st and the 'brilliant fighter flares'; again we were blind markers and, after a bomb run on H2S, we left the target and flew a leg on a south-west heading, and then turned west. The moon was on my right. There was broken cloud below. The mid-upper gunner reported two Ju 88's flying above a cloud layer, parallel to us, – one behind the other with the moon low behind them. They continued on this path at the same altitude as ourselves for a few minutes, which seemed strange since they made no attack. I was curious to see them and raised up in my seat to see for myself. I saw only one but sure enough he had the unmistakable silhouette of a Ju 88 with its box-like, transparent canopy. In a few more moments their function became clear, brilliant pink parachute flares began burning behind us at our level. We must have been one of the first to leave the target and they had used us as a guide to lay flares and mark the route out. In seconds the Wild Boars would be patrolling above the flares to see the bombers silhouetted in their light. Then we noticed another line of flares on our other side. It was as though, to our rear, there had been constructed a brightly lit avenue in the sky. Yet we were not attacked. Could it be that the Ju 88's carrying the flares were the bomber version of that aircraft, bomb bays loaded with flares but not armed with cannon? That was the only explanation I could think of. In operations after that time the first few aircraft took a different route out of the target than did those following. Pilot Officer Pidding and crew, behind us as they left Berlin, had a running battle with an Me 110, both Pidding's gunners expending a lot of ammunition.

On the trip to Nuremberg on August 27th, sandwiched between the Berlin operations, we crossed the Thames east of London, heading south to Beachy Head. We crossed to France near Dieppe, then it was past Amiens, past Luxembourg, and across the Rhine south of Mannheim. From there east to Nuremberg in the old Kingdom of Bavaria, brought into Germany by Bismarck in 1871. We dropped four green TI's and 7000 pounds of bombs on the target and had a brush with a Wild Boar Fw 190 on leaving the city. He came in to attack but the rear gunner kept me informed and I took strong evasive action when he told me to. Neither of us fired; I didn't even see the fighter. We completed the long return journey across Southern Germany and Northern France without incident, but the Squadron lost ED 876 V for Victor, piloted by Flight Sergeant K.C. Turp. Two of our aircraft, piloted by Squadron Leader Hildyard and Pilot Officer King, were shot up over the target. King's hydraulics being ruined – he made a successful belly landing. Flying Officer Chick's target photograph was examined next day with interest; it was said to be probably the finest ever taken at night.

I missed the trip to Mannheim on September 5th due to new crews having filled up our required contribution of fourteen aircraft but Chick went, and got himself coned in searchlights again, this time for eight minutes. We lost Pilot Officer J.H. Price and crew, the fighters having been active in the target area; Price was a fellow Canadian but had not been with us long.

CHAPTER ELEVEN

H2S and 'Abortions'

WE took 'T' for Tommy to Munich on September 6th where some confusion reigned over the target. We left base on a route specially arranged over London to give the people an opportunity to see, in the late sunset, the air power which was hammering Germany on their behalf. We crossed the great city *en route* to Beachy Head, and from there it was south-east, by now in complete darkness, across northern France on a line towards Freiburg. Before reaching that city we turned east across the Rhine and over the source of the Danube, trying to keep Lake Constance and the flak of Friedrickshaven to starboard, but we were off course and were shot at, whether by the Swiss or by the Germans I am not certain. We ran in as blind markers to open the attack, flying at about 10,000 feet since there was solid cloud above that level. I could see the railway station through a break in the cloud and our bomb doors were open when Tolman reported a fighter astern. We now had Flight Sergeant Hicks, a Canadian mid-upper gunner aboard, and he confirmed the sighting. A tall man, Hicks had a deep voice which was always calm. Damn, I thought, just when we were about to bomb! Still, there seemed no choice, it would be stupid to fly straight and level while the fighter lined up his attack; I closed the bomb doors and did a very steep turn to port, since the fighter had now moved to that side. I made a complete circle and we didn't see him again. On the second run in, cloud obscured our vision. We could not have been far from the railway station since we had made only one complete circle since seeing the fighter. Flight Sergeant Hyatt, a new bomb-aimer, could now see target markers. He waited a few seconds and let go our markers which by now really were blind. The attack went astray because the target indicators were barely visible to the main force through the cloud. This was especially true of the vital opening phase, our phase, of the attack. On return to Wyton we found that one of our aircraft had returned early because its navigator had forgotten his computer. The Squadron Operations Book said, 'This speaks for itself and we add no comment.' Squadron Leader C.A.J. Smith, despite the problems with cloud, obtained a target photo within 1,000 yards of the aiming point.

The poor overall results on Munich prompted an investigation the next day by Group. Someone said that the investigation was conducted because bombs had gone down on one of the prisoner of war camps and some of our own men had been killed. We were heartsick to think that this might be true but we knew full well by now that we were causing great casualties every time out. However, in the three and a half years from the Battle of Britain to the time of the invasion, Bomber Command was the only weapon the Allies had which could strike Germany. We had to keep up the pressure. Wing Commander Cousins DSO, DFC, the Group Navigation Officer, came the three miles from Huntingdon to Wyton to interrogate the blind markers. We all knew him, so the atmosphere was informal. He talked to each aircraft's pilot, navigator and bomb-aimer in separate groups of three. He sat with my group, a chart of the Munich area spread on a board on his lap and a pair of dividers in his hand; he was interested in what we had seen before breaking off the bomb run because of the fighter. I began to think that we should have kept on the bomb run, but on later reflection had no doubt that I had done the right thing. If a prisoner of war camp was hit I don't think it was hit by us – unless it was within a mile or two of the Munich railway station.

It was time again for leave. We had flown thirteen operations since the last leave in July. Before going on leave, however, Group Captain Johnnie Fauquier, the CO of 405 'Vancouver' Squadron, which was the sole Canadian Pathfinder Squadron came to Wyton for a visit. I didn't speak with him but Searby said that he was looking for Canadians for flight commanders[1] and pointed out that it was time that I assumed some command responsibility. I said that I didn't particularly want to leave 83 and didn't volunteer. The tide in the affairs of men which, taken at its flood, leads on to fortune, held no fascination for me. I knew that I was only a wartime warrior and had no ambition for higher rank, particularly because as a flight commander or squadron commander one could not fly as much as I was now doing. Squadron commanders, for example,

1. Fauquier had a chat with Garvey who was nearing his 60th trip but Garvey turned down the job. Fauquier's search was quickly ended when Bennett, the Group Commander, found that Reggie Lane of Victoria, B.C. had, in May, completed 45 trips with 35 Squadron. He asked Lane to take over one of 405's flights with a view of replacing Fauquier as Squadron Commander. Lane did this in October, and in January 1944 took command of the Squadron, bringing his total of operational flights to 56 by August 1944. Lane stayed in the RCAF to pursue a distinguished career and retired as a Lieutenant General.

usually flew less than half the scheduled operations. There was a certain safety factor for me in frequent operations and I liked to go quickly from one to the next. In that way one could keep abreast of the rapidly changing defences. People laughed when I said that one could navigate his way around Germany by the guns and searchlights but this was literally true. Each city had its distinctive pattern of flak and searchlights. Operational flying to me was the norm, rather than the exception, and so I felt at ease doing it; I was stimulated by it and was more afraid of cowardice than of death. Fear, in my opinion, was a killer; if one feared death, he quickly found it. I had seen pilots arrive on the squadron like frightened rabbits, soon to disappear, and not all of them were inexperienced. Some came on a second tour after periods as staff officers. It may sound callous but Chick and I often predicted to ourselves how long they would last. Sometimes we told these predictions to each other. We were seldom wrong. One notable exception was a small pilot who shall remain nameless; he was so small that he needed an extra cushion to sit in a Lancaster. I could not have had a good look at him when I predicted that he would not last a month. Chick agreed. We were both wrong. When I finished my operations this little man, who turned out to possess the ferocity of a wolverine, was still going strong.

And so leaving command responsibilities and rank to those who wanted them, I sought instead the type of flying I liked. Promotion was not difficult for those who wanted it, provided they had ability. I learned for example that Al Avant, who had graduated first at Yorkton, was now a flight commander with a DFC, later to be a squadron commander, with a DSO also, on Halifaxes in 6 Group. Al was a fine commander and survived the war to pursue a peacetime career in the RCAF.

There were others on 83 like Chick and myself who survived.[1] Besides those I have mentioned, Squadron Leader Hildyard finished his second tour in August and of course there was Searby, and there was Warrant Officer Jack Finding and Pilot Officer Tolchard, both excellent captains, and there was Pilot

1. The number of aircraft missing or crashed from 83 Squadron during the time I was a member of it was close to the average of 4.34% for Bomber Command at that time. This meant that about 13%, or one in eight, survived 45 operations. The number of crews who survived 45 seemed higher to us on 83 than it actually was because most newly-arrived crews had already done a half tour, or more, before joining Pathfinders.

Officer Hellier, Flight Lieutenant Mason, Squadron Leader Guy Sells, Pilot Officer Britton and Squadron Leader Ambrose Smith, all pilots of great skill.

Ambrose's crew used to complain good naturedly that he never came down from 20,000 feet and got them off oxygen until they were over England. I had no doubt that Ambrose knew precisely what he was doing. Then, too, some others I can recall are Squadron Leaders Tommy Blair and Norman Scrivener, both top flight navigators, as was Squadron Leader Dunk, and there was Ian Meikle, the South African bomb-aimer and Johnnie Johnston, the gunnery leader, all of whom had been decorated. Also there was 'Taffy' Preece, the gunner with the Conspicuous Gallantry Medal. And there was Wing Commander Cyril 'Plunger' Smith, DSO, DFC, the ex school-master, so named for his love of poker, and Wing Commander A.S. Johnson, DSO, DFM and bar, later to become a fleet operations manager of British Airways. These last two pilots got into a ferocious argument in the mess after a couple of drinks one night. They were playing poker in the card room[1] and were comparing years of service in the RAF. I think 'Plunger' suggested that Johnson had joined up because he couldn't get a job in civilian life. This infuriated Johnson who said that Smith had only joined the Air Force as 'a damned draft dodger'. They were serious about such insults and I thought they would come to blows. This was delightful; here were two of the best bomber pilots in Britain, each with distinguished records, calling each other unemployed and draft dodger; only in England at this time could that have happened.

So Chick and I went on leave. As we were leaving the station Searby called us to his office and said that before we left we should go to see the Mayor of St. Ives who wanted a couple of officers to appear at the town's Air Force celebration. We accepted the invitation, or perhaps it was an order, to display ourselves as heroes. After speeches by several officials on a sunny day in the main square of St. Ives, an attentive group of people stood at the town war memorial while the mayor presented us with a brace of pheasant. This was a great present, and a sacrifice by someone in meat-short England. Since we were on leave we weren't going to turn the pheasant over to the Air Force cooks. We went to Chick's home at Maidenhead on the Thames, a beautiful spot just up-river from London. His mother was not at home to cook for us so we decided

1. Gambling in the mess was illegal, so they always insisted they were playing 'bridge'. We, of course, were not familiar with five-card bridge!

to cook them ourselves. We had a bottle of Scotch with which to relieve our parched throats, for cooking pheasant gives one a terrible thirst, and we plucked and cleaned the birds. I knew how to do this and Chick maintained that he was familiar with the stove so we got the birds safely in the oven. Then we told lies for a while and saved the balance of the whisky from going bad. We were sitting in the kitchen and the bottle had been almost drained when we noticed that a great deal of smoke had filled the air. Investigation revealed that the chimney was on fire. So we had a decision to make: should we call the fire department before we ate the pheasant or should we eat the pheasant and then call the fire department. The latter seemed the best course. So we ate those delicious pheasant with bread and cheese in Chick's smoke-filled kitchen, washed down by red wine and Scotch whisky. Not many gourmets have done that.

We spent a few days after that in Cornwall where by a stroke of good fortune we met not one, but two, attractive young war widows sunning themselves on the beach in the late summer heat. It was our clear patriotic duty, said Chick, to bring these pale beauties out of their bereavement. Putting all else aside, we stoically did so.

On our return from leave on September 23rd we were treated to a double-barrelled attack on the Ruhr. Britton and I were blind markers on Darmstadt and the rest of the Squadron went to Mannheim. The weather was excellent and each of the targets was easy to find, particularly Mannheim, at a bend in the Rhine. The marking was accurate on both targets and as a result the bombing was effective. Over Darmstadt I observed a Wild Boar diving into his own searchlights and heavy, bursting flak to get at a Lancaster which was coned. I saw both of them fire their guns but didn't see the outcome of the attack. The I.G. Farben Works suffered damage as did the dock area at the junction of the Rhine and the Neckar. We returned to Wyton without trouble where we found that one of our aircraft had been late in getting airborne because one of its gunners had deserted. A spare gunner had been found having a quiet pint in the mess.

Since I have referred to them frequently, I should say a word or two about military decorations. The British system of decorations was, in my view, elitist and it offended many Canadians for the same reason. There were orders, there were crosses and there were medals. Senior officers got the orders, junior officers got the crosses and other ranks got the medals – for the same thing! The decoration for distinguished flying by junior officers was the Distinguished Flying Cross. The same thing for a senior officer was a Distinguished Service Order and for a non-commissioned officer was a Distinguished Flying Medal. The distinction between officers and men, and between junior officers and senior officers, was further riveted in place by this unwarranted separation. A Warrant Officer, the senior rank of non-commissioned officer, was an exception to the rule; he would be awarded a DFC rather than a DFM for conduct for which the next rank below him, a Flight Sergeant, would get a DFM. While everyone spoke flippantly of decorations, 'Oh I got this one for crossing Piccadilly Circus in heavy traffic', or 'This one came with some cigarettes when I'd done a tour' they were very proud to wear them. Strange, is it not, that a human will risk his life for such baubles? Some will say, 'Oh they weren't risking their life for the decorations, the decorations were incidental to their perseverance, skill and courage'. But that was not always true; I knew people who would and did risk their lives, and sometimes they lost, in pursuit of decorations. Motivational experts would do well to examine this behaviour. The incentive of decorations was far more powerful on both sides than was rank or money – perhaps like notches on a gun or bombs painted on the fuselage, decorations brought recognition, but more, they represented the approval of those in authority. In the British system of monarchy it seemed a splendid tradition to receive a decoration from the sovereign head of state in the presence of friends and loved ones while a military orchestra played lively music. The same would not be true if the decoration were bestowed by a political figure.

Much of the pleasure in receiving a decoration seems to lie in people's recognition of what it is. Like most Canadians, for example, I am but dimly aware of our present system of decorations, and for this reason much of the lustre of receiving one may be lost by its recipient. This merely illustrates, I suppose, that a tradition is not made overnight.

Canada has now established three awards for heroism, both civil and military. They are:

(1) The Cross of Valour, awarded some eleven times since 1972, four of them posthumously.

(2) The Star of Courage.

(3) The Medal of Bravery.

Talk of decorations is a way of mentioning that on September 27th I received the usual 'postagram' signed by Air Chief Marshal Harris saying, 'My warmest congratulations on the award of your Distinguished Flying Cross', and a few days later I received a similar letter from Vincent Massey, the Canadian High Commissioner in London. My home Province, British Columbia, through BC House in London, contributed some cigarettes to the occasion. Lest the reader be concerned that one's mental gyros be toppled by this sudden fame let me mention that from September 3, 1939 to September 1, 1943, 448 DFC's and 248 DFM's were awarded to members of the RCAF. In the next year, ending September 1, 1944 an additional 810 DFC's and 159 DFM's were awarded to members of my Service.

A typical example of conduct leading to an immediate decoration might be that which occurred to an aircraft from the Canadian Thunderbird Squadron over Mannheim, just after the blind markers had gone down. It was piloted by Flight Lieutenant L.N. McCaig with Warrant Officer E.S. Hawkes as rear gunner. The Squadron record book said this:

Immediately after bombs were gone a Ju 88 came in to attack from below and astern. Both gunners opened fire and the enemy aircraft broke off the engagement. A second Ju 88 came in and again the gunners opened fire at about 600 yards. The Ju 88 came on and opened fire at about 500 yards. The gunners observed strikes and pieces fell from the Ju 88 which was claimed as destroyed. However, the Lancaster had also suffered great damage. The hydraulics were shot up – port fin and rudder shot off – rear turret damaged – port wing damaged – two petrol tanks holed – port elevator damaged – inter-com and radio transmitter damaged and the D.R. compass ruined. Both mid-upper and rear gunners received wounds, one in the thigh and the other in the calf, but both continued firing until the enemy aircraft was destroyed. The pilot by superb airmanship managed to keep control of his aircraft and set course for the long journey home. Due to the damage the aircraft flew nose heavy and great strength was needed to maintain altitude. The pilot made a crash landing where medical help was secured for the injured crew members.

McCaig and Hawkes were both awarded the DFC for the night's work. One wonders if the mid-upper gunner got a DFM.

* * *

On September 23rd Chick and I were introduced to someone
who seemed already to be well-known to the mess staff and station
personnel. He was Flying Officer C.P. 'Mac' McDonald, DFC,
DFM. Mac indeed was well known, a strongly built, gregarious
Canadian in the RCAF; he had apparently just that day returned to
the Squadron from neutral Sweden where he had been living since
April 21st. That was the night when on 106 Squadron we had
bombed Stettin and Kelly had been wounded. Mac, then a pilot of
83 Squadron, had been less fortunate than we and, shot up by flak,
had radioed that he was baling out over Sweden where he and his
crew were interned. The Squadron Operations Book states that his
baling out and internment were made known the next day by a
broadcast on Swedish radio. It must have been an indulgent prison
judging from Mac's stories of Swedish hospitality and the liaison
he described with a fair Swedish beauty. In any event he was
repatriated to Britain in the bomb bay of a Mosquito in an exchange
of courtesy between the two countries. On September 29th he was
sent to Bochum with 83 Squadron on a refresher trip when most of
the rest of the Squadron was not operating. Mac didn't get very far.
When Chick and I returned from a night at the movies in
Huntingdon he was seated in the mess, his right leg in a cast, a
tankard of ale in his hand and crutches beside his chair. He told us
that while he had been in Sweden a modification had been made to
the automatic pilot of the Lancaster, changing the method by which
it was disengaged. But no one had told him of this, so when he was
airborne near the Wash *en route* for the Dutch coast he attempted
to disengage the auto pilot and couldn't do it. I don't know whether
or not he tried the fire-axe on it but after a great deal of anguish and
inability to disengage the thing he finally decided that he wasn't
going to fly all the way to Bochum and back on auto-pilot and so
ordered the crew to bale out, which they did. Unfortunately, Mac
landed in a pigsty and fractured his ankle. So there he was, sitting
in the mess telling us this tale of woe. We decided to cheer his
departure from the Squadron with several toasts to an uneventful
convalescence and he left happily on his crutches with our good
wishes ringing in his ears.

On September 27th we did a trip of 4 hours and 15 minutes to
drop yellow flares as a blind marker on Hanover. Severe icing
conditions caused a lot of bombers to return early but approaching

the target the weather was good. The blind markers were not well placed by ourselves and the others and most of the visual markers were not able to see the aiming point and their flares were scattered.

As a result, most of the bombs fell in open country. When we heard of this we rationalised, 'Oh well, you can't always be right.' Ironically, our visual marker, Pilot Officer Britton, got an aiming point photo but no one bombed his markers. Tolchard had a battle with a fighter and Jack Finding had an even more terrible time on this trip. A flak shell blew off the pilot's escape hatch and out flew all the maps and the navigation log. His intercom failed and the crew had to shout to each other. He was hit again on the bomb run and on return to base was guided in, with cloud at 300 feet, by a searchlight playing on the underside of the cloud.

On October 2nd it was Munich again. Situated about 40 miles south of the Danube and 75 miles north of the Brenner Pass, it was the farthest target in south-east Germany. Again we were blind markers and we had a new bomb-aimer now regularly flying with us. He was Flying Officer Sherwood, a very large Englishman and a good bomb-aimer. When we were blind marking he helped Bedell with navigation and in operating the H2S, as well as releasing the bombs.

For some time Bomber Command had felt that the more rapidly an attack could be completed the less chance the fighters had to get to the target in time, or if they did get there the less time they would have for seeking us out. It was therefore decided that the concentration of aircraft over the target should be drastically increased. The risk of collision with our own aircraft and from 'friendly' bombs was accepted and all the attacks in October were scheduled to last no more than 26 minutes. In fact over Munich the attack had been completed within nine minutes of the time at which the German fighter controller correctly diagnosed the target. As a result the missing rate was lowered to 2.3 percent. In the raid on Kassel the following night when we were again blind markers, although the loss was 24 aircraft, (4.4 percent) nine were destroyed by flak, the causes of the loss of eight were unknown and only seven were shot down by fighters. This was the result of confusion created in the mind of the German controller by the dog-leg route.

We entered Europe over the Dutch coast, north of Den Helder, aiming for Hanover, but 30 miles short of Hanover turned south-west and flew for some minutes on that heading and then made another turn south-east for Kassel. The German controller trying to diagnose our destination from the track of the blind markers, first sent the fighters to Hanover and then to Brunswick before he realised that the target was Kassel. For this reason it was important that the blind markers stay on schedule. They were the first to attack and if they were only two minutes early, that was an extra two minutes of fighter attacks for everyone over the target by Wild Boars. Unfortunately, we didn't mark Kassel very well and due to haze the visual markers couldn't identify the target area. Most of the bombs missed the target. We lost Squadron Leader J.R. Hayter DFC and crew in JA 972. We were also saddened by the departure from the Squadron of the beloved 'Plunger' C.A.J. Smith who, though he was ill, wanted to continue flying. The doctor wouldn't let him, and told him that he had flown his last operation. This was a bitter blow to 'Smithy', he being another who had set himself the goal of 60 operations on a Pathfinder Squadron. It was bitter too for the rest of us who were so genuinely fond of him. I don't know what the diagnosis was but he had, I think simply worn himself out in the attempt to realise his difficult goal. Chick, upon his return from Kassel, found an unexploded four pound incendiary stick in his fuel tank. It was still live when the ground crew carefully removed it. Someone above him had dropped a shower of incendiaries and he had flown through it.

On October 5th the first Canadian-built Lancaster, KB 700, was flown on operations by 405 Squadron, just the other side of Huntingdon from ourselves. The Packard-built Merlin was being produced in the United States to Rolls-Royce specifications and these engines were provided for Lancaster airframes made in Canada to re-equip the Canadian 6 Group. 405 Squadron, although it was in the Pathfinder Group, was still a 6 Group Squadron, just as 83 did not lose its identity as a 5 Group Squadron when it went to Pathfinders. The first order in Canada was for 300 Lancaster BX's from Victory Aircraft and these were built from September 1943 to March 1945 and ferried to the United Kingdom. By the end of the war a total of 430 Lancasters had been built in Canada and 10,000 Canadians were involved in their construction.

On October 7th we were again blind markers, this time on Stuttgart; there was simultaneously a force of Mosquitoes attacking Munich as a diversion for the German controller. It worked, the controller sent his fighters to Munich and by the time he got them back to Stuttgart the attack was over. The Command lost only four aircraft. This was a somewhat deceptive introduction to Pathfinder operations for Wing Commander Simmonds who had just arrived on 83 Squadron from Bomber Command and who flew with me that night as second pilot. The route and target were completely covered with cloud; it became an attack with sky markers and he saw nothing. This time it was Garvey's turn to collect an incendiary which landed without detonating in his tail turret. The gunner was offered only aspirin on his return.

It was around this time that the Germans sent an occasional night fighter over the North Sea to inspect us at Wyton and Gravely. They didn't shoot any of us down but caused some consternation with our defences and made us look over our shoulders a little. We wondered what had prompted this activity until, on October 11th, we had a lecture from one Squadron Leader Day, an interrogator of German prisoners on the subject of German interrogation techniques. He told us that a shot-down Pathfinder crew had recently been taken prisoner and had talked about our location. The Germans would like nothing better than to knock down a couple of Pathfinders, he said.

If congestion of aeroplanes over the target was a concern for aircrew, congestion over England after an operation was much worse. Over a target the aircraft were all travelling in the same direction at approximately the same speed, thus reducing the risk of collision but over their bases in England the traffic was fierce. There were airfields in Bomber Command no more than two miles from each other. At Wyton, for example, there was the satellite airfield of Warboys only two miles away. If our aircraft did a left hand circuit, theirs had to do a right hand one on a parallel runway to avoid collision. Approaching either the south or the east coast, homeward bound, one could use 'Gee' for an accurate course to base, and *en route* to Wyton one could read the flashing Morse identification lights of other airfields. We usually stayed at an altitude between 7,000 and 10,000 feet to avoid other bombers. These would lose altitude to 2000-3000 feet at their own airfields as we crossed over them. By this time everyone had his navigation lights on and it was not uncommon to criss-cross the path of other returning bombers. There was no flying control until one reached one's own airfield and reported there to the controller who gave the altimeter setting, a height to fly circling the base, and a turn by number for landing. We were instructed to conserve fuel but nonetheless there was often a race to get to base when one was nearing it and saw other aircraft heading in the same direction. It could be annoying if someone called up to obtain his turn to land while still 30 miles away, when he was not experiencing an emergency. Persons who did this were soon made aware of airborne etiquette and they seldom did it again. Sometimes, for example, when aircraft were damaged or short of fuel, or if carrying wounded, the radio language became saltier than usual. On one occasion the vicar of a church near Wyton, who had been listening on the station frequency to our landing chatter, complained to the station commander that 'these boys are going to their death with blasphemy on their lips'. We were asked to modify our language.

The airfield lighting was good. A circuit was marked out around the field with faint blue lights and one orbited until told to land; these lights ended in a funnel at the runway in use, from the entrance to which one could see the glide path indicator to lead one to the end of the runway. This consisted of lights angled from the end of the runway to the pilot on the approach in such a way that if he was on the correct glide slope he would see a green light – if too high he would see an amber, if too low a red. This was fine if one could see the airfield. However, on the rare occasions when ground fog completely obscured the field an emergency procedure was followed to land at nearby Graveley, using 'Fido', a fog dispersal device. This was a rather remarkable idea and it worked quite well on October 20th, the one occasion when I used it.

Alongside the runway to be used, on both sides, was a pipe some six inches in diameter connected to a large gasoline storage tank. The pipe had upright nozzles sticking from it at regular intervals along its length. When the fog was bad, as it was when we returned and couldn't see Wyton, Fido was turned on and set alight. A sheet of flame two feet high on either side of the runway soon created enough heat to raise the fog one or two hundred feet, enough for us to see to land after a beam approach. The only thing wrong was that Gravely was a Halifax airfield and its glide path indicator was set for the steeper approach angle of that aircraft as compared to the Lancaster. Our pilots on the approach couldn't understand why they were overshooting the glide slope and one Lancaster ran out of runway and ended up in a pasture. But everyone finally landed safely from an operation which, without Fido, could have ended in disaster.

The German night fighters were improving from the chaos at Hamburg. On the night of October 8th over Hanover, for example, fighters accounted for 21 of the 27 aircraft which failed to return. They had laid an aerial flarepath in anticipation of an attack on Bremen but soon scurried to Hanover. The attack was successful in spite of the fighter opposition. We and others again dropped blind markers which were said to be 'extremely accurate' and the aiming point was 'brilliantly illuminated for the visual markers'. The first four visual markers overshot but soon there was a better concentration of green TI's within a half mile of the aiming point as seven visual markers, three from our squadron, got aiming points. These three were obtained by the crews of F/S Hellier, F/L Chick and P/O Tolchard. 340 of the 430 attacking crews got their bombs within three miles of the aiming point. Two square miles of the centre of the city were devastated. Still the Germans refused to leave their cities.

The next attack, on October 18th was to Hanover again. 83 Squadron contributed thirteen crews. Perhaps if we kept it up we could drive the Germans from this city, as we appeared to have driven them from Hamburg. I had with me as second pilot, Squadron Leader Joe Northrup, DFC, AFC, who had flown with an electronic countermeasures flight jamming the German beams in their attacks on England; for this he had been awarded an Air Force Cross. He had also flown a tour on Stirlings with 7 and 15 Squadrons where he had earned his DFC. Joe had joined the RAF as a 'Halton Brat', an apprentice mechanic in 1929 and he appeared to regard me with the stereotype image of Canadians which many English had. Canadian males who read this will be pleased to know that they are regarded as happy-go-lucky men, great gamblers and successful with girls. This image is a derivative of the then British view of Americans as 'overpaid, over-sexed and over here'. Northrup couldn't adjust to my carrying a knife or a pistol on operations, as I invariably did. He regarded this as a wild west exhibition. I let it be known that unarmed persons might be captured by an elderly and toothless police dog when they might easily have escaped to the French underground. Airmen, like other military men, were governed by the code of law which obliged them to attempt to escape if captured. I never resented the sometimes patronising attitude of the English. They, after all, didn't much care for each other, let alone for the non-English.

There was solid cloud over Hanover. We dropped blind markers in what appeared to us to be the correct place and probably got our own bombs down fairly accurately but the markers could not be seen through the cloud by the main force and so when reconnaissance later examined the place it was found that the attack had largely gone astray. Pilot Officer Stiles became the third to pick up an incendiary dropped by another aircraft.

On October 20th it was Leipzig, south and a little west, some 95 miles from Berlin and about 230 miles east of Kassel, in eastern Germany. Here again the markers were dropped blind on H2S but that was not of much use when most of the main force could not see them through the clouds. So, like Hanover, many of the bombs went astray.

Leipzig was a fairly long-range target which took us 7 hours and 10 minutes to complete. Some crews had difficulty with icing and electrical storms. But the fighters had the same weather problems and the overall losses were accordingly low. On 83 we lost Squadron Leader R.J. Manton and crew in JB 154. Manton was a fine pianist, somewhat older than the group of young aircrew who frequently gathered round him at the piano and begged him to play. A sensitive man, we surmised that he was suffering the pangs of unrequited love, for he often played sad music. In the evening, before we took off we asked him to play 'Rustle of Spring', which was one of his favourites. He played it flawlessly and we then dressed and went to our aircraft. We wondered, when he didn't return, if Manton's aircraft had iced up. I learned after the war that he was killed. We also lost Warrant Officer S.G. Hall and crew in JA 731 but I understand that he survived. Two of our crews had been forced to turn back with a variety of troubles, ranging from compasses to instruments, to turrets. Two others were damaged by fighters; one, Pilot Officer Simpson lost half of his tail, his hydraulics, his air pressure, his starboard inner engine and had a burst tyre. He managed to land at Newmarket, on the race-course. Britton, who had just been commissioned, suffered three attacks, losing part of his tail plane, one engine, his flaps, and part of his main plane. His rear turret was knocked out and his upper turret damaged on the first pass. He couldn't hold the control column far enough forward so he got some of the crew to help him hold it while his engineer, F/Lt. Forster, went aft, found the elevator trim wires and adjusted them manually. Britton made a masterful landing with a burst tyre.

Our crew had now been backer-up on six attacks, visual markers on two and blind markers or illuminators on fourteen. We were an experienced marker crew and Group Headquarters seemed keen on adding to our responsibilities. I was asked to go to Huntingdon to see the Pathfinder Group training inspector, Group Captain Hamish Mahaddie, DSO, DFC, a flamboyant Scot who had flown many operations earlier in the war. Seeing him at 8 Group was a lot less formal than the last group headquarters I had visited, while under arrest. He made me welcome and pointed out that since I had now done forty trips, and would be finished at forty-five, he wanted to know what I wanted to do next. I hadn't given a thought to the problem for fear it might tempt fate, so I told him that I thought I would just keep on with 83 for a while. He said, 'Well if that is so, we can get you flying some new equipment.' He didn't tell me what the new equipment was and I really wasn't too concerned; I had more operations to do.

On October 22nd it was Kassel again, with some crews on a diversionary raid to Frankfurt. This time we were expected to make up for the poor job of marking we did on October 3rd. Our crew were to be visual markers.

We encountered 10/10th cloud and electrical storms on the way to and from the target. Balls of fire were observed which hadn't been put up by the Germans. The blue flames of St. Elmo's fire danced around the propellers. One had to be concerned about ice forming on the wings and propellers. We had pulsating rubber de-icing boots for the leading edges of the Lancaster's wings and glycol for the windscreens but ice on the propellers was a concern because it could come off and cut through the cockpit window. The weather cleared over the target but most of the blind markers overshot by one and a half to five miles. Still, for ourselves as visual markers, that turned out to be better than if they had undershot. A couple of blind markers were near the aiming point at five minutes before zero hour and these enabled us, as one of the visual markers, to identify the target and drop our red target indicators with 'extreme accuracy'. Within three minutes at least thirty red markers from six aircraft were burning in a compact group within a half mile of the aiming point. 380 of 444 crews got their bombs within three miles of the aiming point. In the Konigsplatz no building was undamaged. Tremendous industrial damage had been done on both sides of the Fulda River. In fact a firestorm similar to that on Hamburg, had been created. There was hope yet of winning the war with area bombing alone. If the Germans could see what could happen to all of their cities, they might give up or evacuate them. But they did not give up and their fighters fought back. Forty-two of our aircraft were lost, almost 10% of the attacking force; of these about thirty-two were shot down by fighters. One of our squadron was attacked by a fighter and another, F/Lt. Sambridge, was coned by searchlights and hit by flak causing a fire in his port wing which finally burned out.

The Squadron Operations Record Book states on 26 October 1943: 'The preliminary report of the raid on Kassel and Frankfurt came through. The Kassel raid was probably the best attack Pathfinder Force has ever carried out. The illuminating and blind marking were excellent with a slight tendency to overshoot. All nine visual markers identified the aiming point and six have so far been plotted within one mile of the aiming point. From 83 Squadron F/Lt. Thompson had an aiming point and P/O Tolchard and F/Lt. Garvey were within one mile.

The German flying bomb programme suffered this night a devastating blow. Nine of its principal factories including the Fieseler works, manufacturing the first series of the bomb, were forced to evacuate to another site where there was no compressed air, no electricity and no telephones or transport. 91,000 people were rendered homeless and 40% of the work force failed to report to the alternate site. The raid cut off the supply of the bomb's control gear, diving mechanism, compass and other vital parts and represented Bomber Command's greatest contribution to delaying the flying bomb offensive.

By the autumn of 1943 it was standard practice for Bomber Command to fly diversionary attacks on one target while the main force attacked another, or there would be a feint towards one city with the force turning to attack another. Also the radio frequency used by the German controllers was jammed, as was the frequency used by the German fighters.

The Germans countered the jamming of their controllers by increasing their transmission strength. One interesting incident in these electronic countermeasures occurred on November 17th when we went as visual markers to Ludwigshafen, near Mannheim. Bomber Command had a German-speaking person pretending to be a controller broadcasting to the German fighters. As the attack was about to begin he told the fighters to land, which most of them did; we lost only one bomber from the whole force. This was an isolated instance however and the German controllers' running commentaries to place their fighters in the bomber stream, and the German AI equipment were, on the whole, very effective and of course no amount of electronics could conceal a target under attack. Our attack on Ludwigshafen was the last chance which anyone had for a while to do visual marking. The Battle of Berlin opened on November 18th and Berlin was marked wholly blind by H2S.

Much effort was involved in the German fighter commanders predicting the movements of the bomber force. They were obliged quickly to sort the mass of conflicting information deliberately presented to them in the form of spoof attacks by small forces of heavy bombers and by minelaying operations, Mosquito attacks on alternate targets, and of course the dropping of 'window' to simulate a large force in one area while the main force went elsewhere. The ground radar operators, however, soon became adept at distinguishing the real bombing force from the decoys by the number of H2S signals emanating from the heavy bombers. Until the real force could be identified they gambled, firstly upon getting the fighter force airborne at all, since fuel burned orbiting their beacons meant a loss of fighting time. Then the correct beacons had to be chosen and the attack location diagnosed in order to get the fighters quickly into the bomber stream. Usually the choice was narrowed to a general area. Frankfurt – Stuttgart? Mannheim – Karlsruhe? Or would the bombers continue on to Munich, or to Nuremberg? Or perhaps north to Leipzig-Berlin? There was no point in ordering fighters from Berlin to the beacon at 'Ida', south of Aachen, or to 'Otto', east of Frankfurt if the bombers shifted their heading to the North across Holland towards Hanover, better to send them to the beacon at 'Ludwig', north-east of the Ruhr.

For the German aircrew the difficult part of the operation was to get into the stream of bombers. Once there they could begin hunting on their airborne radar, but their own speed was not markedly higher than that of the bombers, hence they were pleased when they found themselves in the bomber stream. In this they were guided by the running commentary of their controllers and by the shadower aircraft. It was even more vital to the Wild Boars that the limited fuel supply of their single-engined aircraft should not be dissipated as they orbited their visual beacons. Usually, as the Pathfinders at the head of the bomber force neared the western frontier of Germany, all or most of the twin-engined night fighters were in the air and were either at, or on course to, their beacons. In minutes they would be vectored between 5,000 and 7,000 metres altitude towards the bomber stream. As the attack developed fighters would be re-routed and soon a force of perhaps two hundred and fifty night fighters would be committed to the attack from airfields as widely separated as Berlin, Northern France, Southern Germany, Denmark and Belgium. The kills would commence. In a typical Me 110 a pilot would take off from his runway and point its nose towards the assigned radio-beacon. Back to back with him would be his radar operator. They might have, in addition to a pair of 2 cm cannon, two 3 cm drum-fed cannon which when fired would dazzle the pilot. These were large enough to blow great pieces of debris from a bomber, sometimes endangering the fighter as well. Later, when Mosquito night fighters became more common, a third man, a gunner was carried. His job was to scan the sky behind for attackers. He had twin-barrelled heavy machine guns.

The radar operator guided his pilot into position by means of his *Lichtenstein* set, comprised of two screens, one for height and the other for bearings. He would navigate his pilot sometimes as close as two hundred metres below and astern the bomber, calling out his distances as he did so. The pilot would then visually identify the bomber and take aim. Usually the radar operator could tell from the size of the blip as they approached whether or not the aircraft was a bomber. Sometimes the pilot made visual contact without the preliminary stalk on radar. The pilot, when he closed, would exercise great care not to direct his fire into the bomb load at short range. He would even trim his aircraft to the attitude he wanted as he took up his position to fire. Sometimes he could discern an H2S scanner in the belly of a bomber but often he would open fire at ranges up to 400 yards. He would press the button which triggered off his cannon and absorb the shuddering recoil as the explosive shells were released. Usually the bomber crew had not seen the fighter even though they had been weaving. If they did, the tail gunner would usually be the one to return the fire. When fuel tanks were hit the flames would lick along the wing almost immediately and the fighter pilot would make a diving turn while the flames mushroomed from an engine and perhaps spread along the fuselage. At this point the bomber would be visible to other bombers in the vicinity and many were witnessed by our crew as the bomber slid into a dive, flames spreading towards its tail before it blew up in the air. If the bomber still had its bombs aboard the explosion would be much brighter. Sometimes, however, the bombs did not go off until the aircraft crashed to earth far below. Occasionally the fighter crews saw dummy-like shapes emerge from the bomber and parachutes open but most often they did not. The fighter crews logged the time and position of the impact for the Luftwaffe ground investigative teams who would verify, if they could, the claims of the fighter crews. When a Pathfinder was shot down that fact was usually evident from the brightly coloured red, green or yellow target indicators which exploded either in the air or on the ground. The fighter crews liked to shoot down a 'master of ceremonies' as they called them.

Martin Becker of I NJG6 was one such fighter pilot. Becker, a highly skilled pilot at night, didn't use the conventional *Von unten hinten* attack. He had started flying night fighters in 1941 and had evolved a variation of that technique wherein he approached on radar in the normal manner to make visual contact with the bomber but then he would fly to one side and below it. He would close the range while staying to the side, keeping the bomber in view against the lighter part of the sky. In this way he usually avoided being seen by the gunners. He would then attack in a skidding pass across and behind the bomber, firing his two 20 mm Rheinmetal-Borsig cannon in a long burst as he went by. He became highly successful at this and on one raid on Frankfurt was the highest scoring Luftwaffe pilot with six bombers shot down. Eight nights later he was again highest scorer on a Nuremberg raid when he destroyed seven. The Nuremberg raid occurred on March 30, 1944 but I mention it here to illustrate the results which could be achieved by a skilled pilot without upward firing guns. Becker finished the war with fifty-seven heavy bombers shot down, the 11th highest-scoring night fighter pilot of the Luftwaffe.

Becker, at the time of the Nuremberg attack, was a *Staffelkapitan* and as usual, was flying an Me 110. His first sighting was of a Halifax below him. He dived after it and unseen by its gunners, took up a steep curve of pursuit firing two quick bursts with his forward firing guns. The Halifax reared like a stricken horse and slipped back in a glide before rolling over, its fuselage on fire; the time was 00:20 hours. Almost immediately Becker saw the shape of another four-engined aircraft three or four hundred metres away; again he banked to the attack and closed. As he fired a long burst the typical orange flames spread along the starboard wing and more flames came from the starboard outer engine. It was a Halifax and as it went into a shallow dive Becker fired another burst at it. It began to go down vertically with great speed and crashed near Frankfurt; the time-00:23 hours. Becker, a few minutes later, saw a Lancaster which he lined up and fired at; it shot out a stream of flame, fell steeply and exploded near Luttich; the time-00:33. At 00:35 he again shot down a Halifax with his forward firing guns. At 00:40 he shot down another, his fifth in twenty minutes. He was getting short of fuel and could feel the intense strain of battle, but soon his radar operator found yet another target and guided Becker to it. He gave it a five second burst and it crashed at 00:50; by this time he had to land at a busy field which was servicing many other fighters. He quietly refuelled, rearmed and took off again, this time under the direction of a ground controller. He was soon directed to another target and shot down a Halifax on its return journey. It crashed near Luxembourg at 03:15 hours.

Hitler summoned Becker to his headquarters in East Prussia and presented him with the Knight's Cross to the Iron Cross.[1]

The reader will note the number of Halifaxes shot down by Becker. Crews flying Halifaxes and Stirlings suffered several periods of unacceptably high casualties. In the autumn of 1942, for example, the operations of Halifaxes in 4 Group were suspended for four weeks because of casualties of between five and ten percent suffered each time out over the previous six months. And in December 1943, the Stirlings of No. 3 Group were permanently suspended from long range operations because of casualties suffered in the previous four months ranging from four to eight percent. And again, in the Battle of Berlin, from November, 1943 to March, 1944, the Halifax II's and V's of No 4 Group suffered losses ranging from four to eleven percent per operation and were permanently suspended from bombing targets in Germany. If a

1. This outline of fighter activities is derived from much fuller accounts thereof in *The Bombing of Nuremberg*, by James Campbell, and *The Nuremberg Raid*, by Martin Middlebrook.

squadron suffered casualties of 7% on each operation the proportion of crews who would survive a tour of thirty operations was only 11%, that is about two crews in eighteen. This meant that the squadron and flight commanders, together with the experienced crews, were rapidly lost and the loss rate would increase because of an unduly high proportion of inexperienced crews.

In late October Searby told me that with Manton missing he didn't have a flight commander for 'A' flight and he asked me to do the job for a while. I of course protested that there were two or three Wing Commanders on the squadron, each of whom was far better equipped than I to be a flight commander. I further argued that I didn't know the first thing about Air Force Administration. Searby was well aware of this, 'You don't have to know', he said. 'Just examine the papers that are presented for your signature and if you agree, sign them. If you don't agree, say so and send them back where they came from.'

And 'Oh yes', he added. 'Make sure that chiefie (the maintenance chief) keeps all the kites in the air.' How I was supposed to do that he did not make clear. But being a flight commander was easy, particularly when he took no part in the briefing and also when there were two Wing Commanders sitting with their feet up in the flight office who could decipher and explain anything that came along – and further, the maintenance chief didn't need any advice or admonition from me about keeping aircraft in the air. All I did was transfer papers from the 'In' basket to the 'Out' basket and sign the pilots' log books to certify that their monthly flying totals were correct. The reason for the shortage of administrators was that we had lost two pilots of senior rank in October and their replacements had not been at Wyton long enough to take over permanent positions. I was, for example, asked to take Wing Commander Porter to Berlin on November 18th to show him the sights. We were blind markers. Our losses turned out to be low on this trip, only nine out of 444, but this was no doubt partly due to the fact that the fighters were busy elsewhere destroying twenty-three bombers on a simultaneous attack by a smaller force on Mannheim-Ludwigshafen, and partly to the appalling weather. Perhaps too we were assisted by our taking the long southern route home. One of our captains, one navigator and several gunners were frost bitten. One of the gunners was my own reliable and keen-eyed F/Sgt. Tolman; we would miss him.

At this time, true to his word, Mahaddie sent to 83 Squadron the first of some new aircraft with an advanced type of H2S. It transmitted on a wave length of three cm rather than the usual 10 cm and the increased power was reputed to give a much clearer definition of topographical features. It was to be used exclusively for target marking and had been rushed to Wyton for the Battle of Berlin. My navigator and bomb-aimer were instructed in the use of the equipment and the CO told me, 'If, when you get to the enemy coast, it is not functioning, bring it back. We have instructions not to risk it falling into the hands of the enemy unnecessarily.' I got the distinct impression that the equipment was more valuable than I was.

Then an incident occurred, about which I have puzzled ever since. On November 22nd we went to our dispersal site for an operation to Berlin; we didn't go to our customary site to the left of the main gate for JA 940 but to one near the maintenance hangar where JB 461 was parked. We had not been able to flight test the machine in the afternoon because people had been working on the new H2S. I was first to get in the aircraft and was walking up the fuselage, parachute in hand, past the racks of machine gun bullets leading to the turrets, when I noticed that the wooden cover over the H2S scanner was not secured; it was sitting awry over its hole. This cover was round and about three feet in diameter; I lifted it up to replace it properly, at the same time looking down into the H2S bubble and saw, clearly visible in the bottom of the antenna nacelle, a large footprint. Someone had stepped on it for certain, but was this by accident, or design? I put it down to carelessness, and thinking that it might not have affected the set's ability to transmit, I started the engines and asked Bedell to check the set on the ground. It appeared to be functioning normally so we took off. But it didn't seem to be working as we gained altitude. Bedell couldn't see the coast-line on it as we passed over the North Sea. Well, maybe it would pick up on the way out I thought. Soon we estimated that we should be crossing the Dutch island of Texel but the set still wasn't working. We then passed the German fighter station at Leuwarden on the north Dutch coast; still the damned thing was not working. Then I saw some flak from what appeared to be Emden on the port beam. Without H2S we had no precise knowledge of where we were and we had already risked the set – it still was not working. So for the first time in forty-four operations I had to turn back. The

Operations Record Book for 22 November 1943 states, 'The crews flying the special aircraft were ordered to return if their equipment was unserviceable and P/O Hellier was the only special crew to reach the target, the other three returning early.' We dropped our bombs near some guns by the radar station on Texel, with no confidence that we hit anything. What a lonely place the intelligence room seemed when we returned. There were only three crews in it. The rest by now had bombed Berlin. My crew that night consisted of the navigator, Bedell, now a Flight Lieutenant; Sherwood, the bomb-aimer, now also a Flight Lieutenant; the wireless operator, Flying Officer Houston; the rear gunner, Pilot Officer 'Taffy' Preece; the flight engineer, Flight Sergeant Belton; and the mid-upper gunner, a fellow Canadian, Flight Sergeant 'Porky' Connors; only two NCO's, the rest officers. Because of the footprint I was not surprised that the H2S had malfunctioned.

We lost Pilot Officer Henderson DFM, and crew that night in JB 424. He had only recently returned to the Squadron after having been shot down and escaping across France to Spain.

The next night we took a different aircraft, again a new one, JB 355 with a new H2S. The target was the same, Berlin, and our instructions were the same. Two of our thirteen aircraft didn't get off and I thought for a moment that we wouldn't also. While waiting for start-up at about 4.00 pm I was standing idly behind the starboard wheel of the aircraft, as was my custom, and I happened to look across the airfield to the north west. To my astonished eyes there appeared a large orange and black flame and a cloud of smoke rising in a puff from the site of one of the Lancasters. I knew in an instant what it was – a fully loaded exploding Lancaster. I yelled, 'Down on the ground', to anyone who could hear, and dived myself between the wheels of our own fully loaded Lanc. The crew hit the nearest dirt and none too soon; the shock wave from the explosion took little more than a second to cross the airfield and reach us but when it did, the Lancaster under which I was sheltering was picked up as though by a giant hand and moved over about two feet. I thought for a moment that the aircraft might topple over or that one of its wheels might land on us. The poor devils in that exploding aircraft, whoever they were! When we got back that night we found that it was JA 686. An armament crew had been working on it when somehow the camera photoflash exploded and up went its fuel tanks and a full load of bombs. It blew an enormous hole in the ground. Four airmen and four civilians were killed and twelve people were injured. In a moment or two the Station Commander came rushing up in his van and told us to get airborne, which of course we were about to do anyway.

Not only was the target the same but so was the route and so was the result; the H2S refused to work, only this time there was no footprint. We dropped our bombs aimlessly again at Texel and returned to Wyton. I was upset by two 'abortions', as we called them, in a row. They were bad for the morale of both myself and the crew. When we returned we found Tolchard's equipment had also failed and he too was compelled to return. Squadron Leader Johnson had engine trouble and had not been able to get airborne.

We lost Wing Commander Raymond Hilton, DSO, DFC and Bar and crew in JB 284 over Berlin on that one. He was well liked by all on the Squadron, having previously done a tour with 83; his wife Betty had been a Wimbledon tennis champion. Hilton had in fact been made Squadron Commander on November 2nd but had been unable, in the short time to November 23rd, to make his presence felt as such. I for one missed Searby's steady presence; he had been posted away on November 4th. Searby, in addition to his flights over the North and South Atlantic as a ferry captain, had completed twenty-four bombing operations before coming to Wyton and had done eleven more as CO of 83 Squadron. After Hilton's loss we had to wait until a new Squadron Commander could be found and sent to Wyton.

On November 26th we were briefed again for Berlin, this time by the southern route across France, then east and northward. Again the H2S refused to function but this time I flew some way into France, determined to risk the wretched thing rather than have it dictate our tactics, but still it would not work. By this time we were far enough inside France that I could see the elliptical pattern of faint blue airfield lights of the fighter station at Abbeville. Bedell confirmed that the lights should indeed be Abbeville's so I decided to bomb it and bring the H2S back. I quickly dropped the Lancaster from 20,000 feet to 8,000, flying in a slow spiral, keeping the lights in view. I was suspicious that perhaps these lights might be a decoy, but I reasoned, 'Decoy for what?' There had not been any night attacks on Abbeville – why would they have a decoy airfield?' Whether decoy or real this piece of real estate received that night a 4,000 pounder and several one thousand pounders down the middle; we kept the TI's on board. I made up my mind then, while on the bomb run and just as the faint blue lights were suddenly switched off that any H2S set that I carried in future, whether working or not, would come along all the way on the operation for which we were briefed.

At about this time 'Taffy' Preece reported from the rear turret that there was a twin-engined fighter astern. As usual I took evasive action; it was a Ju 88 and we did not see it again. It would have been ironic to have been shot down while bombing a target of opportunity.

Preece had started flying with us after the November 18th trip to Berlin when in extremely cold weather Tolman's electrically heated suit had failed him in one foot; as a result he had suffered severe frostbite in two toes and it was thought that he would lose them. Preece had been rear gunner for Searby, so we had known him since our days on 106 Squadron, a very long time ago. Tall, blond, Flying Officer Smeaton and crew in JB 459 were lost on Berlin that night as was P/O Millar and crew. Flying Officer Tolchard, like myself, was again forced to return early with a faulty H2S and Pilot Officer King's H2S had failed on the ground so he had been unable to get airborne.

CHAPTER TWELVE

Night and Day

AIR Chief Marshal Harris in a minute to Churchill on
November 3rd, 1943, said, 'We can wreck Berlin from end
to end if the U.S.A.A.F. will come in on it. It will cost, between us,
400-500 aircraft. It will cost Germany the war.'

But the U.S.A.A.F. couldn't attack a long-range target like
Berlin for another ten months, by which time their fighters were
able to escort the bombers on this long trip. So Bomber Command
undertook the Battle of Berlin on its own.

The losses on the operations in November had been light and
Lord Portal, the Chief of Air Staff, told Churchill that this was
'particularly encouraging'. Churchill's reply was 'All very good. I
congratulate you.' The remark was premature; on December 2nd
the night fighters were very active and shot down most of the forty
bombers that were lost. This was 8.7% of the force sent out.

Our batman, an elderly civilian from Huntingdon, woke Chick
and me early on December 2nd and we soon found that ops were
on. I wanted to do a careful flight test of the H2S, and so before
lunch I assembled the crew at the dispersal site of JB 352 R for
Robert; it was not ready for flight. A civilian radar technician,
actually an electronics engineer, or 'boffin' as we called all such
Air Ministry specialists, together with an airman, were working on
the H2S. I watched them switch the set on and off and examine the
scanner. They seemed dissatisfied but I couldn't understand their
jargon and it was cold, so rather than expose my ignorance I moved
to the crew shack and its stove for warmth.

One of the corporals was saying to a teenage fitter as I came in,
'You'd better watch out for Chiefie, young fellow me-lad – he
acquired a taste for young boys like you when he was in the Middle
East.' The young fitter looked horrified as he sidled out the door,
his back to the wall for the incoming maintenance chief who had
not heard the remark. I asked the corporal why he was scaring the
young 'erk' with lies like that. 'It's all part of his training, sir. He
thinks, because he knows that there's no ring-twitter gauge or left-
handed spanner that he's a qualified fitter. Well, he's got to learn
other things as well', he said with a wink and a vicious grin.

Still the boffin was working on the H2S, now joined by an

engineering officer and the pretty 'RDF bloke'. We couldn't do the air test. Annoying! We would have to assume that everything would be right at take-off time. I went back to the mess to read *Aeroplane* and *Illustrated London News* and wait out the time. Briefing would be at 4.00. The crew list showed a maximum effort. There wasn't much doubt that the target would be Berlin; it had been Berlin at the last four briefings.

We assembled as usual in the briefing room, my crew and I sitting near the front of the room. The Station Commander walked in and the adjutant called us to attention. We stood as usual and the Station Commander asked the adjutant to call the roll of captains, which he did, and each captain responded for his crew. Then the curtain was pulled and without much comment the forecast of Berlin as the target was confirmed. I liked the route-straight in and straight out. To hell with all the usual dog legs. The Station Commander told us who would be marking what. Our crew of course were to be 'special blind markers' with our new H2S. I muttered to myself, 'If the damned thing works'. Then he told us the fuel load and the route markers to be dropped by 156 Squadron, wished us a good trip, and turned the briefing over to Squadron Leader Neal, the Intelligence Officer. Neal was an erudite man, not a member of air crew, whose face, as I have mentioned, had been badly burned. His mouth was a gash set at 45 degrees to a piece of twisted flesh containing two holes for nostrils above which a pair of intelligent grey eyes looked out from under lids which had once been liquefied by flame before settling in their sockets. He told us the anticipated strength of the first and second Luftwaffe fighter divisions and in particular the strength and aircraft types of the *Geschwader* at Leeuwarden. We shouldn't meet much flak *en route* if we stayed on track, as for the defences of Berlin itself, he suggested that we probably knew them better than he did.

The met briefing was next. It was given by a tall, slim man who hadn't a hair on his head. He was a flying officer in his early thirties but looked sixty. He said that there would be cloud over the North Sea, decreasing along the route until there was only thin stratus. Berlin itself should be clear, except for some ground haze and smoke. Icing would be encountered in cloud.

The flying control officer then gave us our start-up times, marshalling instructions, take-off times, recognition colours, the forecast runway to be used and the altimeter setting. The navigators and bomb-aimers moved to their specialised briefing tables to determine flight plans and bomb settings and all the aircrew then returned to the NCO's and Officers' Messes for their flight meal. We had the usual bacon and eggs, the unheard of luxury for ground staff and civilians. Our mess dining room was well equipped. Indeed we had, not long before, hosted the King and Queen at a luncheon where the King, I noticed, had barely touched each course of the carefully prepared meal much to the disappointment of the chef. So our table was fully equipped with silver and china and we ate our toast from silver-plated racks, applied vinegar to our chips from crystal cruets and flavoured our eggs from shining condiment containers. It was all quite civilised. The massive oak tables were covered with white linen, and fresh flowers from some greenhouse in winter adorned its centre. The conversation was casual, perhaps a little strained but nevertheless casual. We were joined by the Mosquito crews who would fly a diversionary raid, taking off an hour after we did and returning an hour earlier due to their great speed.

We dressed in our room in our flying clothes. Chick had a small good luck doll called Harry which he customarily hung from his compass above his instrument panel. This night I hid it from him to see whether or not he was superstitious, but one look at his face as he anxiously searched our room convinced me that I should not cause him anxiety and I quickly 'found' Harry for him. He has it to this day at his home. I put my loaded Smith and Wesson .38 as usual inside the blouse of my battledress. It was as much a talisman I suppose as Chick's doll. We set out to the crew-room where we picked up parachutes, escape kits, Mae West jackets and rations. Then it was a ride in a canvas-covered vehicle to the aircraft dispersals. JB 352 was close to the main hangar and we got out of the vehicle to find the aircraft apparently serviceable; at least the ground crew said that it was. They had the battery cart and fire extinguisher already in position. We waited only a few minutes before getting in. I went first up the ladder and along the narrow fuselage, then climbed over the main spar and turned on the master switch. As I stood by the pilot's seat Sherwood went past me to the bomb-aimer's compartment. The intercom cord from his flying helmet caught in the pitch levers as he went by and he gave it a jerk to free it. I bawled him out for doing so, saying, 'That could have been the undercarriage lever you were jerking. Be careful you don't do that again.' He flushed as he looked back, not accustomed to being scolded like a child.

I put my parachute pack behind the pilot's armour plate, sat in the seat, hooked up my intercom and oxygen hose and fastened the straps of my shoulder harness with the quick release pin. I opened the pilot's side window; the ground crew were ready for starting. They and the engineer and I started each of the four motors and let the oil circulate as they warmed up. The ground crew unfastened the electrical lead from their battery cart, took away the cart and stood by the wings holding the ropes fastened to each of the wheel chocks as I ran up each engine in turn and checked the magnetos; they were perfect. Belton was checking engine temperatures and oil and fuel pressures. As usual we scattered gravel and moisture behind us as we ran up the engines. I called each of the crew to check their intercom and was relieved to hear Bedell report that everything was apparently normal with the H2S. It was taxiing time; I waved away the chocks and advanced the starboard outer throttle for a left turn off the dispersal pad.

The snug fit of the four throttle levers in one's right hand was a comfortable feeling; the outer two flat knobs were curled over the inner two for ease of their separate movement in taxiing but all four were closely spaced so as easily to hold them with the fingers and palm of one hand.

I released the brake, swung the loaded Lancaster on to the perimeter track and, engines idling easily, followed another Lancaster along the narrow pavement to the end of the runway. Others had already moved in behind, navigation lights on, and were following us. I could see other Lancs moving, far across the field. We paraded, like stately geese in procession, to the take-off point of the long runway. There at the side of the runway stood the usual collection of staff, male and female, about twenty in all, to see us off. We waved as we turned into wind and they extended their outstretched arms, fingers in the Churchillian V for Victory sign and waved in return. I looked at Belton whose arm was outstretched in front of my nose. But his middle finger was stuck vertically upward in a rude gesture at the assembled group, and when I swatted his hand away he said, 'I'm just waving to the Station Commander.' We received the flashing green Aldis lamp and I pointed the nose of the Lanc down the runway after the Lancaster ahead, which was now airborne, its navigation lights visible in the blackness. I had done the take-off check and the flaps were down twenty degrees. I held on the brake until the engines were fully wound up, then released the brake. We would need most of the runway. All four Merlins were now roaring like fast, harsh-voiced machine guns. They pulled at the aeroplane when the brake was released. They had their work to do and the propellers were doing it. I opened the throttles fully, the port ones slightly ahead of the starboard, checked the swing, gathered speed and got the tail up – by now the noise from the engines was bouncing off the runway in a high flat scream which abated only slowly as we lifted a couple of feet off the ground at a speed of 100 knots.

Unlike a jet aircraft which when rotated is climbed steeply, these heavily laden, propeller driven bombers were held close to the ground after take-off to build up speed. I soon had 125 knots, retracted the wheels and gently brought the nose up in a climb. At 800 feet I took up the flaps in easy stages and reduced the boost and revs to climbing speed. We climbed away from Wyton at a speed of 135 knots on a course slightly north of east; our nav lights were still on but no lights were visible in the cockpit. I was monitoring the flight instruments by their luminous dials. The lights of three other machines were visible. I was anxious to hear from Bedell whether or not the H2S was working. Sherwood moved aft to a station beside Bedell as we climbed.

In fifteen minutes Bedell reported, 'It doesn't seem to be working, Punch. At least I can see nothing on it.' I decided at that moment that we would go to Berlin, whether it was working or not. We would, if necessary, keep our Target Indicators on board. The Gee was functioning and I was confident that before it was completely jammed by German transmissions, Bedell could get us a course on it for a precise entry of the enemy coast. I said, 'Keep trying Jack, maybe it will pick up. 'We climbed slowly but steadily out over the east coast, high above the North Sea and, nav lights now off, into the predicted cloud. We were on the southern side of a low pressure system with the wind at our back and the area of low pressure, of course, on our left. We would have a strong tail wind assisting us as we entered Europe. If we were lucky we could catch the high side of the low on the return journey and have a tail wind home as well.

Besides Bedell, Sherwood and Belton we had on board, as wireless operator, Flying Officer Houston who, while on only his second flight with us, was an experienced professional. In the tail turret was the gallant 'Taffy' Preece who had completed sixty trips, had shot down two fighters and wore the Conspicuous Gallantry Medal. Why he was called 'Taffy', a Welsh nickname, was not clear to me because he came from Ireland. I was told by another gunner that when Taffy had completed sixty trips he had gone home on leave to Ireland where his father had asked him how many operations he had done. When told sixty, his father had replied, 'You mean the war has been on for four years and you've only worked sixty nights! Get on back and do some more.' The dutiful son did just that. In the mid-upper turret was Warrant Officer 'Porky' Connors, so-named for the usual physical reasons. Porky was of medium height, a tough Canadian with grey eyes, ruddy complexion and a fair moustache. He laughed easily and drank a lot of beer but I had the feeling that he was completely self-sufficient and could fight coolly and courageously. He seemed to trust no one and I was sure that to him I was just a pilot to fly the mount for his guns.

Everyone on board was near the end of his second tour or on a third. Each knew his job well and there was no idle chatter. When out over the North Sea I levelled off the Lancaster and Preece asked if he and Connors could test their guns. I gave the OK and listened to the muffled stutter of the six Brownings as they fired short bursts at a rate of 1,200 rounds per minute. They reported the guns and turrets operating well. This was nice to know as we had picked up a little ice. The outside air temperature was now bitterly cold at – 60°C, and there was danger of the guns freezing.

Bedell gave me a course to steer into Holland and I asked him if the H2S was functioning. 'Sorry, skipper, no joy', he said. Damn, I thought, I could not lightly disobey orders. I should really turn around and take the thing back to base. But I simply couldn't do it. If we make it, I thought, there will be no criticism, and if we don't? Well, we won't be present to account for the decision. I told the crew that we were going to press on and could sense that the vote to do so was unanimous. 'Damn the torpedoes full speed ahead,'[1] seemed somehow appropriate as we plunged across the Dutch coast. Soon I could see route markers dropping on the port quarter some miles behind, lighting the way for the main force. The 110s and the 88s would be close by, but we were fairly high. The advanced H2S equipment had come to us in a factory-new aeroplane and its

1. Attributed to David G. Farragut at the Battle of Mobile Bay, August 5, 1864.

engines were performing beautifully; without any stress we had reached 22,000 feet. We knew that our track and that of the other blind markers would be followed carefully by the German controllers. They would aim the Tame Boars at us, but unless their pilots were mind readers they had to climb up on our course to pursue us, or if already at our height but to one side, they would have to do an intercept. Either way they would end up in something of a stern chase and before encountering R Robert would likely see another of our aircraft behind us or below us. There were some advantages to being a blind marker! Getting over the target first however was not one of them – particularly over Berlin. By the time we got there the flak gunners would know that we were coming and the Wild Boars would be patrolling above the city waiting for the first arrivals. The searchlights were groping the sky at Bremen to the north-west and Hanover to the south-east. We had come out of the cloud and the visibility was good. I noted with some concern that I could see the rivets on the port wing beside me and the stains made on the wing by the exhaust flames. The exhaust pipes too were glowing. There seemed altogether too much light. We had been out about two hours when Bedell came on the intercom, excited. He said, 'Punch the H2S is working – I can see Misburg on it.'

'Misburg?' I asked. 'Where the hell is that?' 'It's just north of Hanover', he said. 'I think we'll be able to bomb on H2S. I'm going to put it on the short range setting and see what it looks like', he added. In a few minutes he confirmed that likely we'd be able to bomb on it. Well, that was a relief. I needn't think up ingenious excuses for when we got back as to why we had risked it.

The flight plan had been based upon strong tail winds and the forecast was correct; we made good speed. We were on track and right on time.

Sherwood was now in the nose fiddling with his bombsight and switch panel in case he could see well enough to bomb visually. I checked the luminous instrument panel and flew my usual weaving pattern. Everything was going well. We roared eastward for another half hour. Then Preece reported a Ju 88 on the port quarter, low at about 400 yards, and he quickly told me, 'Turn port, turn port, go!' I did this violently, without thought or hesitation, the cumbersome Lanc responding well although fully loaded. I looked out anxiously but saw no tracer and heard no firing; there was nothing. The fighter had broken off his attack to the port beam, down. But now

Connors said that he could see a twin-engined aircraft on the starboard quarter at about 400 yards; he was coming in; 'Turn starboard, turn starboard.' I did not wait for the word 'Go! ' There was no gun-fire from either the fighter or ourselves. I tensed, expecting that there would be another pass and that this time we would see some cannon shells, but there were none and we saw nothing. We all peered into the dark, eyes like saucers, but saw nothing. Gradually the tingling on one's head, neck and spine subsided. We resumed course.

There were no lights ahead-not a single searchlight. Berlin was playing possum. But the visibility between small cloud patches by now was excellent. We were cruising in a gentle corkscrew. Soon the searchlights came on – before we got there – and after a few minutes we were into them and all hell was breaking loose. I looked over at the port beam and an aircraft was coned in about twenty searchlights. The time was 20.05. I watched a Ju 88 go after him. He blew up without any tracer being visible from either aircraft. Berlin was darkly visible below. Bedell said that he could see the River Spree on the H2S and gave me a course to steer towards it. Sherwood could see ground detail but there was haze and smoke and he could not identify anything. We would have to bomb blind on H2S. I saw two sets of yellow target indicators go down to port before ours did. But I followed Bedell's directions and opened the bomb doors. Sherwood dropped our TI's and bombs, and as usual I could feel them leave; we shot upward a few hundred feet when the load was gone. I was not aware that the Germans had begun to equip their fighters at this time with radar which could 'home' on our H2S transmissions. But over Berlin it made no difference. The Wild Boars could see us anyway. In fact there was one now ahead on the port side. He was about 2,000 feet below, and climbing. A shower of green target indicators burst below and to one side of him.

Although we had given up the practice of counting and logging the time and position of exploding aircraft, particularly when running in to the target, we nevertheless saw more than twenty of our bombers exploding in the characteristic yellow-orange balls of fire on the route in and out of the target area. I set course west for home. Connors reported that his guns had frozen; they were jammed and wouldn't fire. Too much oil on them he thought; even oil will freeze at – 60°C. I wondered how he knew, unless he had tried to fire them, that they were frozen. Other sets of greens were now visible, well concentrated – and long straight streaks of incendiaries were scarring the ground. The rippling ground smoke mirrored the blast of 4,000 pounders. Photoflashes were popping far below, like cameras at a sporting event. Berlin, in its haze, began to take on a reddish hue. Lone searchlights fingered the sky as we threaded our way through them. I counted to myself, ensuring that I did not fly the same course or height for longer than 17 seconds. In ten minutes we were clear of the city and, looking back, could see that the attack was well under way. We tensed, scanning for fighters on the route back.

We seemed to catch the high side of the low pressure area; Bedell said that we were cruising swiftly. I put the starboard wing tip against Polaris as I had often done before, and adjusted the revs of the four Merlins, so that their conflicting roars would yield one synchronised tune. In an hour we were back in cloud at 20,000 feet and, feeling momentarily secure, I began to reflect upon my role in bomber operations.

Wilkes' announcement, after we had bombed Abbeville on November 26th, that he was finished with ops, had been a shock to me, although I knew that the number of his trips had been running one ahead of my own. He had, of course, not been on my second pilot trips but while I had been doing one of them he had made a trip with another crew, and he had done two with Jack Finding while I was ill in May; so he had finished his second tour.

'Poonch', he said, for his 'u' was different from mine, 'Poonch, it's time for me to stop;' he assumed his best soccer stance, right shoulder forward and down, his head cocked to one side, and his face wearing its characteristic broad smile. What could I say? I knew that his wife would be pleased; he had once brought her to the station and had introduced me to her. She had asked me rather shyly to take good care of him, and I had responded that it was he who was taking good care of me. Now she had him to herself again; he had been screened off ops by Group Headquarters. So I had Houston aboard, an excellent man to be sure, but Wilkes had been with me from the beginning and now I was alone, the last of our original crew who had arrived bright-eyed at Syerston almost nine months ago. Kelly had been wounded, the flight engineer had given up early, the navigator had been Jettisoned, Hanratty had finished after his first tour, Tolman would limp a little in future, and now

Wilkes too was gone.[1] If I flew one more operation I would have completed 46 without counting the boomerangs on Texel.

So be it – I would fly one more; perhaps I could then get on fighters.

* * *

My decision to quit, although I was not conscious of it, had been building up for some time. I had swallowed my doubts, starting with Frankfurt on April 10th when the order to drop an 8,000 pounder through cloud on that city, although dropped with the assistance of Oboe, had upset me and undermined my resolve to attack only military targets. For the next few months, throughout the Battle of the Ruhr, it had seemed possible, with accurate marking by Oboe, to bomb only military objectives. The Krupp works, the submarine pens, the docks on the Rhine, the heavy industrial facilities in the heart of Germany; these were military targets, even if civilians were killed in attacking them. Whatever doubts I had then of the policy we were pursuing would, I thought, be dissipated on a Pathfinder Squadron where we would have H2S equipment with which to hit not just the city of Berlin but the Siemens Electrical Works in Berlin.

Then in early July we had started that monstrous fire in Cologne. I was awed at the sight of flames and smoke to 12,000 feet. But this was nothing compared with Hamburg later that month. After Hamburg we, the aircrew of Bomber Command, became fully aware that the intention of Bomber Command was to smash and burn the cities of Germany, using only the back of our hand to destroy Italian targets. And this became more evident late in August and early in September when, even with H2S, we found that we could not mark targets in Berlin with any precision. We were simply bombing the city and its people. Gone now was the joy of battle. No longer could one exult in a job well done; targets like Peenemunde were few and far between.

1. Wilkes was later to write in a letter, 'I don't think I was ever really scared - a flutter now and then but not scared. The good Lord endowed me with an inbuilt radar system and made me into a two-person man. It was easy for me to forget about everything else. The reason I stopped dead at 45 ops was because my inbuilt radar system said Time to Stop and it has rarely failed me'. After leaving the Squadron, Wilkes went on transport work where he crashed once on take-off, ditched once in the Irish Sea and baled out once. He asserts that it is definitely better to be born 'lucky' than 'rich'.

At the meeting with Mahaddie in late October I had tentatively decided to continue to sixty trips. After all, Garvey had done sixty, straight through, and had been promoted to Squadron Leader and awarded a DSO. I hadn't told Mahaddie this, of course; I simply told him that I wanted to continue on for a while longer. But it was now turning out to be a mistake to have told him that much. He took my decision to continue as reason for training us on the new H2S equipment; Group had wanted its most experienced blind marker crews on it and the equipment had failed on three consecutive occasions. We had not only lost credit for completing three attacks but despite the orders to bring the equipment back, these operations had seemed like returning because of some trivial mechanical trouble or engine failure. I became morose.

But more important, I had become irritated by the presence of two new members of my crew who had not been chosen by me, but had been allocated to fill vacancies. I would have preferred to return to an OTU to select fresh crew members and train them myself, but such was not to be. The crew I now had were worn and drawn-looking veterans with bloodshot eyes; even the eyes of the blond and handsome Taffy Preece were red and sunken, his jaw line tight. Conners' watery red eyes protruded a little and he wore a permanent sneer beneath his moustache. Sherwood seemed introverted and wooden, seeking the company only of his fellow bomb-aimers. Bedell, although still his usual controlled and efficient self, appeared pale from too much time behind the navigator's curtains. Belton alone had retained his good nature but he had suffered a bout or two with alcohol, which he had lost. The happy loyalty of that close knit band of brothers who had come to Wyton was gone. I was flying now with six self-sufficient, tight-lipped gladiators and I didn't like it. I longed for the clean, cold skies of a fighter aircraft, where if one killed, he killed only a killer. I made up my mind to quit. But what was that ahead? Flak!

'Bedell, are we on course? There is flak ahead. What is it?'

'Must be some coastal batteries firing. We're on track and there is no town there', he said.

'I don't give a damn if we are on track; give me a course to steer round that flak – which side should I go?'

'Doesn't make any difference.'

Belton interrupted to say, 'What's the matter with you? I've seen you head through flak ten times that bad'.

I was angry at the inference. 'You bloody fool, don't you know enough yet not to take unnecessary risks?', I asked, not expecting an answer.

'But there's not very much of it', he replied.

'You stick to your goddamn gas gauges', I snapped, 'And I'll fly this aeroplane.'

He retreated, and nothing more was said until we were well out to sea and had dropped low enough to take off our oxygen masks. Belton then handed me a cup of coffee, perhaps as a peace offering. I thanked him and he smiled; the tension had passed.

We were among the early ones back to Wyton. We had set a record; six hours and ten minutes to Berlin and back; the average time on our other Berlin trips had been seven hours and 43 minutes.[1]

At de-briefing I told the Station Commander that the new H2S had not been working at the Dutch coast but that when one got near the target it seemed to function properly. He understood what I meant and turned without comment to the next crew being de-briefed.

The next night, December 3rd, we were scheduled to operate again, but there was a difference in this one. Having decided to make it my last I told Bedell this. I felt that I owed him an explanation but could think of none to tell him. He nodded in apparent understanding; he had several more trips to do. But he went missing, presumed dead, the next month. It is painful even now to think of his loss.

I thought that the target would be Berlin. I was wrong. It was Leipzig. That night as we waited for the time to start engines, I leaned as usual with my left elbow on the huge tyre of the starboard wheel. The air was not cold, despite the time of year but the sky was grey, with only a little light left in the darkening day. So this was to be my last trip? I shuddered to think that it could be my last in more ways than one; then it occurred to me that I probably would finish the trip alive. Really, I must put such thoughts from my mind, but the probability of survival was real, and it kept intruding; I took a deep breath and tried to suppress the thought but the breath fairly exploded from my cheeks and I heard with surprise my own voice saying softly, 'God, let me have strength. I do not ask that I return alive, for that would be selfish, but I do ask for the strength to carry out this trip with precision and courage.' The words seemed torn

1. The Squadrons Operations Record Book states, 'Night fighters were very much in evidence as it was the well worn straight in-and-out route but all our crews returned safely'.

from me against my will. What was this unexpected dialogue with God? I had never prayed in my life; I believed in no deity; I expected no abrogation of the laws of nature on my behalf. Yet there it was! I was talking to God! Could it have been embedded in me by the culture which had nourished me? 'God' must arise from the limitations of man, I thought. 'God' must be a recognition by man that he is finite. All of this was racing through my head. But now it was time to start engines and I turned to climb in the aeroplane.

When we considered the route we were to take to Leipzig it made sense. We went, as usual, on the northern route, as though to Berlin but upon reaching the vicinity of Magdeburg, instead of heading straight on to Berlin, turned sharply south and attacked Leipzig. The target was sky-marked by two of us using the new H2S. We were in JB 355 and this night it paid for itself. When I asked Bedell how it was working we were running towards the target and despite the thick cloud he said, 'I can see a policeman standing on a corner holding up his white glove.' Some of the crews thought the blind marking the best they had ever seen. 'Never before', wrote G/C Dudley Saward, chief radar officer at Bomber Command, 'had a bombing attack been executed with such precision against an unseen target.' During the raid several photos had been taken of the cathode ray tube, 'including', he said, 'one memorable one of the image of Leipzig at a range of about eight miles. The exact resemblance to the map shape of the town was so sell defined that I had a number of copies printed and mounted alongside a map tracing of the town itself.' He sent copies of these with 'a covering letter extolling the effectiveness of this new device, and begging support for speedier supplies', to influential people like Lord Cherwell and Sir Robert Renwick.

I didn't sleep at all the night following my last trip. For the first time in over two years I could permit my mind to think of a possible future but I felt a great sadness and kept hearing the powerful Merlins – they were throbbing – and they kept ringing in my ears, as they often did after an operation.

In a few days the Squadron went to Berlin again without me. I sent a telegram to my mother that I was finished ops so that she could stop worrying for a while.

* * *

On or around December 4th, 1943 the Squadron was handed

over to Wing Commander Abercromby, DFC and Bar who, immediately upon taking command confronted Chick in front of several officers in the mess with the accusation that Chick, so he had heard, was one of the leading exponents of the theory of 'weaving' in order to avoid attacks by enemy fighters. He implied that such flying was cowardly, and said that it was to cease, and that henceforth all pilots of 83 Squadron were to fly straight and level so as to provide a stable platform for their gunners to fire from. He could only have said such a thing because he had given it much thought and was convinced of its truth. He could not have been aware of the German NAXOS radar which homed on a bomber's H2S, or of cannon fired without tracers in *schrage musik* or 'slanting' attacks. None of us was aware of such techniques. Chick, angered by a man who apparently believed the exchange between Cochrane and Saundby about increased firing of .303's, said that he had 'weaved' for over forty ops and wasn't going to change his tactics now and further that our job was to mark targets, not to shoot down enemy fighters. He became so angry with Abercromby that he told him he could fly straight and level if he wished but that he, Chick, would give him only three weeks on the squadron if he did so. He had to be restrained from striking the new commander by the great Yorkshire bulk of A.S. Johnson who grabbed him by the back of the collar and escorted him from the lounge in order to avoid a certain court martial.

Chick finished his operations about a month later with a score of forty-eight, twelve of them to Berlin. He had done three extra trips to finish off the second tour of some of his crew members. He and I have since noted to each other that we were fortunate to finish when we did – 83 Squadron lost thirteen aircraft and crews in January, 1944. Indeed, the whole of the Pathfinder Force, no doubt because of the NAXOS radar sets homing on their H2S transmitters, suffered worse casualties than usual. These were such as to cause Bennett later to write, 'This Battle (Berlin) was indeed the bitterest part of the war for me – I thought that the backbone of the Pathfinder Force was really broken.'

I remained at Wyton over Christmas, at which time Abercromby demanded to know why I was still on the station. He said that it was bad for the morale of the crews to have a tour-expired pilot hanging about. I told him that the RCAF hadn't yet figured out what to do with me. He arranged for me to be sent to an RAF Operational Training Unit while they decided; so I got him to sign my log book and left the station. He was lost a week later, killed in action on January 1, 1944.

Berlin was not wrecked from end to end, although a considerable part of it was destroyed. And the Battle of Berlin did not cost Germany the war; a grinding land campaign had yet to be fought. More than 9,000 bombing sorties were flown during the battle on round trips of about 1,200 miles to Berlin. During the same period approximately 11,000 more sorties were flown against other German cities until the services of Bomber Command were handed over to Eisenhower's command at the beginning of April, 1944. The Battle of Berlin was over. The Main Offensive was over. 3,301 aircraft had been lost during the main offensive.

The overall casualty rate in thirty-five operations in the four months commencing November 18, 1943, and terminating with the Nuremberg raid on March 30, 1944, was 5.2%. 1,047 bombers failed to return from these thirty-five trips, twenty-four of them to Berlin, but the losses on the last raid, Nuremberg, were ninety-five aircraft, 11.8% of the attacking force.

The German night fighter defences had proved that Bomber Command could not maintain a strategic offensive on deep penetrations of Germany. The Luftwaffe had, by January, 1944 fitted the SN-2 radar to most of the Tame Boars to augment the *Lichtenstein* sets. Now the fighters had such a marked superiority over the bombers that bomber crews were instructed not to use H2S, or to use it only for short periods when vitally required for navigation or for blind marking on long range targets. There was no other technique available.[1] But the accuracy achieved against the Ruhr and against Hamburg could not be achieved on long range targets such as Berlin, and the attrition from fighters became too great to sustain. Harris recognised this and in April 1944, in a letter to the Air Ministry said as much. He said that 'The strength of German defences would in time reach a point at which night bombing attacks by existing methods and types of heavy bomber would involve percentage casualty rates which could not in the long run be sustained.' He went on, 'Remedial action is therefore an urgent operational matter which cannot be deferred without grave risk. Already the cost of attacking targets in the Berlin area under weather conditions which give good prospects of accurate and concentrated bombing is too high to be incurred with any

1. About ten months were to elapse before a transmitter called 'Piperack' could be developed and deployed so as to jam the SN-2 sets and it took almost as long before a variation of 'Gee', called 'G-H' was put into service to augment H2S in target marking.

frequency. The only remedy, therefore,' he said, 'is the provision of night fighter support on a substantial scale.'

Too little and too late! Harris was putting on record that which every aircrew member of Bomber Command already knew. Bomber Command could not keep up the pace.[1] There were three reasons for this and they did not include as Bennett suggested, that Bomber Command had balked at the jump. The reasons were, firstly, because the technique for accurate night bombing of long range targets did not exist. Secondly, because the night bomber force did not have the armament with which to defend itself against night fighter technology and schrage musik attacks. And, thirdly, because the Air Council and Fighter Command had failed for three years to meet the challenge of supporting the night bombers with a large force of night fighters and intruders. During the period I had been on a squadron, Bomber Command had lost 2,227 aircraft, about three times its strength.[2]

A few weeks after leaving the Squadron I was in charge of a flight of single engined aircraft making practice attacks on our own bombers. I was out behind the flight shack practising throwing a bayonet at a tree when I was notified that I had been awarded a Bar to my DFC. I was pleased at the news and happy to sew the little silver rosette on my DFC ribbon. There had been some sixty of these awarded to that date to members of the RCAF and a further 146 were awarded from then to the end of the war.

Soon after this the invasion was launched. I was on an instructors' course at the time and observed the massive armada from a training plane. On completion of the course I was instructed to report to Warrington in Lancashire for shipment home to Canada. I reported to the depot with mixed emotions. Although anxious to see my home and family, I knew that in Britain I had lived my finest hour. My heart was with this gentle but valiant people and I grieved to leave them, but my soul was North American, and destiny yet had plans for me.

1. Dudley Saward in his book *Bomber Harris* bristles at the suggestion made by the authors of *The Strategic Air Offensive Against Germany* that the Battle of Berlin was a failure. I agree that it was not a failure but I do not agree with Saward when he said, 'The reference (by Harris) to Berlin losses was a slight exaggeration but it was excusable poetic licence for obtaining what he wanted'. I cannot regard Harris' statement as either exaggerated or poetic licence. It was plain truth!

2. The average operational strength of Bomber Command in January 1943 was 515 aircraft, including 178 Lancasters and 17 Mosquitoes; by March 1944 it has risen to 974 aircraft, including 594 Lancasters and 58 Mosquitoes.

CHAPTER THIRTEEN

The End Game

IT should not be thought that Bomber Command's sole concern had been with area bombing. AVM Cochrane of 5 Group was, throughout the war, a strong advocate of precision bombing, and it was carried out. First Nettleton, with the first Lancasters, led the precision raid on Augsburg. Then about a year later Gibson led 617 Squadron on the successful breach of the Möhne and Eder dams. These operations suffered terrible casualties. Both leaders were awarded the Victoria Cross and both were later killed. The dam raids were to become the most accurate attack of the war. They required the drop by each crew of a special bomb from an altitude of 60 feet while running the Lancasters in over the backed-up water to the dam face. 617 Squadron lost eight of nineteen Lancasters in this attack. Then on February 8 1944 Leonard Cheshire visually marked the Gnome and Rhone aeroplane engine factory at Limoges from very low level, precisely on the aiming point. His 617 Squadron crews bombed with precision from high altitude on the markers and smashed the factory, with no damage at all to the surrounding area. There were however no flak defences. When Cheshire and his deputy Martin tried the same tactics on the Antheor viaduct, which was heavily defended, Martin was literally blasted away by flak and Cheshire was driven away by the ferocious low level flak and searchlights. His Squadron's attack accordingly failed. Cheshire then began marking from a Mosquito rather than from a Lancaster and under his leadership 5 Group tried the low level marking technique on several lightly defended targets: Wesseling, Schollene, Königsberg, Kaiserslautern, Harburg and Heilbronn before trying it on heavily defended targets such as Munich (three times) Brunswick (twice), Wilhelmshaven and Nuremberg. Not surprisingly, the results achieved on the larger targets were similar to those achieved by conventional methods and probably the technique should have been saved for small, hard to hit targets, of which there were many. Cheshire was later awarded a very much deserved Victoria Cross, and by the consensus of most pilots Martin should have received

1. For further details of the precision bombing raids, see *The Strategic Air Offensive Against Germany*, pp 182-189. Of particular interest are the raids, under the courageous leadership of Willie Tait, on the German battleship *Tirpitz*.

the same.[1] But this hard driving, low level marking never became routine and the great leaders of the precision raids, Nettleton, Gibson, Cheshire, Tait and Martin played no role in marking the targets of the main offensive.[1]

Bomber Command, in the six months after the Battle of Berlin, was placed directly under the authority of the Allied Command for support of the invasion of Europe by the bombing of tactical targets. Changes were made in its organisation. 83 and 97 Squadrons were moved back to 5 Group, whence they had come, and the Pathfinder Mosquitoes of 627 Squadron were ordered to accompany them. They moved to Coningsby under Cochrane's Command. Cochrane was a restless and demanding tactician and 5 Group lost no time in perfecting independent methods of attack.

Instead of the Lancaster illuminators, or blind markers, of 83 and 97 Squadrons dropping flares while all flying on the same heading, they were split into two forces. Flare Force One, for example, at eleven minutes before zero hour might drop their 5,000 candlepower illuminator flares while flying on, say, a southerly heading. Flare Force Two might then approach the target at nine minutes before zero hour on a heading at right angles to that of Flare Force One, say on an easterly heading. In this way the risk of overshooting or undershooting the target was minimised because the visual markers, who were coming in behind the flare forces, could see the intersection of the two lines of illuminators. With the target area thus illuminated the Mosquito visual markers could search the area and when one of them thought he had found the aiming point he would yell 'Tally Ho' and drop a red or a green flare on it. The target having been visually marked at four or five minutes before zero hour the marker leader could assess the marker accuracy and, if satisfied, call in the main force at zero hour. If not satisfied he would direct another visual marker to try. Then he would direct the main force to bomb on the red or the green.[2] 5 Group also, when the weather permitted, applied the techniques of offset bombing in cases where the aiming point had become obscured by smoke, cloud or smoke-screens. This method, pioneered by the Americans, of selecting a point which could be

1. Fauquier was the exception to this statement, having been both a precision leader (617 Squadron) and a Pathfinder (405 Squadron).

2. I am indebted to S/Ldr Ken Matheson, DFC & bar, RCAF, a member of 83 Squadron in the summer and autumn of 1944, for this description of their activities then.

seen a short distance from the aiming point, allowed for this distance and thus the attackers were able to strike the obscured aiming point. With these methods the bombers soon became of great assistance to the allied ground forces. However, even with refined marking procedures, the weather continued to be a problem and failures continued to occur as before.

At the end of September 1944 Bomber Command was freed to resume its role of area bombing and this it did in the last six months of the European War to March 1945. The aerial balance of power by this time had shifted dramatically in favour of the bomber. When Holland was taken by the Canadian and British Armies, Oboe stations were set up in their wake, thus bringing into the range of accurate pathfinding many cities which for years had been difficult to mark. Bomber Command switched to daylight operations for a third of its sorties. In 1944, in the six months after the Battle of Berlin, the missing rate fell to 1.5% and in the last eight months of the war it fell to.9%.[1] After the devastating overkill of Dresden on February 13, 1945, consideration was given to the halting of area bombing and it was stopped the next month in March 1945.

Thus the war ended without a way having been found, except in circumstances of complete air supremacy, of marking accurately and consistently at night the long range targets in Germany; this, despite all of the efforts of the Pathfinders, and of 5 Group, and of numerous Air Ministry and other civilian technicians. Had such a way been found the war against Germany would undoubtedly have been won by bombing alone, just as ultimately it was against Japan.

These remarks should not be interpreted however to mean that the bombing offensive against Germany was a failure. Far from it. Controversy still rages on this question but certain patterns are now obvious. Shortly after the war, when the appalling damage which had been wrought by the British and American bombers upon Germany first became apparent, and when Japan had been stricken by atomic bombs, the conscience of the world, until then stilled by the vicious struggle, arose again. Critics maintained that cities should not have been bombed;[2] it would have been preferable apparently, that the Allies lose an extra half million men in order to

1. The number of operations required to complete a tour was increased as a result of the reduced casualty rate.

2. The Oxford historian, A. J. P. Taylor, was among those who deplored the results of what he called 'indiscriminate bombing'. Unfortunately he prescribes no standards for what he might regard as discriminate bombing.

win the war 'cleanly'. Some people, including Clement Atlee and Sir Stafford Cripps deplored the bombing of 'non-military targets', though they had themselves participated in developing the policy for the 'undermining of the morale of the German people to a point where their capacity for armed resistance is fatally weakened.' How did they expect such weakening to be accomplished? By cutting off the German ration of oranges and bananas? The official history of the bombing offensive[1] produced voluminous statistics showing the miracles of production accomplished, despite the bombing, by the German war economy. One wonders what might have been accomplished by the Germans had they not been bombed? For this information one must speak to the Germans themselves. And lest anyone be in doubt, let him consult the diaries of Dr. Goebbels or the interrogation of Albert Speer, Hitler's Production Minister.[2] And in this connection the part played by the American heavy bombers in daylight attacks, particularly in 1944 and 1945, cannot be over-emphasised; Albert Speer thought them the most dangerous of all attacks because they followed a definite system of assault on industrial targets. He says it was such attacks which finally caused the breakdown of the German armaments industry. If I do not write of them it is only because I did not participate in them. Strategic bombing by day and night played almost as large a part in the war against Germany as it did against Japan, and ultimately it was the sword of Damocles in both cases.

At the war's end some 600,000 people had been killed by the bombing of Europe, while Britain and the U.S. suffered 120,000 aircrew killed in the same attacks. The latter number comprised 55,000 RAF and Commonwealth aircrew (including 10,000

1. *The Strategic Air Offensive Against Germany,* HMSO, 1961

2. This interrogation was carried out by S/Ldr Tooth of the Combined Intelligence Objectives Sub-Committee, 18 July 1945, and is contained in Appendix 37 of the official history cited in preceding footnote. Speer states that if, after the first attack on Hamburg, such attacks had been repeated on six other German cities, the will to sustain armaments manufacture and war production would have been crippled. He also expressed the opinion that strategic bombing alone could have rendered Germany defenceless had it been directed on the chemical industry. He points to the complexity of a chemical plant, stating that if damaged the entire plant must be restored before the chemical production, which is a self-contained unit, can pass through all its stages. In other industrial processes, work could be re-commenced with the undamaged machine tools shortly after the attack, and the factory concerned could take up production again in successive stages.

3. Surprisingly, the per capita losses suffered by New Zealand and Canada were greater than those suffered by Great Britain. See Appendix 'B'.

Canadians of the RCAF)³ and 65,000 of the 8th and 9th U.S.A.A.F.

As I have suggested, this narrative would be incomplete without reference to the American air offensive in daylight because it, more than anything else, finally achieved air supremacy for the Allies in Europe. A review of the events leading up to this will be helpful.

The British had switched to night bombing early in the war because they found that their unescorted bombers were no match for the German day fighters. On December 18, 1939, twenty-two Wellington bombers attacked German naval targets in daylight at Wilhelmshaven. They were intercepted by German fighters at Heligoland and twelve of them were destroyed. This was to be no exception. In May and June of 1940 RAF Blenheims and Battles were shot to pieces in daylight in France by the German fighters. In the Battle of Britain the same fate in daylight was suffered by the Germans. Even with fighter support their day bombers were destroyed. Those single-engined German fighters of the highest performance hadn't the range to fight the RAF fighters effectively over England and the German twin-engined fighters were shot down.

The RAF, when its turn came to take the offensive in 1941, switched to night bombing. This resulted in the policy of area bombing which I have described. But the switch to night bombing was really an act of desperation. It was an alternative to achieving air supremacy and thus contained within itself the seeds of its own defeat. Since it evaded the issue of air supremacy it must ultimately lose it. I do not criticise the British for this. They had no alternative at the time, and they had vowed to fight in any manner they could. But there should be no illusions now as to what happened then. Most people at the time did not regard night bombing as self-defeating. Probably Harris and his Group Commanders did not, but many of us remembering Richthofen, Mannock, and Bishop, regarded it as a poor substitute for air supremacy. Manfred Von Richthofen wrote in 1918, '...Clausewitz has already said that in war nothing else makes sense but the destruction of the opposition. The mastery of the air in war is won through nothing other than battle, that is shooting down the enemy. It is only in the fight that the battle is won.'¹

I have said that the Air Council and Fighter Command failed to meet the challenge of supporting the night bombers but, of course, the problem was initially that of Bomber Command to specify. In

1. *The Red Baron*, London, 1980

1940 some people still thought it possible to bomb in daylight, without fighter escort; certainly the Americans thought it possible as late as mid-1943 when the Luftwaffe taught them otherwise.

Twenty percent of the RAF bombing sorties in 1940 were made in daylight. These suffered an unacceptable 5% casualty rate.[1] Bomber Command in 1941 shifted almost completely to night bombing, increasing the total number of sorties flown by 60% but reducing the number of those flown in daylight to 12% of the total. The number missing or crashed at night in 1941 was close to 4%, a barely sustainable figure. Ominously that figure rose by the end of 1942 to 5%. This should have prompted drastic action, for in concrete terms a 5% casualty rate meant that only one in five members of bomber air crew had a statistical chance of surviving 30 trips.

Perhaps the challenge was not met because Harris had taken command of Bomber Command in late February 1942, and his attention, of necessity, was focused upon increasing the size and the bombing effectiveness of the Command. A field commander cannot do everything. But it is sad to reflect that a good mind like Bennett's was shortly thereafter directed to increasing the effectiveness of bombing, without an equally good mind and large resources being focused upon defensive armament and fighter support. The final responsibility for this must be left with the Air Council.

It was obvious to the most junior member of aircrew in 1942 that Fighter Command, after the Battle of Britain, was no longer an effective weapon; it had been forged for defence and had served magnificently in that capacity but its efforts to follow Trenchard's fiat to 'use the scouts offensively' failed. The intensity of British fighter activity remained generally low, until the time of the invasion. Some measure of this can be seen in the fact that throughout the war, in excess of 100 German pilots on all fronts, shot down more than 100 aircraft each, while the highest scoring Allied pilot shot down forty-one.

The sweeps in strength for three years by fighters across France and the Low Countries were able to accomplish little. Even when

1. In Appendix 42 of the official history the authors conclude that although it may continue to operate, the effectiveness of a strategic bomber force might become unacceptably low, due to the lack of experienced crews, if losses of 5% were suffered over a period of three months' intensive operations. This conclusion is, of course, not applicable to a present or future war, which might not last three months, nor to a strike force in which effectiveness is not a function of experience.

light bombers were dispatched in daylight to harass and interdict the Germans in these areas, the fighters of the Luftwaffe did not rise to the bait and do battle. Why should they? 'Let them believe that they are accomplishing something,' said the Germans in effect. 'While we concentrate our fighters against the real threat, the bombers. Better that they should not direct their minds to defending their bombers.'

It is probably not a well-known fact but there were enough surplus single-engined fighters and pilots in Britain at this time to have provided every bomber in Bomber Command with its own fighter escort. Where was the difficulty in developing long-range single-engined fighters? Lindbergh had flown in 1927 from New York to Paris in a single-engined aircraft. The Americans when faced with a similar problem, soon developed a long-range fighter, the Mustang, for use in daylight. Certainly the Germans were managing to fly their single-engined interceptors over long distances at night. And there was no shortage of skilled, night instrument pilots who were willing and able to provide an escort for bombers in much the same way that destroyers provided escort for capital ships. I suggest that some remedial techniques could have been tried when such large resources of airframes, engines and pilots were so readily available in Fighter Command. I realise, as General Eisenhower once observed, that 'All hindsight is 20–20 vision', but in retrospect the continued separation of Fighter Command and Bomber Command was analogous to the Admiralty having placed its destroyers in one task force and its capital ships in another, with the former saying to the latter, 'Good luck to you – I wish I could be of help.'

Fortunately, the game was not yet over. Just as the German night fighters were demonstrating their supremacy by night, the U.S.A.A.F. was beginning to assert its strength by day. And they did it as Richthofen had said it must be done – in battle.

Strange perhaps that Bomber Command was becoming unable to fly by night but the U.S.A.A.F. could do so by day? Not so strange when you examine the facts. It is necessary to look at the early experience of the U.S.A.A.F. in Europe. When the U.S. 8th Air Force arrived in Europe in 1942 its members were strong advocates of precision daylight bombing but they had no fighters capable of escorting their bombers to and from the long-range targets in Germany. So they decided to defend their bombers so well, by means of defensive armaments that they could dispense with fighter support. At least that was the theory. They mounted a formidable arsenal of half-inch machine guns in their B-17 Flying Fortresses – one which, had it been possessed by Bomber Command, might have enabled us to give a better account of ourselves in the solitary fighting of the night time. But even in massed daylight formations American bombers found that they could not operate except on short-range targets, such as the submarine pens in France. Only on these operations could they be supported by their own Thunderbolt fighters and the British Spitfires.

When the Americans in 1943 attempted to attack German targets in daylight beyond the range of their own and the British fighters they suffered terrible losses. Regensburg! Schweinfurt! On Schweinfurt 291 Fortresses, by the time they reached Aachen, had travelled as far as their fighter escort could go. The Germans knew this and that was where their fighter attack began. Sixty Fortresses were shot down, more than 20% of the attacking force. A disaster! An additional 138 Fortresses were damaged. On four attacks within six days 148 American bombers were lost. It was clear that even heavily armed bombers could not operate alone in daylight against a strong, skilled and determined fighter force. In considering what the Americans did next, let us not forget that in similar circumstances in 1940 and 1941, first the British and then the Germans admitted the loss of air supremacy and switched from day bombing to night bombing. It has been said of the Americans that they did not switch to night bombing for the reason that they could not – that their crews, '...highly trained in the formation tactics of day bombing, had little training, and most of them none at all in the navigational problems of night flying.[1] This to me does the Americans a double injustice; it not only underestimates their ability to adjust to the operational situation, it detracts from the courage it took to do what they did next. I submit that if I and my navigator could complete a night bombing GTU in two months, when prior to that time the navigator had done little navigation at night and I had not even flown the aircraft, I am quite certain that a fully trained Fortress crew could have learned night navigation and night bombing in six weeks. (The American B-29 offensive against Japan was switched from day to night bombing in less than six weeks.) The same author said that the 8th Air Force could not

1. Noble Frankland, *The Bombing Offensive Against Germany*, p 78

have converted to night operations because the 'Fortresses gave out very conspicuous exhaust flames'. One wonders if that author ever flew behind a Wellington or a Stirling or a Mark II Lancaster at night, each of them like the Fortress equipped with radial engines. He would undoubtedly have seen conspicuous exhaust flames. Or he could have viewed the few Fortresses which were modified by the RAF with exhaust flame traps to fly at night.[1] The Americans, to their everlasting credit, did not waver when their unescorted daylight attacks failed. They were determined to drive the German fighters from the skies and the instrument with which they accomplished this was the superb P-51 Mustang, produced for the U.S.A.A.F. by accident.

A first cousin of the famous AT-6 Harvard Trainer, the Mustang had been produced by North American Aviation on order for the RAF. The U.S.A.A.F. tested it and found it wanting. But Rolls-Royce engineers determined that the only thing wrong with it was that it was under-powered. Its Allison engine was not sufficient and its maximum speed was only 365 mph at 15,000 feet. So Rolls-Royce tried the Merlin 61 in it, and then tried the Packard-built Merlin in it and that is where the Mustang took off – straight up. Speed increased as it climbed, from 375 mph at 5,000 feet to 455 mph at 30,000 feet. At 35,000 feet it would still do 440 mph. It could go faster than the Focke Wulf 190 by 50 mph up to 28,000 feet and above that by 70 mph. It could out-turn both the Messerschmitt 109 and the Fw 190 and could out-dive them both. For years German fighter pilots had out-dived their adversaries in order to escape. Now there would be no escape by diving. The P-51's rate of roll was faster than the 109G and almost as good as the 190's. But as an additional bonus it could carry long-range fuel tanks with a loss of speed of only 35 mph, and with them it could fly as far as the bombers could go.[2] 14,000 Mustangs were eventually built. They first went into action in December 1943 and quickly made their presence felt over Germany. Not only that, but by flying long-range escort for the Fortresses they enabled huge numbers of Spitfires, many of which had been sitting idle for three

1. Frankland was a war-time navigator who completed a tour of bomber operations as a Flight Lieutenant and was awarded a DFC. After the war he obtained an MA and a Ph.D and assisted Sir Charles Webster in putting together the authorised history of the bombing offensive.

2. I have taken the Mustang performance figures from those quoted by Noble Frankland in The *Bombing Offensive Against Germany*, p 81.

years, to become useful on the short-range portion of the escort service. In February 1944 the 8th Air Force resumed its long-range attacks. In March of 1944 its bomber casualties were down to a figure which could be sustained, 3.5 percent. Later in 1944 huge daylight air battles took place, the like of which the world had never seen before, and has not seen since. Perhaps 800 Mustangs and Thunderbolts would escort 1,300 Fortresses to Berlin where they would be met by 900 German interceptors. The skies of Europe were filled with the condensation trails of 3,000 aircraft in a single engagement. And after engaging in battle in shifts the returning Mustangs would strafe the German airfields on their return journey. Allied fighters ranged far ahead of the bombers to hunt down the enemy fighters and to break up their formations before they reached the bombers.

The American fighter pilots were fine team flyers. Two of them, Don Gentile and John Godfrey, shot down twenty-three and eighteen German aircraft respectively and destroyed seven and eighteen respectively by strafing. They took turns at flying either lead or number two, and both men were fine deflection shots. They even invited German attacks by flying slowly together and when pursued would quickly split, climb and loop back on their pursuer. Churchill called them Damon and Pythias.

In six months the fighters could dare the German fighters to take off, and with the advancing Allied armies progressively taking possession of their bases, the task of the Luftwaffe became impossible. The Junior Birdmen of America had also grown up.[1]

1. Many North American youngsters first learned the principles of flight from a syndicated series called 'Junior Birdmen of America'.

CHAPTER FOURTEEN

Checkmate

THE afternoon of May 8th 1945 in Oxford. A fine day. The bells of the square church tower some 20 yards from my tiny attic room are deafening. Study is impossible. I look out of the window and see the huge, swinging masses of bronze creating the clamour. The sound waves are almost visible. People are hurrying out of buildings, and between the bells I can hear shouting below. I know what it is. The whole world knows what it is.

I am reading Modern Greats at Lincoln College. Philosophy, Politics and Economics. I have just returned from a session with my tutor and still have in one hand an essay on Plotinus as I unbutton my tunic with the other. Plotinus, born in Egypt, was thought to be of Roman birth. At least Rome, which failed to produce much in the way of philosophy before St. Augustine, claimed him as one of her own. He was not my favourite philosopher.

Seven years have elapsed since Dr. Knebelman, fresh from the Institute of Advanced Studies at Princeton had arrived at Washington State. He had fired my 17-year-old imagination with small papers on the theory of numbers and with gossip about Einstein. I think now of Knebelman's strong, hawk-like visage and his love for the austere geometry of Riemann and Lobachevsky. What am I doing in Oxford? I suppose it is the war. I want to think about politics and economics and the causes of wars. But Plotinus seems far removed from all of this. So too seems that tall, kindly, white-haired man in the padded chair of his book-lined study. He probes my knowledge of Plotinus attempting to see what is original and what plagiarised. I could tell him. Very little of it is original. But then very little of anything is original.

The bells come to a stop and in the distance I can hear a military band. I button up my tunic again. It has changed in appearance since Gieves made it. A sympathetic tailor in Oxford has managed to convert it to a civilian jacket. Still blue in colour, its wings, medal ribbons, belt, rank and pockets are gone. Its lapels have been widened and tapered and the shiny gold buttons have been replaced with grey ones, shaped like bones. I wear a beige shirt and tie and brown shoes. Over all I put on the short, black academic gown of a person *in statu pupillari* and start down the stairs to observe the commotion.

Upon my return to Canada from England (I was one of the first to return) I had entered another world, an almost foreign one it seemed. When I telephoned my mother from Ottawa her voice sounded flat and nasal. Did I once sound like that? Would I again? People I had known all my life were strangers. The young males I knew who were still at home avoided my eyes or apologised in one way or another for their continued existence. This saddened me. I was not nearly so confident as they that I had chosen the right route.

I was sent to a fighter squadron on Vancouver Island. But the air was noticeably free of Japanese. When the opportunity came I accepted a request to sell war bonds in industrial plants in BC. The public speaking experience would do me good. So I became an Air Force dummy, on display, telling people how Brian Slade had been killed. They cried when they heard tell of him and bought war bonds. But the thought of my friends still fighting in Europe had a strange effect. It was not conscience, but I felt that I had to go back to England. I had to see how I felt about Jean and perhaps I had to fight again. But Ottawa would not let me go. It would be bad publicity, they said, if a returning airman were sent back to Britain and killed. And so before the year 1944 had ended I had written a careful letter to my Command Headquarters threatening to resign my commission if I were not sent back to Britain. The Air Force, to my surprise, gleefully took up my offer, relieved to be rid of the unfamiliar problem of a disgruntled fighting man. They quickly released me with a pat on the back and a few dollars in my pocket, and I immediately entrained for Halifax.

Ordinary civilians could not buy passage to Britain at this time so I would have to find a berth as a seaman. There were no union problems in joining a crew it seemed. Seamen, for obvious reasons, were in short supply. The U-boat offensive had resumed and 150 U-boats, now virtually all equipped with snorkel, were operating in the Atlantic. Upon enquiry at the hiring hall I was sent for an interview with the captain of the steamship *Delilian*, a small freighter of 4,000 tons. A convoy was putting itself together in the harbour.

The skies were clear but the air was bitterly cold as I walked up *Delilian's* gangplank in the dazzling morning sunshine. I moved forward to the captain's cabin, noting as I went the huge icicles hanging from the ship's hawser. Rats would have a slippery time boarding the vessel by that route.

I had never seen men chained before. I could hardly believe my eyes but there on the deck two men wearing only thin clothing to ward off the penetrating cold were chained to the ship's railing outside the captain's cabin. They were dishevelled, shivering and sullen. I shifted sideways to get by them and knocked on the door. The captain, a cheerful and corpulent Scot, was seated in a high-backed chair. He felt obliged to explain the presence of the chained men. 'The filthy scum have been into the cargo of Scotch', he said, not even looking towards the men who were visible through the open door. 'Come in and shut the door. I'm waiting for the Halifax police to lock them up.' I shut the door. 'Stokers they are,' he said. 'So I'm short two men. Can you stoke a boiler?'

'Stoking' to me was synonymous with shovelling and I thought that almost all ships now burned oil. Wrong again it seemed. I said 'Yes, I think so, sir.' If Eugene O'Neill's *The Hairy Ape* could shovel coal I could too.

'Good,' he grunted. 'We've just brought a cargo of Scotch from Glasgow. It's in the warehouse now and we're loaded, ready to sail. You can report to the 2nd engineer.' He paused to examine me. 'But they say you were an Air Force officer.' He looked puzzled. 'You can't live aft with that scum in the fo'c'sle. I'll see that you get a cabin in the officers' quarters.' His tone softened. 'My son is an Air Force officer,' he said. 'In the Far East.' The interview was over.

In a few hours we were at sea outside the harbour thrashing along at eight knots. Before the day was out a gale had come up and the ship, being small, wallowed in the huge troughs, periodically plunging into mountains of water. I could not see the convoy. The spray extracted by the wind from the wave tops stung my face as I shovelled accumulated ashes from the boilers over the side. The 2nd engineer appeared during the second watch and showed me how to 'fasten a rope round your waist and secure it so you won't get washed overboard.'

The Atlantic, as I shovelled, began appearing rhythmically down the deck from the bow, each time taking a great bite from the pile of ashes. This was much more efficient than my shovel. I decided to let the waves do the job while I became seasick. Soon the frigid sea had swept the deck clean and I could go to my cabin to die.

But the 2nd engineer, also a Scot, refused me permission to die. Next morning he got me out of my bunk. I could not eat, of course. 'What you need is exercise,' he said. 'Come with me,' and he led me through the engine room, past two great clanking connecting rods for the high and low pressure cylinders and up to the coal bunkers. Handing me a shovel he pointed to the greater part of a coal mine. 'Shovel that down the chute of that hopper until it's full,' he said.

A watch is four hours and I had the hopper full in two, so assuming that I was to continue working, I began to fill the neighbouring hopper. It was almost full when the watch ended and a wiry little Glasgow Scot appeared shirtless from the heat of the boilers to inspect the hoppers. He was delighted. 'I see you've filled mine too, Canada,' he said. 'That's verra gud o' ye. The next watch has nothing to do. You deserve a reward. Here, have a dram,' he said pulling a small bottle of Black and White Scotch from his hip. 'Tak a big swig,' he said. 'We've got gallons o' the stuff in the fo'c'sle. We dinna land all the cargo for you North Americans.' He winked as he took a guzzle himself and handed me the bottle.

He was right. In a couple of days I asked the captain if I could move aft to sleep in the fo'c'sle and he granted permission. I was concerned that the stokers and seamen would resent my special status in an officer's cabin and I had visions, from their scowls at work, of ending up over the side of the ship. It would be better I thought to be one of them. So I moved aft, and on looking over the fo'c'sle the source of the whisky supply became evident. Everyone had four or five large bottles and several small ones under his mattress. There were even bottles under mine when I took possession of the single bunk which ran athwartship. All the other bunks ran fore and aft. My stoker friend grinned as he pointed to the whisky. 'There was a loose board you see in the side of the warehouse in Halifax. We waited until the cargo had been off-loaded and put in the warehouse you see. For stealing on a ship is a verra serious offence you know.'

'And stealing from the warehouse is no laughing matter either,' I replied. 'You're lucky you weren't handcuffed to the railing too.' They must by this time have accepted me as one of them or they'd not have told me the story. I was convinced of my acceptance a week later when we hit another patch of foul weather. The bunk athwartship rolled ferociously as the ship ploughed into the waves and it pitched from head to foot as the ship rolled from side to side. They had saved the worst bunk in the fo'c'sle for me and could scarcely conceal their delight at my discomfort. One of them said, 'Never mind Canada, you'll be able to hear the torpedoes better if you're awake when a sub attacks.' I thought of this on the next watch when the Navy began dropping depth charges. (They said it was a practice exercise). It sounded, from the engine room, like huge steel hammers were hitting the side of the hull.

Before we docked in London (it had taken three weeks to cross the Atlantic) I had become a good stoker and had earned, after deduction for food and lodging, about fifteen pounds, but I cannot say that I could function in heavy weather as all the crew, including the ship's cook, could. Once while bouncing off the passage walls en route to the galley in heavy seas I saw the cook approaching down the passage at an angle of thirty degrees from the vertical. He had a bucket of water in each hand and didn't spill a drop. I suspected that this, together with a strong stomach, were the criteria of a good seaman.

In early February, before reaching Britain, we learned that the Soviet forces of General Zhukov had reached the Oder, opposite Berlin and had halted to re-group. The British and Canadians were near Nijmegen advancing to the Rhine. The Germans had been expelled from Belgium and the 3rd Army to the south had moved into Germany east of the Our. I knew that once the Rhine was crossed Germany was finished. My services would not be of much assistance to General Eisenhower it seemed. I decided not to join the RAF.

After docking I signed off the ship's articles and spent a couple of days in Bournemouth. This, in retrospect, was the beginning of the end with Jean. Seeing her again I knew that deeper reasons than confusion about her underlay my decision to return to Britain. It was not just that the war was here and consequently that a part of me was here also. It was some kind of intellectual thing. It came from *Mort d'Arthur, Hurrah for Merry Sherwood* and *Ivanhoe*. It came from *Chums* and *Boy's Own Annual*. It came from my maternal grandparents and later from Russell's introduction to *Mathematical Philosophy*.

On the occasions I had flown over Oxford or Cambridge the thought of attending one of these great schools had come strongly to mind. I decided now to try to enter Oxford. It had a tradition with Canadians because of the Rhodes Scholarships.

With no misgivings whatever as to my meagre qualifications I presented myself. Needless to say the dons were not greatly impressed. I was admitted to Lincoln, one of the smaller colleges, not from admiration for my academic élan but out of gratitude, it seemed, for my fighting generation. I was soon into the Oxford life, but only on the surface. There were few veterans there as yet. My fellow students were boys and I quickly became frustrated with Plotinus, suffocated by Locke and bored with Adam Smith. One needn't go to a University to read these men, I thought. One could read them as I had Spinoza. In my own time. Then I overheard a philosophy student say, or hear that over at the other place (Cambridge) Bertrand Russell is lecturing on non-demonstrative inference, and he's giving general lectures as well.' That sounded more like it. Perhaps I should go to Cambridge.

The bells began to ring again as I came down the stairs and entered the street. People were dancing, crying, shouting, laughing and singing. They were drinking too, and climbing, jumping, hugging and kissing.

We were soon in the square and the bells stopped again. The band was entering from a side street. It too stopped and formed up in parade formation. The bandmaster signalled, the band started to play and the crowd began with one voice to sing 'Land of Hope and Glory, Mother of the Free'. I came to attention in military fashion. Tears were running down my cheeks as I tried to swallow the sobs which shook my chest. The deadliest war in human history was over. God help the Japanese now.

I watched the happy crowd for a few moments then returned to my tiny attic room. I packed my books and the few possessions I owned and left Oxford, with no word of goodbye to anyone. Perhaps next term I would go to Cambridge.

THE END

APPENDIX A
BOMBER COMMAND

Monthly Table of Sorties Dispatched and Aircraft Missing or Crashed

		Sorties		Missing		Crashed		Totals (%)	
		NIGHT	DAY	NIGHT	DAY	NIGHT	DAY	NIGHT	DAY
1939	September	83	40	2	12	3	0	6.0	30.0
	October	32	0	2	2	2	0	12.5	—
	November	15	4	0	0	1	0	—	—
	December	40	119	0	17	0	2	—	16.0
1940	January	38	6	0	0	0	0	—	—
	February	54	4	1	0	2	0	5.8	—
	March	239	53	5	1	6	0	4.6	1.9
	April	489	167	18	15	8	0	5.3	9.0
	May	1,617	802	21	49	3	3	1.5	6.5
	June	2,484	812	26	31	7	1	1.3	3.9
	July	1,722	616	40	32	3	4	2.5	5.8
	August	2,188	417	52	18	11	0	2.9	4.3
	September	3,141	98	65	1	21	0	2.7	1.0
	October	2,242	172	27	1	32	0	2.6	0.6
	November	1,894	113	50	2	34	0	4.4	1.8
	December	1,385	56	37	2	25	0	4.2	3.6
1941	January	1,030	96	12	3	12	1	2.3	4.2
	February	1,617	124	16	2	32	2	3.0	3.2
	March	1,728	162	35	4	36	0	4.1	2.5

	April	2,249	676	56	23	12	7	3.0	4.4
	May	2,416	273	39	20	14	3	2.2	8.4
	June	3,228	531	76	22	15	3	2.8	4.7
	July	3,243	582	91	55	28	3	3.7	11.8
	August	3,354	468	121	35	45	5	5.0	8.5
	September	2,621	263	76	14	62	1	5.3	5.7
	October	2,501	138	68	17	40	1	4.3	13.0
	November	1,713	43	83	0	21	0	6.0	—
	December	1,411	151	36	7	16	0	3.1	4.6
1942	January	2,216	24	56	0	32	0	4.0	—
	February	1,162	252	18	15	14	1	2.7	6.3
	March	2,224	131	78	2	21	0	4.4	1.5
	April	3,752	246	130	13	29	2	4.2	6.1
	May	2,702	105	114	1	21	0	5.0	0.9
	June	4,801	196	199	2	39	1	5.0	1.5
	July	3,914	313	171	19	22	0	4.9	6.1
	August	2,454	186	142	10	16	5	6.4	8.1
	September	3,489	127	169	6	39	0	6.0	4.7
	October	2,193	106	89	14	27	0	5.8	3.4
	November	2,067	127	53	11	23	0	3.7	8.6
	December	1,758	200	72	16	22	2	5.3	9.0
1943	January	2,556	406	86	15	18	3	4.1	4.4
	February	5,030	426	101	6	22	3	2.4	2.1
	March	5,174	284	161	7	25	1	3.6	2.8
	April	5,571	316	253	12	24	1	5.0	4.1
	May	5,130	360	234	19	27	4	5.1	6.4

June	5,816	0	275	0	15	0	5.0	—
July	6,170	0	188	0	31	0	3.5	—
August	7,807	0	275	0	33	0	3.9	—
September	5,513	0	191	0	34	0	4.1	—
October	4,638	0	159	0	21	0	3.9	—
November	5,208	0	152	0	48	0	4.0	—
December	4,123	0	170	0	47	0	5.3	—
1944 January	6,278	0	314	0	38	0	5.6	—
February	4,263	45	199	0	21	0	5.2	—
March	9,031	18	283	0	39	0	3.6	—
April	9,873	10	214	0	25	0	2.4	—
May	11,353	16	274	0	29	0	2.7	—
June	13,592	2,371	293	12	30	0	2.4	0.5
July	11,500	6,293	229	12	29	4	2.2	0.3
August	10,013	10,271	186	36	22	1	2.1	0.3
September	6,428	9,643	96	41	15	0	1.8	0.4
October	10,193	6,713	75	52	26	0	1.0	0.8
November	9,589	5,055	98	41	34	0	1.4	0.8
December	11,239	3,656	88	31	43	0	1.2	0.8
1945 January	9,603	1,304	121	12	57	0	1.9	0.6
February	13,715	3,685	164	9	60	0	1.6	0.2
March	11,585	9,606	168	47	76	10	2.1	0.6
April	8,822	5,001	51	22	25	6	0.9	0.5
May	360	1,863	3	0	0	1	0.9	0.6

1939-45 (Those shown as crashed were damaged so badly by fighters, flak or other causes that they were written off).

APPENDIX B

BOMBER COMMAND AIRCREW KILLED, 1939-1945

COUNTRY	POPULATION (1940)	CASUALTIES		PERCENTAGE OF TOTAL CASUALTIES	CASUALTIES AS A PERCENTAGE OF POPULATION
Britain	46,889,000	38,462	– RAF	69.2	0.082
Canada	11,506,655	9,919	– RCAF	17.8	0.085
Australia	6,929,691	4,050	– RAAF	7.3	0.059
New Zealand	1,491,484	1,679	– RNZAF	3.0	0.113
Poland	35,000,000	929	– Polish	1.7	—
		500	– Other	1.0	
		55,539	– Total	100.0	

APPENDIX C
The Author's Operational Flights

1943			TARGET	DUTY CARRIED OUT
1.	March	11	Stuttgart	Bombing (2nd Pilot)
2.		12	Essen	Bombing (2nd Pilot)
3		22	St. Nazaire	Bombing – Visually
4		27	Berlin	Bombing – Visually
5		29	Berlin	Bombing – Visually
6.	April	10	Frankfurt	Bombing – Blind
7		13	Spezia	Bombing – Visually
8.		14	Stuttgart	Bombing – Visually
9.		16	Pilsen	Bombing – Visually
10.		18	Spezia	Bombing – Visually
11.		20	Stettin	Bombing – Visually
12.		30	Essen	Bombing – Blind
13.	May	4	Dortmund	Bombing – Visually
14.		12	Duisburg	Bombing – Visually
15.		13	Pilsen	Bombing – Visually
16.	June	12	Bochum	Bombing – Visually
17.		21	Krefeld	Bombing – Visually
18.	July	3	Cologne	Back-Up Marker
19.		12	Turin	Bombing – Visually
20.		27	Hamburg	Bombing – Visually
21.		29	Hamburg	Back-Up Marker
22.	August	2	Hamburg	Back-Up Marker
23.		7	Turin & Genoa	Back-Up Marker
24.		10	Nuremberg	Back-Up Marker
25.		14	Milan	Visual Marker
26.		15	Milan	Visual Marker
27.		17	Peenemunde	Blind Marker
28.		23	Berlin	Blind Marker
29.		27	Nuremberg	Back-Up Marker
30.		31	Berlin	Blind Marker

1943		TARGET	DUTY CARRIED OUT
31. Sept.	3	Berlin	Blind Marker
32.	6	Munich	Blind Marker
33.	23	Darmstadt	Blind Marker
34.	27	Hanover	Blind Marker
35. Oct.	2	Munich	Blind Marker
36.	3	Kassel	Blind Marker
37.	7	Stuttgart	Blind Marker
38.	8	Hanover	Blind Marker
39.	18	Hanover	Blind Marker
40.	20	Leipzig	Blind Marker
41.	22	Kassel	Visual Marker
42. Nov.	17	Ludwigshafen	Visual Marker
43.	18	Berlin	Blind Marker
44.	22	Berlin	Bombed Texel
45.	23	Berlin	Bombed Texel
46.	26	Berlin	Bombed Abbeville
47. Dec.	2	Berlin	Special Blind Marker
48.	3	Leipzig	Special Blind Marker

APPENDIX D

CASUALTIES – REPORTED MISSING OR CRASHED (*indicates killed*)

NO. 106 SQUADRON, SYERSTON, NOTTS.

1.	12/13 March 1943	Lancaster R 5749	F/Sgt. A. L. McDonald* and crew
2.	29/30 March 1943	Lancaster ED 596 'H'	S/Ldr. E. L. Hayward DFC* and crew
3.	3/4 April 1943	Lancaster ED 542	Sgt. T. J. Ridd* and crew
4.	8/9 April 1943	Lancaster W 4156	Sgt. J. L. Irvine* and crew
5.	14/15 April 1943	Lancaster ED 752	F/Lt. L. C. J. Brodrick and crew – PoW
6.	30 April/1 May 1943	Lancaster ED 451	Sgt. S. Abel* and crew

NO. 83 SQUADRON, WYTON, HUNTS.

7.	4/5 May 1943	Lancaster R 5629 'J'	Sgt. J. R. Leigh* and W/Cdr. J. R. Gillman* (2nd Pilot) and crew
8.	12/13 May 1943	Lancaster W 4955 'R'	F/Lt. L. A. Rickinson DFC and crew
9.	13/14 May 1943	Lancaster W 4981 'F'	Sgt. A. S. Renshaw* and crew
10.	11/12 June 1943	Lancaster R 5686 'G'	S/Ldr. J. E. Swift DFC and crew – PoW
11.	12/13 June 1943	Lancaster ED 603 'L'	F/O E. A. Tilbury* and crew
12.	16/17 June 1943	Lancaster ED 907 'H'	P/O C. Murray* (RCAF) and crew
13.	18 June 1943	Lancaster ED 439	F/Sgt. M. K. Cummings *RAAF and crew – crashed near Grantham.
14.	21/22 June 1943	Lancaster ED 997 'R'	F/Sgt. D. W. C. Fletcher* and crew
15.	21/22 June 1943	Lancaster EE 121 'K'	P/O H. Mappin* and crew
16.	22/23 June 1943	Lancaster W 4982 'O'	Sgt. M. E. Rust* and crew
17.	29/30 July 1943	Lancaster R 5625 'D'	P/O K. A. King and crew – crashed at Sibson
18.	23/24 August 1943	Lancaster ED 984 'A'	F/Lt. I. C. B. Slade* DFC and crew
19.	23/24 August 1943	Lancaster JA 927 'O'	P/O J. A. Reid *and crew
20.	27/28 August 1943	Lancaster ED 876 'V'	F/Sgt. K. C. Turp* and crew
21.	5/6 September 1943	Lancaster JB 118 'R'	P/O J. H. Price*(RCAF) and crew

22.	29/30 September 1943	Lancaster JB 187 'R'	F/O C. P. McDonald DFC, DFM (RCAF) and crew –bailed out.
23	3/4 October 1943	Lancaster JA 972	S/Ldr. J. E. R. Hayter* DFC and crew
24	20/21 October 1943	Lancaster JB 154 'A'	S/Ldr. R. J. Manton* and crew
25.	20/21 October 1943	Lancaster JA 701 'E'	W/O S. G. W. Hall* and crew
26	23/24 November 1943	Lancaster JB 424 'B'	P/O R. Henderson *DFM and crew
27	23/24 November 1943	Lancaster JB 284 'C'	W/Cdr. R. Hilton* DSO, DFC and bar, and crew
28.	26 November 1943	Lancaster JA 686	Aircraft blew up at Wyton (no aircrew casualties)
29	26/27 November 1943	Lancaster JB 459 'T'	F/O A. B. Smeaton* and crew
30	26/27 November 1943	Lancaster JA 913 'G'	P/O K. R. G. Millar* and crew
31.	16/17 December 1943	Lancaster JB 344	P/O F. E. McLean (RAAF) and crew–crashed on return
32.	1/2 January 1944	Lancaster ND 354 'A'	W/Cdr. W. Abercromby* DFC and bar, and crew
33.	2/3 January 1944	Lancaster JB 355 'J'	F/O F. C. Allcroft* DFC and crew
34.	2/3 January 1944	Lancaster JB 114 'Q'	F/Lt. L. W. Munro* (RNZAF) and crew
35.	2/3 January 1944	Lancaster JB 453 'F'	P/O E. B. Stiles *(RCAF) and crew
36	20/21 January 1944	Lancaster ND 414 'K'	S/Ldr. A. P. Jones and crew – PoW
37.	20/21 January 1944	Lancaster JB 461 'L'	F/Lt. K. King DFC (RAAF) and crew – POW
38	20/21 January 1944	Lancaster ED 974 'Y'	P/O G. 1. Ransom* (RCAF) and crew
39	21/22 January 1944	Lancaster JB 488 'X'	F/O J. C. H. Davies* and crew
40.	21/22 January 1944	Lancaster JB 365 'G'	F/O W. K. Hutton*(RAAF) and crew
41.	27/28 January 1944	Lancaster JB 724 'V'	F/Lt. S. H. Alcock* DFC and crew
42	28/29 January 1944	Lancaster JA 967 'S'	F/Lt. H. R. Hyde* and crew
43	28/29 January 1944	Lancaster JB 412 'B'	P/O W. Simpson and crew – PoW
44.	30/31 January 1944	Lancaster JB 352 'C'	F/Lt. A. H. J. Sambridge* and crew

The normal crew was comprised of pilot, navigator, bomb-aimer, flight engineer, wireless operator, mid-upper gunner and rear gunner (7 men). I have included crews lost in January 1944, (although I had by then left 83 Squadron) because most of the captains were known to me.

APPENDIX E

OPERATIONS RECORD BOOK

83 Squadron, Pathfinder Force, RAF Wyton

SUMMARY OF EVENTS – 14/8/43 to 31/8/43
(Permission to reproduce this material given by the Keeper of Public Records)

PLACE	DATE	SUMMARY OF EVENTS.
Wyton	14.8.43	Practice bombing and 'Y' training were the order of the day this morning. Night Flying tests in preparation for the evening work occupied most of the afternoon. 14 aircraft are on but two were unable to take off, S/Ldr Hildyard and S/Ldr. Manton. The crews operating 'V' F/Sgt. Turp, 'F' P/O Shipway 'W' W/O Finding, 'Y' P/O King, 'J' S/Ldr. Sells, 'L' F/O Chick, 'A' F/Lt. Mason, 'Q' F/Lt. Garvey, 'T' F/O Thompson, 'X' P/O Reid, 'E' G/Capt. Searby and 'M' S/Ldr. A. B. Smith. All crews returned safely and another pin was knocked from under the feet of tottering Italy. The target was Milan.
	15.8.43	Crews were resting after the previous night's operations, there was no training during the day; at night 13 crews paid a return visit to Milan and all returned safe and sound.
	16.8.43	'Y' training and practice bombing were proceeded with but squadron activity was slight. Stand down from operations.
	17.8.43	A fine day with normal work up to about 10.00 hours when a target came through that even the route and other details were with held from all but the CO. Details were late through, the armourers had to wait until after lunch; loads and suspense grew apace. The attack was on Peenemunde and the following Captains were detailed to attack: 'W' G/Capt. Searby who was MC and controlled the raid throughout. He was attacked by night fighters

but staved them off through good crew drill
and co-operation. 'M' S/Ldr. A. B. Smith, 'O'
P/O Reid, 'V' F/O Chick, 'U' S/Ldr. Manton,
'F' S/Ldr. Sells, 'A' F/Lt. Slade, 'K' P/O
Shipway, 'G' S/Ldr. Hildyard, 'E' F/Lt.
Mason, 'B' F/S Turp, 'C' P/O Allcroft, 'X'
W/O Finding, 'T' F/O Thompson, 'Y' P/O
King. F/O Chick returned early. The crews
were unanimous in their opinion that the raid
was a great success. The following is a special
report by G/Capt. Searby: – 'On the approach
to the target across the Danish Islands the
weather was clear and no difficulty was
experienced in map reading; thus it was
hoped that the same conditions would prevail
over the target. Rugen Island was clear apart
from one or two small patches of cloud, and
on approaching Rugen Island, a layer of very
thin cloud sheet, estimated to be between two
and three thousand feet was seen to cover the
small promontory. On reaching the target
area, and before any Markers had been
dropped, we made a run across and were able
to discern the target reasonably well through
the thin cloud layer. After turning left across
the sea and flying parallel to the shore, the
first Reds were seen to fall at Zero – 5, and it
was considered that they had slightly overshot
the aiming point. A second bunch of reds fell
a few minutes later and then Yellow was seen
to fall between the two, and as near as could
be judged this Yellow marker was very well
placed. Green markers fell almost
immediately on the Yellow, and instructions
were broadcast to the Main Force aircraft to
bomb these Green Markers. More Reds were
dropped and some of these were observed to
fall into the sea, and Backers Up were warned
by broadcast of this fact. Backing up
continued, and Greens were observed to fall

into the sea. A third broadcast informed the Main Force that this was so, and they were to bomb the Greens which lay to the right, as it was estimated these were on the target. Two more runs across the target by our own aircraft confirmed this and whilst we were over the target more Greens overshot. A fourth broadcast informed the Backers Up that they had overshot and other Backers Up were instructed to watch their bombing runs and not to overshoot. A sixth broadcast to the Main Force instructed them to ignore the Southerly Greens, which had overshot, and bomb those lying to the North. This was repeated. Another run across showed that the second aiming point was well covered but some Reds were still falling into the sea, and Backers Up were warned of this. At 00.42 hours another broadcast informed Backers Up that they must endeavour to avoid any Green Markers falling into sea. Another run across showed that both aiming points were still being bombed, and fires were seen breaking out, and in the case of the large target, to be going well. There is no doubt that the woods were burning, and it was difficult to differentiate. Further instructions were given to the Main Force to carry on bombing Greens, and a broadcast informed them that the attack was going well despite the smoke screens. These smoke screens were put into operation very soon after the attack started, and were very effective. They were located to the east and north-east of the target area, and the generators could be plainly seen. One more broadcast was made urging the Main Force to watch their bombing, to make steady runs, and carry on bombing Greens. During the whole of the time, our aircraft was over the target area, seven runs were made across

the target, and many aircraft were seen shot
down. Fighter activity was intense, and we
saw twin engine and single engine fighters
clearly silhouetted against the fires below.
There were a small number of heavy flak
guns, the most troublesome to us being
located approximately one mile out to sea, (a
flak ship) due east of the promontory. This
gun fired consistently at us as we circled left
away from the target to make another run.
Other heavy flak guns were seen to be firing
from the western shore in the neighbourhood
of the aerodrome. After making the last
broadcast we circled right with the main
stream, and a few miles from the target were
engaged by a twin engine fighter. This fighter
was first seen below, when the rear gunner
fired four bursts directly at him. He then
attacked from the starboard side, when a
sharp turn was made in the direction of the
attack, and the mid-upper gunner got in a
burst as he passed below: his own fire was
inaccurate. The aircraft was claimed as
damaged. A large mass of fire was observed
in the target area, which did not seem to be
consistent with the size of the target, and
these fires were observed until well past
Langeland on the way home. In this particular
area there was much fighter activity and
several more aircraft were seen to go down.
Light flak guns too, were very much in
evidence, and there can be no doubt that some
aircraft were employing very bad tactics
indeed in flying low across these Islands.'

Wyton 18.8.43   Ops stand down. Training for crews not
                  operating on previous night. Fighter
                  affiliation for P/O's Pidding and Davis.

       19.8.43   Ops laid on in morning with a special target
                  for u/t blind markers. It came as a complete
                  surprise when the operation was cancelled at

briefings The CO paid special tribute to the crews partaking in the Peenemunde raid which from recent reports to hand was an outstanding success. At 09.00 hours there was a lecture on tactics by G/Capt. Searby. Two fighter affiliation exercises by S/Ldr. Manton and P/O Pidding.

20.8.43   Ops stood down. Maximum training and drogue firing, F/Sgt. Turp, P/O King, S/Ldr. Johnson and crews. W/Cdr. Shaw, air to sea firing. Clay pigeon shooting. Buses for ground and air crews to Cambridge.

21.8.43   Stood down again. At 11.00 hours a crew conference was held in the briefing room at which new and old raid tactics were discussed. There were many valuable suggestions and the arguments were keen. Everybody's grouse was given an airing including of course Sergeants' Messing. On the whole grouses were few and everything went to show we are a 'happy' Squadron. In the afternoon a complete stand down, all crews resting with the exception of P/O King who flew to Feltwell to demonstrate 'Window'. Early bus to Cambridge in the afternoon.

22.8.43   'Stood down' is getting monotonous. Just another opportunity for maximum training, air to sea firing, testing new guns in 'K'.

23. 8.43   Ops laid on. Two areas given in morning but as one was Berlin the other was given very little thought. At briefing the crews showed great enthusiasm as this target had been expected daily and now was their chance to hit right at the nerve centre of Germany. The route chosen was not popular and the majority of Captains would have approved a much shorter route. There were 16 crews captained by 'W' W/Cdr. Shaw, 'M' F/O Chick, 'Y' P/O King, 'V' F/Sgt. Turp, 'G'

S/Ldr. Hildyard, 'J' S/Ldr. Sells, 'A' F/Lt. Slade, 'K' F/Lt. Mason, 'E' S/Ldr. Smith, C. A. J., 'U' S/Ldr. Manton, 'O' P/O Reid, 'F' P/O Shipway, 'T' F/O Thompson, 'X' F/Lt. Garvey, 'B' Sgt. Stiles, 'C' F/Sgt. Henderson. Once again 83 Squadron helped to lead the attack. There was an unfortunate and unforeseen failure of our 'Y' equipment which led the attack to develop approx. 6 miles W of actual A/P. The success of the raid was not due to our accurate bombing but to the Germans for building so large a city. The first aircraft in were amazed to find that the flak was not forthcoming as expected. The searchlights were numerous and Jerry's set up was as near daylight as he could make it. It soon became clear that the night fighters were up in great number and were predominant in the defence. Aircraft were being shot down on all sides as they became illuminated. W/Cdr. Shaw was chased immediately after his bombing. At the time he was listening for the MC's broadcast and could not therefore hear his mid-upper's instructions, but his continuous weave completely foxed the fighter who could not make up his mind when to attack and broke off for easier game. We had the sad misfortune to lose two very fine crews. F/Lt. Slade who joined this squadron last April and was one of our first trained 'Y' crews with F/Lt. MacPherson, navigator; the whole crew had done many sorties together and were without doubt one of our leading crews. P/O Reid had not been with us long but was a sound type of Captain and showed great promise of things to come this was his 10th trip with PFF and he really liked this type of work. We certainly suffered a severe loss including F/Lt. Turner, gunnery leader of 'A' Flight, F/Sgt. Lewis, flight engineer, and one of the Squadron's oldest members.

24.8.43 Ops stood down. Very little activity but training for crews not operating the previous night. Bus to Cambridge in evening. A wild rumour that P/O Reid had landed in Sweden, but this proved to be a P/O Read.

25.8.43 Stood down. Aircrew had conference re flying clothing, rations and general comfort. Intensive training. Our CO G/Capt. Searby was awarded the Distinguished Service Order (Immediate) for his magnificent leadership on the Peenemunde raid.

26.8.43 Ops were laid on but scrubbed very early. Film show to aircrew on a very wet morning indeed totally unsuited to flying. In the afternoon all available crews were shown the American film on Venereal Disease. No flying at all during the day. Our CO, S/Ldr Sells and Scrivener and F/Lt. Johnson visited an American Unit to impart information on Night Bombing Tactics. We have all the clues if anybody ever had.

27.8.43 Ops on Nuremberg. 16 aircraft detailed to attack captained by 'W' W/Cdr. Shaw, 'G' S/Ldr. Hildyard, 'J' S/Ldr. Sells, 'F' P/O Shipway, 'U' F/O Chick, 'K' F/Lt. Mason, 'Y' P/O King, 'R' P/O Price, 'D' Sgt. Millar, 'Q' F/Lt. Garvey, 'V' F/Sgt. Turp, 'T' F/O Thompson, 'B' P/O Tolchard, 'X' P/O Pidding, 'E' S/Ldr. Johnson, 'C' F/Sgt. Henderson. This was S/Ldr Johnson's first trip as Captain with us and he has F/Lt. Wilmot's old crew. This was P/O Tolchard's first trip with us. This appears to have been a fairly successful prang and we had a glut of photographs, F/O Chick's being the finest probably that has ever been taken at night. The defences were again depending on masses of night fighters with very occasional predicted heavy flak. Again the majority of our aircraft were shot down in the target area. S/Ldr. Hildyard was coned and hit by flak on his first run and was compelled to jettison his HE and come in again for a good run to drop his T.l.'s. All 'Y' equipment aircraft tested their equipment, dropping a 500 or 1,000 lb. on Heilbronn. F/Lt. Mason and P/O King were visual markers at 14,000 ft., but were unable to locate actual aiming point so reverted to role of Backers. P/O King was shot up over the target and his hydraulics became u/s. On attempting to land one leg of his undercart was down but the other refused. He was obliged to crash land and did so very successfully, none of his crew were hurt. Again we suffered loss. F/Sgt. Turp failed to return; nothing was heard from him after take-off. We shall miss him and his crew who had valuable experience with the Pathfinder Force.

28.8.43   Ops stand down. The photographs last night were exceptionally good and it should be put on record that W/Cdr. Shaw even got one. W/Cdr. Shaw has been steadily trying for some time to achieve a photograph and was almost convinced that a straight and level bombing run paid no dividends in this respect.

29.8.43   Ops stand down. Maximum training, aircraft recce, lecture for gunners. H2S bombing exercise and dinghy drill.

30.8.43   Cloud base interfered with our efforts of training for the day, but nevertheless we did some pretty hard training.

31.8.43   To complete a very successful month we were briefed to attack Berlin. 16 crews were detailed captained by 'G' S/Ldr. Hildyard, 'M' S/Ldr. Smith, A. B., 'J' S/Ldr. Sells, 'W' F/O Chick, (F/Sgt. Rathbone 2nd Pilot) 'K' P/O Shipway, 'T' F/O Thompson, 'F' F/Sgt. Britton, 'L' P/O Finding, 'D' Sgt. Millar, 'E' S/Ldr. Johnson, 'R' P/O Price, 'Q' F/Lt.

APPENDIX E 227

Garvey, (P/O Davies 2nd Pilot) 'X' P/O
Pidding, 'C' F/Sgt. Henderson, 'B' P/O
Mercer, 'U', P/O Tolchard. A new route was
appreciated and according to reports quite
satisfactory. P/O Finding had trouble with
both his starboard engines and bombed Texel,
a last resort target. The remainder
successfully carried out the mission, but once
again it appears the attack fell mainly to the
west of the target and the whole affair was far
below our expectations. The new Jerry tactics
of concentrating fighters over a well
illuminated target presents us with a new
problem. There was 7-9/10ths low strata over
the target and Jerry dropped some particularly
fine illuminating flares bang on track to
counter his decreased illumination of
searchlights. P/O Finding had an encounter
with an ME.IIO, both gunners going into
action, but no claim. This is his 2nd combat in
a very short period with this squadron. S/Ldr.
Hildyard (Flight Commander 'A' Flight) F/Lt.
Hacking, (Nav.) F/Lt. Coleman, (Bombing
Leader) and W/O Goldie all completed their
second tours. Their work for the squadron has
been exemplary; we shall indeed miss their
keen co-operation.

APPENDIX F

Summary of No. 83 Squadron's History

Formed at Montrose	7th January, 1917
Proceeded overseas	6th March, 1918
Returned to England	14th February, 1919
Disbanded at Hawkinge	31st December, 1919
Reformed at Turnhouse	4th August, 1936

War Duties

Night Bombing	Bombing
March to November 1918	September 1939 to May 1945

Commanding Officers

Major J. C. Quinnell	6.2.17
Major V. A. Albrecht	16.5.17
Major E. L. M. L. Gower	1.3.18
Major S. W. Price	28.7.18
Captain C. S. Stonehouse	14.1.19
F/Lt. A. W. Vincent	27.8.36
S/Ldr. D. A. Boyle	2.1.37
S/Ldr. L. S. Snaith, AFC	11.7.37
W/Cdr. R. B. Jordan	21.8.39
W/Cdr. L. S. Snaith, AFC	1.10.39
W/Cdr. J. C. Sisson	9.6.40
W/Cdr. D. A. Boyle, AFC	3.12.40
W/Cdr. W. W. Stainthorpe	16.2.41
W/Cdr. R. A. B. Learoyd, VC	28.2.41
W/Cdr. H. V. Satterly	20.6.41
W/Cdr. S. O. Tudor, DFC	6.9.41
W/Cdr. Crichton-Biggie	14.4.42
W/Cdr. J. R. Gillman	10.2.43
G/Capt. J. H. Searby, DSO, DFC	9.5.43
W/Cdr. R. Hilton, DSO, DFC, and Bar	2.11.43
W/Cdr. W. Abercromby, DFC, and Bar	4.12.43
G/Capt. L. C. Deane, DSO, DFC	3.1.44
G/Capt. J. A. Ingham, DSO, DFC	28.8.44
W/Cdr. F. Osborne, DFC, AFC	10.6.45
W/Cdr. R. F. Smith	26.11.45
S/Ldr. B. J. Hooper, DFC	6.1.47

Locations

Montrose	Scotland	7.1.17
Spittlegate	England	Jan. 1917
Wyton	England	Sept. 1917
Narborough	England	12.12.17
St. Omer	France	6.3.18
Auchel	France	7.3.18
Franqueville	France	2.5.18
La-Moussoye	France	10.10.18
Estrees-en-Chaussee	France	26.10.18
Serny	France	13.12.18
Hawkinge	England	14.2.19
Turnhouse	Scotland	4.8.36
Scampton	England	14.3.38
Wyton	England	15.8.42
Coningsby	England	18.4.44
Hemswell	England	30.11.46

BIBLIOGRAPHY

The events related in this book are contained in RAF Squadron records made over 40 years ago, but it was not until 1973 that these records became available to the public and I did not learn of their availability until 1982, at which time I ordered copies from the Public Record Office in London. These, together with my flying log book and the books appearing below, have formed my source materials. In particular I have relied upon the official history, shown first on the list. I would like also to express my debt to my friend, Brian Goulding, without whose encouragement and assistance this book would not have been published and my debt too to Anita Pelletier for her great patience and typing skills.

The Canadians at War; 1939/45, vols. 1 & 2, Readers Digest (Canada), 1973

The RCAF Overseas, 3 vols. 'The First Four Years', 'The Fifth Year', 'The Sixth Year', Toronto U.P., 1945

Aders, Gebhard, *The History of the German Night Fighter Force; 1917-1945*, Crecy, 1993

Bennett, Donald T. C., *Pathfinder*, Frederick Muller, 1958, Goodall, 1983

Bishop, William A., *Winged Warfare*, Bailey Brothers & Swinfen

Campbell, James, *The Bombing of Nuremberg*, Allison & Busby

Constable, T. J., *Horrido*, MacMillan

Currie, Jack, *Lancaster Target*, Goodall, 1997

Frankland, Noble, *The Bombing Offensive Against Germany*, Faber, 1965

Garbett, Mike, & Goulding, Brian, *The Lancaster at War*, Ian Allen, 1971

Garbett, Mike, & Goulding, Brian, *The Lancaster at War 2*, Ian Allen, 1979

Hastings, Max, *Bomber Command*, Dial Press, 1979

Hinchcliffe, Peter, *Schnaufer*, Crecy, 1997

Irving, David, *The Rise and Fall of the Luftwaffe*, Little Brown & Co.

Johnen, Wilhelm, *Duel Under The Stars*, Crecy, 1994

Johnson, John E., *Full Circle*, Bantam, 1980

MacDonald, Sandy A. F., *From The Ground Up*, Aviation Services Corp., Ontario

Middlebrook, Martin, *The Battle of Hamburg*, Allen Lane, 1980

Middlebrook, Martin, *The Nuremberg Raid*, Allen Lane, 1980

Middlebrook, Martin, *The Peenemunde Raid*, Allen Lane, 1982

Robertson, Bruce, *Lancaster – The Story of a Famous Bomber*, Argus Books 1977

Rudel, Hans-Ulrich, *Stuka Pilot*, Ballantine, 1967

Saward, Dudley, *Bomber Harris*, Buchan & Enright, 1984

Soames, Christopher, *Fighter Aces*, Hamlyn, 1975

Speer, Albert, *Inside The Third Reich*, Avon Books

Ulanoff, Stanley M., *The Red Baron*, Doubleday

Verrier, Anthony, *The Bomber Offensive*, Batsford, 1968

Webster, Charles & Frankland, Noble, *The Strategic Air Offensive Against Germany*, HMSO, 1961